P9-APM-958

THE OFFICIAL®

1997
BLACKBOOK
PRICE GUIDE OF
UNITED STATES
PAPER
MONEY

TWENTY-NINTH EDITION

BY MARC HUDGEONS, N.L.G.
AND TOM HUDGEONS

HOUSE OF COLLECTIBLES • NEW YORK

© 1996 by Random House, Inc.

H This is a registered trademark of Random House, Inc.

All rights reserved under International and Pan-American Copyright Conventions.

Published by: House of Collectibles
201 East 50th Street
New York, New York 10022

Distributed by Ballantine Books, a division of Random House, Inc., New York, and simultaneously in Canada by Random House of Canada Limited, Toronto.

Manufactured in the United States of America

ISSN: 0195-3540

ISBN: 0-876-37935-8

Cover design by Kristine Mills
Cover photo by George Kerrigan

Twenty-Ninth Edition: July 1996

10 9 8 7 6 5 4 3 2 1

CONTENTS

OFFICIAL BOARD OF CONTRIBUTORS

The author would like to express a special thank you to:

W.R. "Bill" Rindone, Bank Notes North West, PO Box 238, Lake Oswego, OR 97034, for his collaboration and Market Review,

Colonel Grover C. Criswell, Confederate Currency Expert, Criswell Publications, Salt Springs, FL 32134, for his pricing collaboration and photographs,

and **Dawn Haley and Larry Felix at the Department of the Treasury,** Bureau of Engraving and Printing, Washington, D.C., for the articles on the BEP.

PUBLISHER'S NOTE

The Official ® Blackbook Price Guide of United States Paper Money is designed as a reference aid for collectors, dealers, and the general public. Its purpose is to provide historical and collecting data, as well as current values. Prices are as accurate as possible at the time of going to press, but no guarantee is made. We are not dealers; persons wishing to buy or sell paper money, or have it appraised, are advised to consult collector magazines or the telephone directory for addresses of dealers. We are not responsible for typographical errors.

NOTE TO READERS

All advertisements appearing in this book have been accepted in good faith, but the publisher assumes no responsibility in any transactions that occur between readers and advertisers.

1997
BLACKBOOK
PRICE GUIDE OF
UNITED STATES
PAPER
MONEY

MARKET REVIEW
by W.R. "Bill" Rindone

"Unprecedented growth" would be the first two words that accurately describe the current paper money climate. As a snowball rolling downhill continues to collect momentum, so does the interest in U.S. currency.

Before looking at today's market, a reflection on the past would be in order. The greatest collection of U.S. currency ever assembled was known as the "Grinnell" collection, after its owner and long-time syngraphist Albert Grinnell. It was so large that it was sold at auction in four segments between 1944 and 1947, and contained an unprecedented variety of Large and Small Size Notes. Many of these notes were, and are, of great rarity. Last year we saw several of the better-known examples once again on the auction block. To say that they were well received would be to understate the truth, and if Barney Bluestone, who cataloged the original Grinnell auctions, had been on hand he would truly have been amazed at the interest displayed by today's collectors.

Auction prices showed a steady climb over the past several months and it is unlikely that they will slow in the future. Although the cost/value of notes continue to increase, there are still many areas which would have to be considered bargains. An example of that would be the 1915-18 Federal Reserve Bank Notes. Most of the issues are very limited, with only two to twenty examples of each recorded to date, and yet the price is remarkably low. We recently sold a Chicago $10 graded Fine for $300. Considering that only a dozen have been recorded, this is an example of a great rarity which is available at bargain prices. When I mention "bargain" prices, I use the term only in relationship to true rarity. If a U.S. coin with identical rarity came up at auction, I would expect the sale price to be in the high five figures, NOT in the low threes.

Although interest is at an all-time high, the collectible currency field should continue to expand for many years. The greatest source of problems now and in the future for dealers will be acquiring enough new material to satisfy those entering the hobby. Because this is a collector-based field, note prices have stayed reasonable and reflect the actual value of the items being sold. Unlike other fields where a collectible item may sell at XXX, its real liquid value may only be a small fraction of the price paid. Even then it may be dependent upon the number of these a dealer is carrying in stock. However, in rare currency, a note purchased by a collector at a retail price is usually highly liquid at close to the figure paid. With very few exceptions a dealer is seldom overstocked on any single item. In the rare instance where that occurs, it is very easy to pick up the phone and immediately move any excess material. Generally speaking, hoards of notes do not exist, and most buys are of one to three notes. Those of us fortunate enough to have been in the field for several years rely on our old customers to sell us material not commonly available. It is indeed a pleasure to purchase or repurchase any collection. Whether the collection is five or twenty years old the sellers normally realize substantial profits.

Collectible paper is today being pursued by a wide range of enthusiasts. History students find great interest in the circumstances under which some issues appeared. An example of that would be the 1869 (and later the 1880) $10 issue of legal tender. After the note's release it was discovered that the eagle on the front of the note had been cleverly designed and engraved. When inverted the eagle has the appearance of a jackass. At the time of authorization a wide chasm existed between the political parties, much as it does today, and this symbol represented the Democratic political party. Although a major stink was raised in Congress, the eagle was allowed to stand as first engraved. Collectors today still refer to this $10 Note as the "Jackass Note." We know that some recent hoards (twenty to fifty notes) were most probably part of bank holdups dating back to the time of Jesse James or, more recently, Bonnie and Clyde. The notes may have been hidden in case of capture or they may be nothing more than money that was set aside in a wall or attic for a rainy day. What happened to the original owner can only be conjecture, but it is safe to say that a story exists behind every note that passes through our hands.

Some hobbyists are enamored with the engravers art. Many of the early federal notes are indeed magnificent works of art. Few who have viewed the paintings on the reverse of the 1865 First Charter National Currency issue or the 1896 Educational series would argue that point. They, as do others, stand as the culmination of the engravers art at a time when they also represented the culture of a young nation to the older, well-established countries of Europe.

Other enthusiasts approach National Currency issues from a geographical interest. They attempt to acquire notes from all the state capitals or perhaps just the issuing banks of a particular state or county. Still others approach from various themes such as collecting only $2 Notes or one of each "type." We recently purchased a major collection whose theme was the matching of all the recent specimen issues reprinted by the Bureau of Engraving and Printing. For this purpose we required one each (front and back) of the original issues. Most of the notes were high grade and extremely rare. Pairs of crisp Uncirculated $100 1882 Brown Backs, 1905 Technicolor $20 Gold, $10 and $20 Treasury Notes, and other rarities abounded. Themes vary and may run from a signature collection of Treasurers/Registers to a collection as esoteric as notes with ships or those by a particular engraver or printer. Whatever the interest, it only serves to add spice to a great hobby.

Currently the following market conditions prevail:

Large Size Type Notes: (1861–1923 series). Better notes are scarce and all notes, regardless of grade, are collectible. Dealer stocks are very low and those of us who have good representation and variety owe it to collections we helped form several years ago. Auction houses find that even if a large collection surfaces it is quickly absorbed and many buyers go away empty-handed. It is not unusual to bid on thirty or forty lots and receive notice that none of the bids were successful. Over the past few years, the true rarity of high denominational ($100–$1,000) notes has come to light. Few records had been kept as to the rarity of these issues. With a central reporting system we now know that very few exist. Among the 1875/1880 Legal Tender, the census ranges from one to twenty examples, depending on the given signature combination, and this includes several that have been impounded in museums such as the Smithsonian. Another very scarce issue that is disappearing from the marketplace is the 1880 series Silver Certificates ($10–$100). Though never commonly available, very few are now offered. This area (Large Size Type) of collecting has the greatest pressure and demand of any issues. It will be interesting to look back in another ten years and remember when. . . .

Small Size Type Notes: (1928–present). Interest continues to build with the release of new designs by the Bureau of Engraving and Printing. This is the first major change to occur in Small Size Notes is the last sixty-eight years! Specialized material such as emergency (Hawaii/North African) issues or 1929 Federal Reserve Bank Notes find ready homes. The amount of material available in all series prior to 1963 has been found to be a great deal less than previously thought. As recently as three years ago it was thought that an unlimited supply of Legal Tender (red seal) or Silver Certificates (blue seal) existed. We now know that it just isn't true, and that today's collectors would be wise to quickly acquire any Small Size issues they might desire for the future.

Error Notes: This is a highly specialized field that seems to surge at times. Recent demand has been so high that price levels have substantially advanced. Anything out of the ordinary is rapidly salted away. Recently a pair of 1981 $1 Federal Reserve Notes bearing the same serial number were auctioned at $3,100. It would appear that each new price level scares off a high percentage of buyers. After a reasonable period of acclimatization, interest again peaks up and eventually soars to new levels.

Fractional Currency: Interest has been stable for about two years and advances are moderate. It is still an area where a "type set" can be put together for very little money. Rarer issues remain in high demand as there are quite a few collectors who are trying to complete sets.

Obsolete Notes: (1800–77) Obsolete Notes are so-called as most of the banks issuing them eventually went broke. They are also known as "Broken Bank" Notes. Nowhere else can such a profusion of colors, vignettes, and denominations be found. Because of the wide variety available, most collecting is done on a theme basis. Nowhere else in the realm of currency collecting can such historical items be purchased for so little. Notes are generally available in the $5–$20 range for circulated specimens and the $15–$35 range for Uncirculated examples. It is possible to collect notes of almost every denomination. Notes of 4¢, 6 1/4¢, 12 1/4¢, 90¢, $1.75, $2.50, $3, etc. are readily available. The market in this field is such that any unusual, rare, or pretty notes are avidly sought after.

MPC (Military Payment Certificates): These have a substantial following among collectors. They are, as a rule, very pretty and, with the exception of certain key issues, quite available and reasonably priced for today's collector. Issued between March 1947 and March 1973, they were used by armed services as currency in local areas at times of conflict. It is a very stable market at the present time.

Colonials: Colonials were issued principally by U.S. colonies between the early 1700s up to, and shortly after, American independence. Although they generally lack pretty vignettes or colors, they do represent some very strong historical episodes. Notes printed in Benjamin Franklin's printing or designed by Paul Revere are available. All were hand-signed and many of the signers were well-known people of that time period, such as signers of the Declaration of Independence and the U.S. Constitution. Others were with George Washington or later became senators or distinguished war heroes. Although a steady demand exists for these items, they are neither expensive nor scarce. Examples from common colonies generally run between $30 and $125, depending upon condition.

Related Fields: In recent years, there has been a growing interest in *Early Checks* (1802–1900). Many of them have beautiful vignettes or represent ghost towns, etc. *Financial Documents* are of great interest to currency collectors and such material finds a ready home. *Autographs of Famous People* is another up-and-coming field. Signatures of presidents and other historical people are avidly sought.

The entire spectrum of currency-related materials is extremely healthy. Will it stay that way? Past history says it will, and what better way to be involved in the history of a nation than with its money. Money still represents the affluence that attracts worldwide interest to this most prosperous of all nations.

INTRODUCTION OF THE 1996 SERIES CURRENCY

The following is reprinted with permission of the Department of the Treasury, Bureau of Printing and Engraving, Washington, D.C.

There will be no recall or devaluation of U.S. currency already in circulation. The United States always honors its currency at full face value, no matter how old.

The new $100 Notes, the first in the series, were released for circulation in early 1996. The new designs of lower denominations will be introduced later, one at a time, at intervals of approximately six to twelve months. As older notes reach the Federal Reserve from depository institutions, they will be replaced by the newer notes.

This multiyear introduction of the new currency is necessary because of the time-intensive processes involved in engraving and producing the new designs. Sufficient inventory will be produced to ensure worldwide availability of the new series.

The Bureau of Engraving and Printing has provided machine manufacturers with new notes so they can prepare vending machines, ATMs, and other cash-handling equipment. While machine manufacturers will have to make modifications to accommodate the new bills, they will have a broader field of machine-readable features from which to choose to authenticate currency.

In conjunction with the Federal Reserve, the Treasury Department will conduct a worldwide public education campaign with two primary objectives: communicate to the general public that there will be no recall or devaluation; and provide information about authenticating the new series to the public as well as central banks, depository financial institutions, other cash handlers, and law enforcement agencies.

THE NEW DESIGN

The new currency is the same size and color as the old notes, with the same historical figures and national symbols. "In God We Trust" and the "Legal Tender" wording also is the same on the new bills. This continuity will facilitate public education and universal recognition of the design as genuine U.S. currency—an important consideration since there will be dual circulation of the old and new currencies around the world.

- **A larger, slightly off-center portrait is the most noticeable visual change.** The larger portrait incorporates more detail, making it easier to recognize and more difficult to counterfeit. Moving the portrait away from the center, the area of highest wear, will reduce wear on the portrait.
- **Shifting the portrait off-center will provide room for a watermark, making it harder for counterfeiters to print.** The watermark depicts the same historical figure as the portrait.
- **Serial numbers on the new currency differ slightly from old currency.** The new serial numbers consist of two prefix letters, eight numerals, and a one-letter suffix. The first letter of the prefix designates the series (for example, Series 1996 will be designated by the letter A). The second letter of the prefix designates the Federal Reserve Bank to which the note was issued. In addition, a universal Federal Reserve seal is used, rather than individual seals for each Reserve Bank.
- **The use of a unique thread position for each denomination will guard against counterfeiting.**

Among the other counterfeit deterrent features are color shifting ink, microprinting, and concentric fine-line printing:

- *Color shifting ink* changes from green to black when viewed from different angles. This feature is used in the numeral in the lower right-hand corner.
- The numeral in the lower left-hand corner incorporates

microprinting, a printing technique using lettering that can be read with a low-powered magnifier. Extremely small print ("USA 100" on the $100 bill) appears as a thin line to the naked eye and yields a blurred image when copied. On the $100 bill, similar microprinting is also used on the lapel of Benjamin Franklin's coat.

- The background of the Franklin portrait on the $100 note incorporates the technique of *concentric fine-line printing*, as does the background of the picture of Independence Hall on the reverse side. This type of fine-line printing is difficult to properly resolve on scanning equipment and to accurately replicate by other means of printing.

Although all denominations of currency will have security features, the number of features vary according to denomination. The $100 Note has a full package of features, while the $1 Note will have fewer and less sophisticated features. The basic appearance of all denominations will not vary.

HISTORY OF THE REDESIGN

Until the late 1920s, U.S. currency was redesigned frequently. There also were several types of notes in circulation: United States Notes, National Bank Notes, and Silver Certificates. Since the introduction of the Series 1928 Federal Reserve Notes, changes in the design, including the use of microprinting and a security thread in Series 1990, have not affected the overall architecture of U.S. currency.

The counterfeit-deterrent features added in Series 1990 were the first step in responding to advances in reprographic technologies. Although these features have proven effective and will be retained, additional measures are necessary to protect against future threats posed by continued improvements in copy machines and scanners. The new design, beginning with Series 1996, is the culmination of a five-year study aimed at staying ahead of the counterfeiting threat and is part of a continuing process to protect U.S. currency.

Authority to change currency design and security features rests with the Secretary of the Treasury, but Congress has been informed throughout the redesign process. The New Currency Design Task Force, comprised of representatives from the U.S. Treasury Department, Federal Reserve System, U.S. Secret Service, and the Bureau of Engraving and Printing (BEP), made its recommendations to the Advanced Currency Deterrence Steering Committee which then made recommendations for the new design and security features to the Secretary of the Treasury. A National Academy of Science (NAS) Committee on Counterfeit Deterrence Features conducted complementary but separate studies.

More than 120 security features were examined and tested, including those submitted in response to a BEP solicitation, those used in other world currencies, and those suggested by the NAS. Evaluation criteria included impact on security, proven reliability, ability to be manufactured in large quantities, and durability over time. Among the features evaluated were holograms, color shifting films, thread variations, color patterns, and machine-readable enhancements.

PRE-EXISTING SECURITY FEATURES

SECURITY THREAD

A security thread is a thin thread or ribbon running through a Bank Note substrate. It is a versatile feature, with many types currently available, including microprinted, metallic, magnetic, windowed, and embedded. The thread will glow red when held under an ultraviolet light. This characteristic makes it impossible to copy with a color copier that uses reflected light to generate an image. Using a unique thread position for each denomination guards against certain counterfeit techniques, such as bleaching ink off a lower denomination and using the paper to "reprint" the bill as a higher value note. The unique position also can be used by currency-accepting equipment to determine the value of the note, especially if the threads are machine-detectable. This security feature, which first appeared in

Series 1990 currency, is included in the new design; however, its position will shift according to the currency denomination for the reasons mentioned previously.

MICROPRINTING

This print appears as a thin line to the naked eye, but the lettering can easily be read using a low-power magnifier. The resolution of most current copiers is not sufficient to copy such fine print. On the newly designed $100 bills, microprinting appears in the lower left corner and on Benjamin Franklin's lapel.

Serial Numbers: The serial number is a combination of eleven numbers and letters on the front of the note in the upper left and lower right. An additional letter has been added so that no two bank notes of the same denomination have the same 11-character serial number.

Federal Reserve Seal: Instead of designating the Federal Reserve district from which a note was issued, the new universal seal now represents the entire Federal Reserve System. A letter and number near the serial number identify the issuing Federal Reserve Bank.

Concentric Fine-Line Printing: This series of fine lines is very difficult to reproduce with color copiers, computer scanners and other traditional printing technologies. It is used on both sides, for the background behind both Benjamin Franklin's portrait on the front and Independence Hall on the reverse.

The use of color reproductions was authorized by the Secretary of the Treasury. Color reprints are prohibited.

Microprinting: Because they're so small, microprinted words are extremely hard to replicate without blurring. Originally located around the portrait of 1990 Series Notes, microprinting has been modified for the new design. Examples of microprinting, which can be read under magnification, now can be found in two places on the front. "USA 100" is microprinted within the number in the lower left hand corner, while "United States of America" appears on Benjamin Franklin's lapel.

Portrait: Since most people focus on the portrait to verify a note's authenticity, the enlargement of the portrait of Benjamin Franklin makes it easier to recognize, while the added detail in the design makes it harder to duplicate. The portrait is now off-center, providing room for the watermark and security thread. Also, this modification reduces the wear and tear on the portrait caused by folding bank notes in half.

Watermark: A watermark has been added on the right front side of the note depicting the same historical figure as the portrait. This watermark portrait is only visible when held up to a light source and does not reproduce on color copiers or computer scanners.

Color Shifting Ink: Color shifting ink changes color when viewed from different angles. This ink is used to print the number in the lower right-hand corner on the front of the currency. The ink looks green when viewed straight on, but changes to black when the paper is held at an angle.

Security Thread: This polymer thread is embedded vertically in the paper and indicates each bill's denomination. The words on the thread can be seen only when held up to a bright light but cannot be duplicated by photocopiers or computer scanners. In the 1990 Series Notes, the security thread appeared only on the left side of a bank note. Now, to improve authentication, the thread is in a unique position in each denomination in which it is used. As an additional enhancement to currency authentication, the new security thread will glow red when held under an ultraviolet light.

NEW FEATURES

TO DETER COUNTERFEITING WITH ADVANCED COPIERS, SCANNERS, AND PRINTERS.

SECURITY THREAD

Embedded polyester strip with repeated USA 50 or USA 100 in an up-and-down pattern. Visible when held to light. Cannot be reproduced in reflected light of copiers. In new Series 1990 $50 and $100 notes.

MICROPRINTING

"The United States of America" printed repeatedly on sides of portrait. Letters too small to read without a magnifier or for distinct copier reproduction. In new Series 1990 $50 and $100 notes.

FEDERAL RESERVE SEAL

Issuing Federal Reserve Bank. Code letter same as first letter in two serial numbers.

PORTRAIT

Lifelike portrait distinct from fine, screenlike background.

PAPER

Cotton and linen rag paper has strong, pliable "feel." No watermarks.

SERIAL NUMBERS

Two serial numbers distinctively styled and evenly spaced. Ink color same as Treasury seal. No two notes of *same series* and denomination have same serial number.

BORDER

Border's fine lines and lacy, web-like design distinct and unbroken.

FIBERS

Tiny red and blue fibers embedded in paper.

TREASURY SEAL

Sawtooth points sharp, distinct, and unbroken. Seal's color same as two serial numbers.

ENGRAVED PRINTING

Engraved plate printing gives new note embossed "feel."

DENOMINATION

Note's value on corners same as over Treasury seal.

THE HISTORY OF
U.S. PAPER MONEY

Reprinted with permission of the Department of the Treasury, Bureau of Printing and Engraving, Washington, D.C.

In the early days of the nation, before and just after the Revolution, Americans used English, Spanish, and French money.

1690 Colonial Notes. The Massachusetts Bay Colony issued the first paper money in the colonies which would later form the United States.

1775 Continental Currency. American colonists issued paper currency for the Continental Congress to finance the Revolutionary War. The notes were backed by the "anticipation" of tax revenues. Without solid backing and easily counterfeited, the notes quickly became devalued, giving rise to the phrase "not worth a Continental."

1781 Nation's First Bank. Also to support the Revolutionary War, the Continental Congress chartered the Bank of North America in Philadelphia as the nation's first "real" bank.

1785 The Dollar. The Continental Congress determined that the official monetary system would be based on the dollar, but the first coin representing the start of this system would not be struck for many years.

1791 First U.S. Bank. After adoption of the Constitution in 1789, Congress chartered the First Bank of the United States until 1811 and authorized it to issue paper bank notes to eliminate confusion and simplify trade. The bank served as the U.S. Treasury's fiscal agent, thus performing the first central bank functions.

1792 Monetary System. The federal monetary system was established with the creation of the U.S. Mint in Philadelphia. The first American coins were struck in 1793.

1816 Second U.S. Bank. The Second Bank of the United States was chartered for twenty years until 1836.

1836 State Bank Notes. With minimum regulation, a proliferation of 1,600 local state-chartered, private banks now issued paper money. State bank notes, with over 30,000 varieties of color and design, were easily counterfeited. That, along with bank failures, caused confusion and circulation problems.

1861 Civil War. On the brink of bankruptcy and pressed to finance the Civil War, Congress authorized the U.S. Treasury to issue paper money for the first time in the form of noninterest bearing Treasury Notes called Demand Notes.

1862 Greenbacks. Demand Notes were replaced by United States Notes. Commonly called "Greenbacks," they were last issued in 1971. The Secretary of the Treasury was empowered by Congress to have notes engraved and printed, which was done by private banknote companies.

1863 The Design. The design of U.S. currency incorporated a Treasury seal, the fine line engraving necessary for the difficult-to-counterfeit intaglio printing, intricate geometric lathe work patterns, and distinctive linen paper with embedded red and blue fibers.

1865 Gold Certificates. Gold Certificates were issued by the Department of the Treasury against gold coin and bullion deposits and were circulated until 1933.

1865 Secret Service. The Department of the Treasury established the United States Secret Service to control counterfeits, at that time amounting to one-third of circulated currency.

1866 National Bank Notes. National Bank Notes, backed by U.S. government securities, became predominant. By this time, 75 percent of bank deposits were held by nationally chartered banks. As State Bank Notes were replaced, the value of currency stabilized for a time.

1877 Bureau of Engraving and Printing. The Department of the Treasury's Bureau of Engraving and Printing started printing all U.S. currency, although other steps were done outside.

1878 Silver Certificates. The Department of the Treasury was authorized to issue Silver Certificates in exchange for silver dollars. The last issue was in the Series of 1957.

1910 Currency Production Consolidated. The Department of the Treasury's Bureau of Engraving and Printing assumed all currency production functions, including engraving, printing, and processing.

1913 Federal Reserve Act. After 1893 and 1907 financial panics, the Federal Reserve Act of 1913 was passed. It created the Federal Reserve System as the nation's central bank to regulate the flow of money and credit for economic stability and growth. The system was authorized to issue Federal Reserve Notes, now the only U.S. currency produced and 99 percent of all currency in circulation.

1929 Standardized Design. Currency was reduced in size by 25 percent and standardized with uniform portraits on the faces and emblems and monuments on the backs.

1957 In God We Trust. Paper currency was first issued with "In God We Trust" as required by Congress in 1955. The inscription appears on all currency Series 1963 and beyond.

1990 Security Thread and Microprinting. A security thread and microprinting were introduced, first in $50 and $100 Notes, to deter counterfeiting by advanced copiers and printers.

1994 Currency Redesign. The Secretary of the Treasury announced that U.S. currency would be redesigned to incorporate a new series of counterfeit deterrents. The new notes were issued in 1996.

COLLECTING PAPER MONEY

Paper money can be a fascinating hobby. Though of more recent origin than coinage, U.S. paper money exists in enormous varieties and can be collected in many ways.

Potential specialties are numerous. The following is not by any means a complete list.

1. Series collecting. Here the collector focuses upon a certain series of notes, such as the $5 1863–75 National Bank Notes, and attempts to collect specimens showing each of the different signature combinations, points of issue, seal colors, or whatever varieties happen to exist in the series. This may sound restrictive but, as an examination of the listings in this book will show, most series are comprised of many varieties. Generally, the older the series, the more difficult or expensive will be its completion, while certain series include great rarities beyond the budget range of most collectors. The cost can be brought down somewhat if one does not demand the finest condition but is content to own an example of the note in whatever condition he can reasonably afford. It should be pointed out, though, that in reselling paper money there is generally a greater loss—or smaller profit—on notes whose condition is less than Very Fine.

2. Set collecting. Sets are groups of notes of different denominations, issued at the same time (or approximately the same time), which were in current circulation together.

3. Place or origin collecting. Collecting notes by the city whose Federal Reserve Bank issued them.

4. Signature collecting. Collecting one specimen of every note bearing the signature of a certain Secretary of the Treasury.

5. Confederate currency collecting. The notes issued for use within the Confederate States of America during the Civil War.

6. Portrait collecting. By the individual or individuals depicted on the note. This is sometimes known as topical collecting.

7. Freak and oddity collecting.

8. Fractional currency collecting.

Imagination, especially if placed into use in a coin shop well stocked with paper money, will suggest further possibilities. All is fair; there are no strict rules on what makes a worthwhile collection, so long as the material included is not seriously defective or of questionable authenticity.

Don't expect to build a large collection rapidly. Paper money is not comparable to stamps, where a beginner can buy a packet of 1,000 different stamps and instantly have a sizable collection. Nor should the size of a collection be regarded as a mark of its desirability or worth. Many prizewinning collections contain fewer than a hundred pieces; some consist of only two or three dozen. Direction and quality count much more in this hobby than weight of numbers. Collectors seeking to own a large collection generally end up with one whose only recommendation is its size. It may impress beginners but is not likely to be regarded highly by more experienced collectors.

PUBLICATIONS

Get a global perspective on paper money collecting from *The Bank Note Reporter*. This monthly tabloid is devoted entirely to U.S. and world paper money, notes, checks, and all related fiscal paper. Find current prices for national and international bank notes, plus an active buy/sell marketplace. *12 monthly issues are $29.95.*

The *Numismatic News* delivers weekly news and information on coin and paper money collecting with exclusive reports from the hobby's only full-time Washington Bureau. Accurate retail/wholesale value guide, current events, and up-to-date calendar make this the most comprehensive numismatic forum available. *52 weekly issues are $29.95.*

The *Standard Catalog of World Paper Money*, 1st Edition, Volume 3, Modern Issues, keeps pace with changing world politics while charting world paper money from 1960 to date. Focus your collection on this active period with up-to-date market valuations. *600 pages and 5,000 photographs for $29.95.*

The *Standard Catalog of World Paper Money*, 7th Edition, Volume 1, Specialized Issues, focuses on 250 years of specialized world paper money issues from over 370 note issuing authorities. More than 17,000 notes are cataloged and priced to cover your interests. *1056 pages and 8,000 photographs for $60.00.*

The *Standard Catalog of World Paper Money*, 7th Edition, Volume 2, General Issues, enhances the series' reputation. Get the reference for nationally circulated Legal Tender since 1700. 22,000+ notes, including emerging nations currency. *1,200 pages and 10,000 photographs for $55.00.*

For more information, please contact:

Krause Publications
700 East State Street
Iola, WI 54990
Phone 715-445-2214, Subscription Services 715-445-3775,
ext. 257

COLLECTING ORGANIZATIONS

PROFESSIONAL CURRENCY DEALERS
ASSOCIATION (PCDA)

Looking for a reliable paper money dealer? . . . Collecting rare paper money can be an enjoyable hobby. Imagine being able to own an example of fractional currency printed during the Civil War era, or a National Bank Note issued by a financial institution in your own state.

Whatever your collecting interests, the members of the Professional Currency Dealers Association (PCDA) will be pleased to assist and guide you. The members of this prestigious trade association specialize in virtually all the areas of paper money collecting.

Once you've started to collect, it can sometimes be a challenge to locate a dealer with a significant inventory. Members of the PCDA are the market makers for currency collectors. Whatever your interest, a PCDA member is certain to be able to supply you. Whether you are a beginner on a limited budget or an advanced collector of many years' experience, you can be certain that you'll find fair, courteous, and reliable treatment with a member of the Professional Currency Dealers Association.

For a free copy of the PCDA membership directory, write to:

Professional Currency Dealers Association
PO Box 573
Milwaukee, WI 53201

Your personal copy of the PCDA directory, listing members by their specialty areas, will be sent to you promptly via first class mail.

THE SOCIETY OF PAPER MONEY COLLECTORS (SPMC)

The Society of Paper Money Collectors (SPMC) invites you to become a member of our organization. SPMC was founded in 1961 with the following objectives: encourage the collecting and study of paper money and all financial documents; cultivate fraternal collector relations; furnish information and knowledge; encourage research about paper money and financial documents and publish the resulting information; promote legislation favorable to collectors; advance the prestige of the hobby of numismatics; promote rational classification of exhibits and encourage participation by our members; encourage realistic and consistent market valuations.

The bimonthly magazine *Paper Money* is issued to all members. For a sample copy and membership information, write to:

Ron Horstman
PO Box 6011
St. Louis, MO 63139

RECOGNIZING THE
VALUABLE NOTES

Every note ever issued by the U.S. government is worth, at minimum, its face value. This applies even to notes of which one-third is missing. Whether a note is worth *more* than its face value—to collectors and dealers in paper currency—depends chiefly upon its age, condition, scarcity, and popularity among hobbyists.

All obsolete notes (such as Silver Certificates) are worth more than face value when the condition is Crisp Uncirculated (or CU as it is called by collectors). Many notes, hundreds in fact, have premium value even in lower grades of condition due to their scarcity. The premium on a collectible note may be double or triple face value or more. There are early $1 Notes worth more than one thousand times face value. While 19th century notes tend to be more valuable, as fewer were printed and saved, notes of considerable value did occur among those of the 20th century.

A note may be valuable as the result of belonging to a series in which all had limited printings, such as the historic 1862 United States Note. This type of valuable note is, of course, the easiest for a beginner to recognize, as the notes look very different compared to those of the present day.

Conveniently, notes have dates on them, and an early date is yet another indicator of possible value. But even without dates and size differences there would be little difficulty in distinguishing an early note. The earlier the note, the more it will differ in design, color, and other details from later currency. It may picture an individual no longer shown on notes, such as Robert Fulton, Samuel Morse, or James Garfield. It may have the portrait on the back instead of the front. The portrait may be to one side rather than centered. The serial numbers may not be where they are normally found. Such notes are instantly recognizable as being very old. They, in fact, look so unlike moderncurrency that some noncollectors take them for stock or bonds or something other than legal tender.

A noncollector often believes that the value of old paper money is linked to its serial numbers. While a serial number can contribute to value, it is well down the list of ingredients for valuable notes. Among specimens of very high value, the serial number is hardly ever of consequence.

What is? Quite often the signatures. The signatures on a note play a very considerable role in the collector's world. If notes did not carry signatures, or if the signatures were never changed, the paper money hobby would be a mere shadow of what it is today. To cite just one example, the 1902 series of $10 National Bank Notes without dates yielded fifteen different varieties for the hobbyist to collect. Every one of them is a signature variety! Take away the signatures and all would be identical. Nothing changed but the signatures, yet they changed fifteen times. A rarity was created, too: the Jones-Woods combination is worth about three times as much as any of the other fourteen. If you did not look at the signatures and were unaware of the rarity of this particular combination, you would surely fail to pick this note out of a batch of 1902 $10 National Bank Notes. There is absolutely nothing remarkable by which to notice it.

There are many other notes on which the signatures are vitally important. The 1875 Bruce-Jordan combination on the $5 National Bank Note is so rare that pricing it is difficult. The other eight signature combinations from this series, while definitely of value, are not in that class.

The color of the seal, which has varied on notes in the 19th and 20th centuries, is seldom a major factor in value. In most cases where it appears to be a factor, some other element is, in fact, responsible for the note's value. An example of this is the $2 United States Note of 1878 with red seal and signatures of Scofield and Gilfillan. It is quite a bit more valuable than any $2 United States Note with a brown seal, leading many people to think that the seal color is a factor in its value. The rarity of this note derives from the signature combination. Another was issued with the same date and same red seal, but with signatures of Allison and Gilfillan. Its value is less than one-tenth as much.

However, there are a few cases in which the seal color makes a great difference in value, so it should not be totally dismissed. The $1 United States Note of 1878 with a maroon seal is valuable, while the same note with a red seal—identical in all other respects—is worth sharply less.

The date appearing on a note can be a value factor, not just by indicating the note's age. There may be two or more variations of the note that are distinguished by the date. In the case of Federal Reserve Notes (the only notes still being printed), the district of origin can influence their value. In some series there were not as many printed for Kansas City or Dallas as for New York or Chicago, and the scarcer ones have gained an edge in collector appeal and value. This applies to an even greater extent among National Bank Notes, which involved literally thousands of local banks across the country.

It's safe to say that paper money should be carefully examined. When examined by a person who knows what he's looking for, there is little chance of a rarity slipping by undetected.

BUYING PAPER MONEY

Browsing in coin shops is the usual way in which beginners start buying paper money. Just about every coin dealer—and many stamp dealers—stock paper money to one degree or another, from a single display album with elementary material to vaults filled with literally millions of dollars worth of specimens. Be observant of condition when shopping from dealers' stocks. There is really no excuse for unsatisfactory purchases from shops—the buyer has ample opportunity for inspection. Don't buy in a rush. Get to know the dealer and become familiar with his grading practices. Some dealers will grade a specimen higher than another dealer, but this may be offset by the fact that they charge a lower price.

Bargains. Is it possible to get bargains in buying paper money? To the extent that prices vary somewhat from dealer to dealer, yes. But if you're talking about finding a note worth $100 selling at $50, this is unlikely to happen. The dealers are well aware of market values, and the slight price differences that do occur are merely the result of some dealers being overstocked on certain notes or, possibly, having made a very good "buy" from the public. What may appear to be a bargain will generally prove, on closer examination, to be a specimen in undesirable condition, such as a washed bill on which the color has faded.

Auction sales. Many coin auctions feature selections of paper money, and there are occasional sales (mostly of the postal-bid variety) devoted exclusively to it. There is much to be said for auction buying if you have some experience and know how to read an auction catalog.

Shows and conventions. Paper money is offered for sale at every coin show and exposition. These present excellent opportunities to buy, as the dealers exhibiting at such shows are generally out-of-towners whose stock you would not otherwise have a chance to examine. As many sellers are likely to be offering the same type of material, you have the opportunity to make price and condition comparisons before buying.

CARING FOR YOUR COLLECTION

Paper money is not at all difficult to care for, store and display attractively. It consumes little space and, unlike many other collectors' items, runs no risk of breakage. Nevertheless, it is important that the hobbyist give some attention to maintenance, as a poorly kept collection soon becomes aimless clutter and provides little enjoyment.

There is not much question that albums are the favorite storage method of nearly all paper money enthusiasts. In the days before specially made albums with vinyl pocket-pages, collectors used ordinary scrapbooks and mounted their specimens with philatelic hinges or photo corners. This, of course, may still be done, but such collections do not have the advantage of displaying both sides of the notes. Furthermore, the use of gummed hinges may leave marks upon removal, whereas specimens may be removed and reinserted into vinyl-page albums without causing the slightest blemish. We especially recommend the albums and "currency wallet" sold by Anco Coin & Stamp Supply, PO Box 782, Florence, AL 35630.

Faded color. There is no known restorative for faded color.

Holes. It is suggested that no effort be undertaken to repair holes, as this will almost certainly result in a further reduction in value.

Missing corners. Missing corners can seldom be restored in a manner that is totally satisfactory. The best that can be done is to secure some paper of approximately the same color and texture, trim a small piece to the proper size, and glue it in place as described below. If a portion of printed matter is missing, this can be hand-drawn, in ink, after restoration. Obviously, this kind of repair is not carried out to "fool" anybody, but simply to give a damaged specimen a less objectionable appearance.

Repairs to paper money. Repair work on damaged or defaced paper money is carried out strictly for cosmetic purposes; to improve its physical appearance. Repairs, even if skillfully executed, will not enhance the value of a specimen, as it will still be classified as defective. Amateurish repair efforts can very possibly make matters worse.

Tears. Tears can be closed by brushing a very small quantity of clear-drying glue to both sides of the tear, placing the note between sheets of waxed kitchen paper, and setting it under a weight to dry. A dictionary of moderate size serves this function well. Allow plenty of drying time and handle gently thereafter.

Wrinkles. Wrinkles, creases, and the like can sometimes be improved by wetting the note (in plain water) and drying it between sheets of waxed paper beneath a reasonably heavy weight—five pounds or more. This should not be done with a modern or recent specimen if there is danger of losing crispness.

Many ills to which paper money falls prey result from not being housed in a suitable album, or any album at all. Framing and mounting present some risk, as the item may then be exposed to long periods of direct sunlight, almost sure to cause fading or "bleaching" of its color.

SELLING YOUR COLLECTION

Selling to a dealer. All dealers in paper money buy from the public, but not all buy every collection offered to them. Some are specialists and are interested only in collections within their fields of specialization. Some will not purchase (or even examine) collections worth under $100, or $500, or whatever their line of demarcation happens to be. Obviously, a valuable collection containing many hard-to-get notes in VF or UNC condition is easier to interest a dealer in than a beginner-type collection. If a dealer is interested enough to make an offer, this is no guarantee that another dealer would not offer more. In the case of a collection worth $50,000, offers from several dealers might vary by as much as $5,000. This is not an indication that the dealer making the lowest offer is unscrupulous. Dealers will pay as much as the material is worth to them, and one dealer may be overstocked on items that another badly needs. Or one dealer may have customers for certain material that another doesn't. For this reason it makes good sense, if you choose to sell to a dealer, to obtain several offers before accepting any. But should you sell to a dealer at all? The chief advantage is quick payment and reduced risk. The price may not be as high as would be obtained at auction, however, depending on the property's nature and pure luck.

Selling by auction. Auction selling presents uncertainties but at the same time offers the possibility of gaining a much better return than could be had by selling to a dealer. It is no easy matter deciding which route to follow. If your collection is better than average, you may be better advised to sell by auction. This will involve a waiting period of, generally, four to six months between consigning the collection and receiving settlement; over the summer months it may be longer. However, some auctioneers will give a cash advance, usually about 25 percent of the sum they believe the material is worth. In special circumstances a larger advance may be made, or the usual terms and conditions altered. One auctioneer paid $100,000 under a special contract, stipulating that the money was not to be returned regardless of the sale's outcome or even if no sale took place. But this was on a million-dollar collection. Auctioneers' commissions vary. The normal is 20 percent, but some houses take 10 percent from the buyer and 10 percent from the seller. This would appear to work to the seller's advantage, but such a practice may discourage bidding and result in lower sales prices.

Selling to other collectors. Unless the owner is personally acquainted with a large circle of collectors, this will likely involve running ads in periodicals and "playing dealer," which runs into some expense. Unless you offer material at very favorable prices, you are not apt to be as successful with your ads as are the established dealers, who have a reputation and an established clientele.

INVESTING

1. Buy only specimens in V.F. (Very Fine) or better condition.

2. Be sure the notes you buy are properly graded and priced in accordance with their grade.

3. Avoid Federal Reserve Notes of the past thirty years. These have been stockpiled by dealers to such an extent that their value is not likely to show dramatic increase.

4. For investment purposes it is usually wise to avoid the very highly specialized types of notes. Investment success depends on continued growth of the hobby, and most new collectors will buy the standard items.

5. Do not seek quick profits. It is rare for an investment profit on paper currency to occur in less than five years. When holding five years or longer, the possibility of a profit is much greater.

6. Notes recommended by their sellers as investments are sometimes the worst investments. Learn about the paper money market and make your own selections.

7. Do not invest more than you can afford. Tying up too much capital in investments of any kind can be hazardous.

GLOSSARY

BROKEN BANK NOTE (a.k.a. obsolete note)

Literally, a Broken Bank Note is a note issued by a "broken" bank—a bank that failed and whose obligations could therefore not be redeemed. It may be presumed, by those who recall passing of legislation establishing the Federal Deposit Insurance Corporation, that banks failed only in the financial panic of 1929. During the 19th century, bank failures were common, especially in western and southwestern states. These were generally small organizations set up in frontier towns which suffered either from mismanagement or a sudden decline in the town's fortunes. Some collectors make a specialty of Broken Bank Notes.

DEMAND NOTES

Demand Notes have the distinction of being the first official circulating paper currency of this country, issued in 1861. There are three denominations: $5, $10, and $20, each bearing its own design on front and back. Demand Notes arose out of the coinage shortage brought about by the Civil War. A total of $60,000,000 in Demand Notes was authorized to be printed, amounting to several million individual specimens. Though this was an extraordinary number for the time, it was small compared to modern output, and only a fraction of the total survived. These notes were signed not by any specially designated Treasury Department officers, but a battery of employees, each of whom was given authority to sign and affix his name by hand in a slow assembly-line process, two signatures to each note. Originally the spaces left blank for signatures were marked "Register of the Treasury" and "Treasurer of the United States." As the persons actually signing occupied neither of these offices, they were obliged to perpetually add "for the . . ." to their signatures. In an effort to relieve their tedium, fresh plates were prepared reading "For the Register of the Treasury" and "For the Treasurer of the United States," which required nothing but a signature. This created a rarity status for the earlier specimens, which are now very desirable collectors' items.

ENGRAVING

Engraving is the process by which designs are printed on U.S. paper money. Engraving involves the use of a metal plate, traditionally copper, into which the design is drawn or scraped with sharp-bladed instruments. Ink is smeared over the surface and allowed to work into the grooves or lines comprising the design. The ink is then cleaned away from raised portions (intended to show blank in the printing). The engraving is pressed against a sheet of moistened paper, and the ink left in these grooves transfers to the paper, resulting in a printed image. When done by modern rotary press, it's a fast-moving process.

FEDERAL RESERVE BANK NOTES

Federal Reserve Bank Notes were issued briefly in 1915 and 1918. Like National Bank Notes they were secured by bonds or securities placed on deposit by each Federal Reserve Bank with the U.S. government. While issued and redeemable by the member banks of the Federal Reserve system, these notes are secured by—and are obligations of—the government.

FEDERAL RESERVE NOTES

Federal Reserve Notes, the notes in current circulation, were authorized by the Federal Reserve Act of December 23, 1913. Issued under control of the Federal Reserve Board, these notes are released through twelve Federal Reserve Banks in various parts of the country. Originally they were redeemable in gold at the U.S. Treasury or "lawful money" (coins) at a Federal Reserve Bank. In 1934 the option of redemption for gold was removed.

FREAK AND ERROR NOTES

These are bills which, by virtue of error or accident, are in some respect different from normal specimens. See the chapter on Error or Freak Notes.

GOLD CERTIFICATES

When gold coinage became a significant medium of exchange, the government decided to hold aside quantities of it and issue paper notes redeemable by the Treasury Department. The first Gold Certificates for public circulation were released in 1882. The series lasted until the era of small-size currency, ending in 1928. In 1933 all were ordered returned to the Treasury Department for redemption, including those in possession of collectors. A new law in 1964 permitted their ownership by collectors, though they can no longer be redeemed for gold.

LARGE SIZE CURRENCY

Large Size currency is the term generally used to refer to U.S. notes issued up to 1929, which were somewhat larger in size than those printed subsequently. The increased size permitted more elaborate design, which seldom fails to endear Large Size currency to beginners. Some of the earlier examples (especially of the 1870s, 1880s, and 1890s) are works of art. Though economic considerations were mainly responsible for the switch to a reduced size, there is no doubt that today's notes are far more convenient to handle and carry. Large Size notes are sometimes referred to as "bedsheet notes."

NATIONAL BANK NOTES

This is the largest group of notes available to the collector. They were issued from 1863 to 1929 and present collecting potential that can only be termed vast. More than 14,000 banks issued notes, in all parts of the country. While the approach to collecting them is usually regional, sets and series can also be built up, virtually without end. The National Banking Act was instituted in 1863, during the Civil War, to permit chartered banks to issue and circulate their own currency. Printing was done at the U.S. Government Printing Office and the designs were all alike, differing only in names of the banks, state seals, bank signatures, and the bank's charter number. Each charter bank was limited to issuing currency up to 90 percent of the value of bonds that it kept on deposit with the government. Charters remained in force for twenty years and could be renewed for an additional twenty years. National Bank Notes circulated in the same fashion as conventional currency and, thanks to the bond-deposit system, gained public confidence. The financial panic of 1929, which brought ruin or near-ruin to many banks, put an end to National Bank Notes.

NATIONAL GOLD BANK NOTES

These notes were issued exclusively by California banks during the 1870s under the same terms as ordinary National Bank Notes, their values backed by bonds deposited with the government. Events surrounding their origins form a unique chapter in the history of American economy. Following the discoveries of substantial quantities of gold in California in the late 1840s, that metal soon became the chief medium of local exchange, largely because it was more readily available in that remote region than coinage. Later, when gold coins and tokens began to circulate heavily in California, banks became so swamped with them that they petitioned Washington for authority to issue Gold Notes that could be substituted for the actual coinage. On July 12, 1870, Congress voted favorably on this measure, giving the right to issue such notes to nine banks in California and one in Boston. The Boston bank, Kidder National Gold Bank, appears not to have exercised its right, as no Gold Notes of this institution have been recorded. The California banks wasted no time in exercising their authority, the result being a series of notes ranging from $5–$500. All were printed on yellow-toned paper so as to be instantly identifiable. The banks issuing these notes were permitted to redeem them in gold coins.

REFUNDING CERTIFICATES

Refunding Certificates, a sort of hybrid between currency and bonds or securities, were issued under a Congressional Act of February 26, 1879. These were notes with a $10 face value which could be spent and exchanged in the fashion of ordinary money but drew interest at the rate of 4 percent per year. The purposes behind Refunding Certificates were several. They were chiefly designed to encourage saving and thereby curb inflation, which even at that time was becoming a problem. Also, they provided a safe means of saving for persons who distrusted banks (safe so long as the certificates were not lost or stolen), and, probably more important, were readily obtainable in areas of the country not well served by banks. In 1907 the interest was halted. Their redemption value today, with interest, is $21.30.

SERIAL NUMBER

The serial number is the control number placed on all U.S. paper bills, appearing below left-center and above right-center. No two bills in the same series bear repetitive serial numbers. The use of serial numbers is not only an aid in counting and sorting bills as printed, but a deterrent to counterfeiting.

SIGNATURES

The inclusion of signatures of Treasury Department officials on our paper bills, a practice as old as our currency (1861), began as a mark of authorization and as a foil to counterfeiters. The belief was that the handwriting would be more difficult to copy than an engraved design. Persons whose signatures appear on notes did not always occupy the same office. From 1862 to 1923, the two signers were the Treasurer and the Register (or Registrar as it appears in old writings) of the Treasury. Subsequently, the Treasurer and the Secretary of the Treasury were represented. These signatures are of great importance to collectors, as some notes are relatively common with certain combinations of signatures and others are rare. A "series" collection is not considered complete until one obtains every existing combination, even though the specimens may be in other respects identical.

SILVER CERTIFICATES

Silver Certificates were authorized in 1878. America's economy was booming at that time, and the demand for silver coinage in day-to-day business transactions outdistanced the supply. Silver Certificates were not intended to replace coinage but to create a convenient medium of exchange, whereby the government held specific quantities of Silver Dollars (later bullion) and agreed to redeem the notes or certificates against them. In 1934 the Treasury Department ceased redemption of these notes in Silver Dollars, and on June 24, 1968, redemption in all forms was ended. The notes are still, however, legal tender at their face value. When printing of Silver Certificates was discontinued, a flurry of speculation arose and many persons began hoarding them. This was done not only in hope of eventual redemption for bullion but in the belief that such notes would become valuable to collectors. Though Silver Certificates are popular with hobbyists, they have not increased sufficiently in price to yield speculators any great profits—especially since many collectors saved specimens in circulated condition.

STAR NOTES

United States Notes, Silver Certificates, and Gold Certificates sometimes have a star or asterisk in place of the letter in front of the serial number. Federal Reserve Notes and Federal Reserve Bank Notes have it at the end of the serial number. These notes are known as "Star Notes."

When a note is mutilated or otherwise unfit for issue, it must be replaced. To replace it with a note of the same serial numbers would be impractical, and Star Notes are therefore substituted. Other than having their own special serial number and a star, these notes are the same as the others. On United States Notes and Silver Certificates, the star is substituted for the prefix letter; on Federal Reserve Notes, for the suffix letter. All defective notes are accounted for and destroyed by burning them in an incinerator.

Large stars after the serial number on the 1869 Series of United States Notes, and 1890 and 1891 Treasury Notes, do not signify replacement notes as are known in later and present-day Star Notes.

Serial numbers on early Large Size Notes were preceded by a letter and were ended by various odd characters or symbols. These characters are not known to have any significance, except to show that the number was terminated, and prevented any elimination or addition of digits. The suffix characters were replaced by alphabet letters on later issues of notes.

TREASURY OR COIN NOTES

Treasury Notes were authorized by Congress in 1890. Their official title was Coin Notes, as they could be redeemed for silver or gold coins. The series did not prove popular and was discontinued after the issue of 1891.

TREASURY SEAL

The Treasury Seal is the official emblem of the U.S. Treasury Department, which has appeared on all our currency since 1862. It is missing only from the early Demand Notes, issued in 1861, and some Fractional Currency. Two versions have been employed, distinguished readily by the fact that one (the original) bears a Latin inscription, while the current Treasury Seal is in English. The basic motif is the same, a badge displaying scales and a key. The original Seal, somewhat more decorative, was in use until 1968.

UNITED STATES NOTES

Also known as Legal Tender Notes, this substantial and ambitious series followed Demand Notes and constitutes the second earliest variety of U.S. paper currency. There are five distinct issues, running from 1862 to 1923. Though United States Notes are all "Large Size" and their designs not very similar to those in present use, they show in their successive stages the evolutionary advance from this nation's first efforts at paper money to its currency of today. The first issue is dated March 10, 1862. Denominations are $1, $2, $5, $10, $20, $50, $100, $500, $1,000, $5,000 and $10,000. Individuals portrayed included not only presidents but other government officials: Salmon P. Chase (Lincoln's Secretary of the Treasury), Daniel Webster, and Lewis and Clark. Some of the reverse designs are masterpieces of geometrical linework. A number of rarities are to be found among Legal Tender Notes, but in general the lower denominations can be collected without great expense.

WILDCAT NOTES

Wildcat Notes are the notes that were issued by so-called "wildcat banks" in the era of State Bank Notes before the Civil War. Numerous banks sprang up around the middle part of the 19th century, mostly in the west and southwest, operated by persons of questionable integrity. Some never had capital backing and were instituted purely as a front for confidence swindles. After issuing notes, the bank shut down, its directors disappeared, and owners of the notes were left with worthless paper. As news traveled slowly in those days, the same persons could move from town to town and work the scheme repeatedly. Notes issued by these banks, or any banks that became insolvent, are also called Broken Bank Notes. Apparently the origin of the term "wildcat" derives from public sentiment of the time, which held that owners of such banks had no greater trustworthiness than a wild animal. "Wildcat" may also refer to the rapid movement of swindling bank officials from one locality to another.

DEPARTMENT OF THE TREASURY, BUREAU OF ENGRAVING AND PRINTING

Reprinted with permission of the Department of the Treasury, Bureau of Printing and Engraving, Washington, D.C.

THE U.S. GOVERNMENT'S SECURITY PRINTER

- Since October 1, 1877, all U.S. currency has been printed by the Bureau of Engraving and Printing, which started out as a six-person operation using steam-powered presses in the Department of the Treasury's basement.
- Now 1,800 Bureau employees occupy twenty-five acres of floor space in two Washington, D.C. buildings flanking 14th Street. Currency and stamps are designed, engraved, and printed twenty-four hours a day on thirty high-speed presses. An additional 700 Bureau employees are at the Western Currency Facility in Fort Worth, Texas, where currency is printed sixteen hours a day, five days a week, on ten high-speed presses.
- In 1995, at a cost of 3.8 cents each, over 9 billion notes worth about $129 billion was produced for circulation by the Federal Reserve System. Ninety-five percent will replace unfit notes and 5 percent will support economic growth. At any one time, $200 million in notes may be in production.
- Notes currently produced are the $1 (45 percent of production time), $5 and $10 (12 percent each), $20 (26 percent), $50 (2 percent), and $100 (3 percent).
- The Bureau also prints White House invitations and some 500 engraved items, such as visa counterfoils, naturalization documents, commissions, and certificates for almost seventy-five federal departments and agencies.

TOURS

- The Bureau of Engraving and Printing is one of the most popular tourist stops in Washington—over 700,000 visit the printing facility each year.
- Free twenty-minute guided tours are offered Monday through Friday, 9 A.M. to 2 P.M., except for federal holidays and the week between Christmas and New Year's. Tours start on Raoul Wallenberg Place (formerly 15th Street). During the summer months (June–August) afternoon tours are given from 4 P.M. to 7:30 P.M.
- Visitors can see press runs of 32-note currency sheets, examiners overseeing production to ensure high-quality notes, the application of Federal Reserve and Treasury seals, and 4,000 note "bricks" being readied for distribution to Federal Reserve Banks.
- Beginning in the fall of 1995, tours of postage stamp production also can be taken.

VISITORS CENTER

- At the Visitors Center, history, production, and counterfeit exhibits showcase interesting information about U.S. currency.
- Many unique items can be purchased at the sales counter. Items include uncut currency sheets of thirty-two, sixteen, or four $1 notes; $150 worth of shredded currency in plastic bags that are sold for $1; engraved collectors' prints; souvenir cards; and Department of the Interior Duck Stamps.

MAIL ORDER SALES

- Persons wishing to receive notes on new Bureau products or to order by mail can write: Mail Order Sales, Bureau of Engraving and Printing, 14th and C Streets, S.W., Room 513-M, Washington, D.C. 20228. Credit card purchases of Bureau products are available by calling (202) 874-3316, Monday through Friday, 8 A.M. to 3:30 P.M.

THE FEDERAL RESERVE BANKS

Reprinted with permission of the Department of the Treasury, Bureau of Printing and Engraving, Washington, D.C.

The Federal Reserve System is divided into twelve Federal Reserve districts, in each of which is a Federal Reserve Bank. There are also twenty-four branches. Each district is designated by a number and the corresponding letter of the alphabet. The district numbers, the cities in which the twelve banks are located, and the letter symbols are:

1-A—Boston	5-E—Richmond	9-I—Minneapolis
2-B—New York	6-F—Atlanta	10-J—Kansas City
3-C—Philadelphia	7-G—Chicago	11-K—Dallas
4-D—Cleveland	8-H—St. Louis	12-L—San Francisco

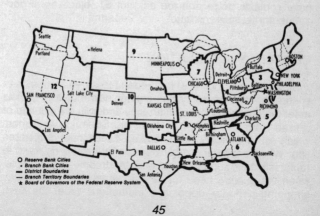

FEDERAL RESERVE SYSTEM

The Federal Reserve System was created by the Federal Reserve Act, which was passed by Congress in 1913, in order to provide a safer and more flexible banking and monetary system. For approximately 100 years before the creation of the Federal Reserve, periodic financial panics had led to failures of a large number of banks, with associated business bankruptcies and general economic contractions. Following the studies of the National Monetary Commission, established by Congress a year after the particularly severe panic of 1907, several proposals were put forward for the creation of an institution designed to counter such financial disruptions. Following considerable debate, the Federal Reserve System was established. Its original purposes were to give the country an elastic currency, provide facilities for discounting commercial credits, and improve the supervision of the banking system.

ECONOMIC STABILITY AND GROWTH

From the inception of the Federal Reserve System, it was clear that these original purposes were aspects of broader national economic and financial objectives. Over the years, stability and growth of the economy, a high level of employment, stability in the purchasing power of the dollar, and a reasonable balance in transactions with foreign countries have come to be recognized as primary objectives of governmental economic policy.

CURRENCY CIRCULATION

An important function of the Federal Reserve System is to ensure that the economy has enough currency and coin to meet the public's demand. Currency and coin are put into or retired from circulation by the Federal Reserve Banks, which use depository institutions as the channel of distribution. When banks and other depository institutions need to replenish their supply of currency and coin—for example, when the public's need for cash increases around holiday shopping periods—depository institutions order the cash from the Federal Reserve Bank or Branch in their area, and the face value of that cash is charged to their accounts at the Federal Reserve. When the public's need for currency and coin declines, depository institutions return excess cash to the Federal Reserve Bank, which in turn credits their accounts.

UNFIT AND COUNTERFEIT NOTES

The Federal Reserve Banks and the U.S. Department of the Treasury share responsibility for maintaining the physical quality of U.S. paper currency in circulation. Each day, millions of dollars of deposits to Reserve Banks by depository institutions are carefully scrutinized. The Reserve Banks are responsible for receiving, verifying, authenticating, and storing currency and shipping it as needed. Currency in good condition is stored for later distribution. Worn or mutilated notes are removed from circulation and destroyed. Counterfeit notes are forwarded to the U.S. Secret Service, an agency of the Treasury Department.

FEDERAL RESERVE NOTES

Virtually all currency in circulation is in the form of Federal Reserve Notes, which are printed by the Bureau of Engraving and Printing of the U.S. Treasury. The Reserve Banks are currently authorized to issue notes in denominations of $1, $2, $5, $10, $20, $50, and $100. Coins are produced by the Treasury's U.S. Mint.

CASH TRANSFERS

Currency and coin are used primarily for small transactions. In the aggregate, such transactions probably account for only a small proportion of the value of all transfers of funds.

32-SUBJECT SHEET LAYOUT

All U.S. currency is now printed with thirty-two subjects (notes) to a large sheet. The first printing is the green back. The second printing is the face of the note, in black. This includes the portrait and border, the series year, the check letter and quadrant number, two signatures, and the face plate number. The sheet is then cut in half vertically for the third printing. This includes the black Federal Reserve seal, the four Federal Reserve district numbers, the green Treasury seal, and two green serial numbers.

The 32-subject sheet is divided into four quarters called quadrants for numbering and other controls. Each quadrant has its own numbering sequence for the eight notes, with serial numbers advancing by 20,000 to the next note. The quadrant number and check letter in the upper left section indicate the first, second, third, or fourth quadrant and the

FIRST QUADRANT			**THIRD QUADRANT**		
A1 A00000001A	A100	E1 A00080001A	E100	A3 A00320001A	A100	E3 A00400001A	E100
B1 A00020001A	B100	F1 A00100001A	F100	B3 A00340001A	B100	F3 A00420001A	F100
C1 A00040001A	C100	G1 A00120001A	G100	C3 A00360001A	C100	G3 A00440001A	G100
D1 A00060001A	D100	H1 A00140001A	H100	D3 A00380001A	D100	H3 A00460001A	H100
A2 A00160001A	A100	E2 A00240001A	E100	A4 A00480001A	A100	E4 A00560001A	E100
B2 A00180001A	B100	F2 A00260001A	F100	B4 A00500001A	B100	F4 A00580001A	F100
C2 A00200001A	C100	G2 A00280001A	G100	C4 A00520001A	C100	G4 A00600001A	G100
D2 A00220001A	D100	H2 A00300001A	H100	D4 A00540001A	D100	H4 A00620001A	H100
SECOND QUADRANT			**FOURTH QUADRANT**		

position of the note in the quadrant. In the lower right corner the position letter is shown again with a plate number. On the back of the note the same small number in the lower right is the back plate number.

NUMBERING SYSTEM

The system of numbering paper money must be adequate to accommodate a large volume of notes. For security and accountability purposes, no two notes of any one class, denomination, and series may have the same serial number. The two serial numbers on each note have a full complement of eight digits and an alphabetical prefix and suffix letter. When necessary, ciphers are used at the left of the number to make a total of eight digits.

Whenever a numbering sequence is initiated for United States Notes or Silver Certificates, the first note is numbered A 00 000 001 A; the second A 00 000 002 A; the hundredth A 00 000 100 A; the thousandth A 00 001 000 A; and so on through A 99 999 999 A. The suffix letter A will remain the same until a total of twenty-five groups, or "blocks," of 99 999 999 notes are numbered, each group having a different prefix letter of the alphabet from A to Z. The letter "O" is omitted, either as a prefix or as a suffix, because of its similarity to zero. The 100 000 000th note in each group will be a Star Note, since eight digits are the maximum in the mechanical operation of numbering machines.

At this point, the suffix letter changes to B for the next twenty-five groups of 99 999 999 notes, and proceeds in the same manner as the suffix letter A. A total of 62,500,000,000 notes could be numbered before a duplication of serial numbers would occur. However, it has never been required to number that many notes of any one class, denomination, and series.

The Federal Reserve Notes printed for the twelve districts are numbered in the same progression as United States Notes and Silver Certificates, except that a specific alphabetical letter identifies a specific Federal Reserve district. The letter identifying each district is used as a prefix letter at the beginning of the serial numbers on all Federal Reserve Notes and does not change. Only the suffix letter changes in the serial numbers on Federal Reserve currency.

PORTRAITS AND BACK DESIGN ON SMALL SIZE NOTES

DENOMINATION	PORTRAIT	BACK DESIGN
$1	Washington	Great Seal of the United States
$2	Jefferson	Monticello
$5	Lincoln	Lincoln Memorial
$10	Hamilton	United States Treasury
$20	Jackson	The White House
$50	Grant	United States Capitol
$100	Franklin	Independence Hall
$500	McKinley	FIVE HUNDRED
$1000	Cleveland	ONE THOUSAND
$5000	Madison	FIVE THOUSAND
$10,000	Chase	TEN THOUSAND
$100,000	Wilson	ONE HUNDRED THOUSAND

DATING U.S. CURRENCY

Unlike coins, the date is not changed each year on U.S. currency.

The date appearing on all notes, large or small, is that of the year in which the design was first approved or issued. For instance, Large Size $1 United States Notes of the Series 1880 were issued with the same date until the new Series 1917 was issued. There was no further date change until the Series 1923.

The same rule applies to Small Size Notes. However, in this case a letter is added after the date to designate or indicate a minor change in the main design or probably a change in one or both of the signatures. For example: the $1 Silver Certificate of 1935 was changed to 1935-A because of a change in the size of the tiny plate numbers appearing in the lower right corners of the face and back of the note. It was changed again from 1935-A to 1935-B in 1945 when the signatures of Julian/Morganthau were changed to Julian/Vinson. Subsequent changes in signatures continued in the 1935 Series to the year 1963 when the signatures of Smith/Dillon terminated the issue with the Series 1935-H. Therefore, these notes were issued for twenty-eight years bearing the date 1935.

NEW TREASURY SEAL

FORMER DESIGN:
The former design had the Latin inscription *Thesaur. Amer. Septent. Sigil.,* which has several translations. It was the Seal of the North American Treasury.

NEW DESIGN:
This new design drops the Latin and states THE DEPARTMENT OF THE TREASURY, 1789. First used on the $100 Note of the Series 1966.

52

GRADES AND CONDITIONS
OF PAPER MONEY

CONDITION

The physical condition of a note or bill plays an important role in determining its value. There are many notes that have no premium value beyond face value in ordinary condition but are valuable or moderately valuable when uncirculated. Even in the case of scarce early specimens, the price given for an Average example is generally much less than that commanded by Fine or Very Fine condition.

Defects encountered in paper money include:

Creases, folds, wrinkles. Generally the characteristic that distinguishes uncirculated notes from those that almost—but not quite—qualify for such designation is a barely noticeable crease running approximately down the center vertically, resulting from the note being folded for insertion into a wallet or billfold. It may be possible, through manipulation or storage beneath a heavy weight, to remove evidence of the crease; but the knowledge that it once existed cannot be obliterated.

Discoloration. Discoloration is not as easy to recognize as most defects, but it must be classed as one. A distinction should be made between notes printed from underinked rollers and those which originally were normally colored but became "washed out." Sometimes washing is indeed the cause; a well-intentioned collector will bathe a note, attempting to clean it, with the result that its color is no longer strong. This should not happen if warm water is used, without strong cleanser. Atmospheric conditions may play some part in discoloration.

Foxing. Fox spots may sometimes be observed on old notes, especially those of the pre-1890 era, just as on old paper in general. They seem more common to foreign currency than American, but their presence on our notes is certainly not rare. These are tiny brownish-red dots, caused by an infestation of lice attacking the paper fibers.

Holes. Holes are more likely to be encountered in early paper money than specimens of recent origin. In early years it was customary for Federal Reserve Banks to use wire clips in making up bundles of notes for distribution to banking organizations, and these clips or staples often pierced the bills. Another common occurrence years ago was the practice of shop clerks and cashiers in general to impale notes upon holders consisting of nails mounted on stands.

Missing pieces. Missing pieces is a highly undesirable defect which, except in the case of rare specimens, renders the item valueless to collectors. Even if only a blank unprinted corner is torn away, this is called a missing-piece note and hardly anyone will give it a second glance.

Stains. Notes sometimes become stained with ink or other liquids. If the specimen is commonplace and easily obtainable in Very Fine or Uncirculated condition, it will be worthless with any kind of stain. In a note of moderate value, its price will be hurt to a greater or lesser degree depending on the stain's intensity, size, nature, and the area it touches. A stain in an outer margin or at a corner is not so objectionable as one occurring at the center or across a signature or serial number. Ink stains, because of their strong color, are generally deemed the worst, but bad staining can also be caused by oil, crayon, "magic marker," and food substances. Pencil markings, which frequently are found on bank notes, will yield to ordinary erasing with a piece of soft "artgum" worked gently over the surface and brushed away with an artist's camel-hair brush. Most other stains cannot be so easily removed. With ink there is no hope, as any caustic sufficiently strong to remove the ink will also injure the printing and possibly eat through the paper as well. Oil stains can sometimes be lightened, though not removed, by sprinkling the note on both sides (even if the stain shows only on one) with talcum powder or other absorbent powder, placing it between sheets of waxed kitchen paper, and leaving it beneath a heavy weight for several days in a room where the humidity is not unduly high.

Tears. Tears in notes are very common defects, which may be minute or run nearly the whole length of the bill. As a rule the paper on which American currency is printed is fairly rugged and will not tear as readily as most ordinary paper, but given careless or hurried handling anything is possible. An old worn note is more apt to tear in handling than a new one. Repaired tears are more common in the world of paper money collecting than may be generally supposed. A clean tear—one which does not involve loss of surface—can be patched so as to become virtually unnoticed, unless examined against a light or through a strong magnifying glass. X-ray examination will reveal repairs when all else fails.

CONDITION STANDARDS

The following condition standards have been used throughout this book and, with slight variations depending upon individual interpretation, are generally current in the trade.

Uncirculated—UNC. A specimen that for all appearances has not been handled or passed through general circulation; a crisp fresh note in "bank" condition. There may be minor blemishes, such as a finger smudge or pinhole, but if these are in any respect severe the condition merits description as "Almost Uncirculated." There is not much satisfaction to be taken in a note fresh and crisp that has gaping holes and fingerprints. Obviously, an 1870 Uncirculated note should not be expected to match a 1970 in appearance or feel.

Almost Uncirculated—A.U. In the case of modern or semimodern notes, this is generally taken to mean a specimen that shows no evidence of having passed through general circulation but, because of some detraction, fails to measure up to a rating of Uncirculated. The problem may be finger smudges, counting crinkles, a light crease, a fold along one or more of the corners, or pinholes. But if more than one of these impairments is present, the item would surely not deserve a classification of Almost Uncirculated.

Extremely Fine—X.F. A note exhibiting little evidence of wear from handling, but not so perfect or near-perfect as to qualify for a rating of Uncirculated or Almost Uncirculated. On a used note issued before 1900 there may be clear evidence of circulation, but no disfiguring marks.

Very Fine—V.F. A Very Fine note has experienced some circulation but escaped without "being mangled." It is still clean and crisp, and its creases are not offensive.

Fine—F. Here the scale begins sliding down. It is obvious that, being the fifth in rank of condition grades, Fine notes are quite a good deal removed from Uncirculated. They have been handed around pretty thoroughly and suffered the normal consequences, but still are without serious blemishes such as tears, missing corners, serious stains, or holes.

Very Good—V.G. A well-circulated note bearing evidence of much folding, creasing, and wrinkling. It may possibly be lightly stained, smudged, or pin punctured, but major defects—such as a torn-off corner—would drop it into an even lower category.

Good—G. Heavily circulated, worn notes that are possibly stained or scribbled on, edges could be frayed or "dog-eared." There may be holes larger than pin punctures, but not on the central portion of design. This is the lowest grade of condition acceptable to a collector, and only when nothing better is available. Unless very rare, such specimens are considered space-fillers only.

Average Buying Prices—A.B.P. The Average Buying Prices given here are the approximate sums paid by retail dealers for specimens in Good condition. As selling prices vary, so do buying prices, and, in fact, they usually vary a bit more.

RECORD KEEPING

For your convenience, we suggest you use the following record-keeping system to note condition of your paper money in the checklist box:

◻ FAIR	☒ VERY GOOD	◻ VERY FINE	☒ ALMOST UNC
◻ GOOD	◻ FINE	☒ EXTREMELY FINE	■ UNCIRCULATED

ABOUT THE PRICES
IN THIS BOOK

Prices are compiled from offerings made by dealers and from auction sale results. In all cases (except for the Average Buying Price) the prices are retail selling prices. While prices are current at the time of publication, the market can be influenced by buying or selling trends, causing prices to change. All prices, except in the case of seldom-offered rarities, are averages, calculated from numerous sales. The actual prices charged by any individual currency dealer may be slightly higher or lower than those indicated in this book. In any given sale various factors play a role, such as whether the seller is overstocked on notes of that type.

HOW TO USE THIS BOOK

The *Official Blackbook Price Guide of United States Paper Money* provides a convenient reference to prices of all standard U.S. currency, old and new, as well as many unusual issues.

Notes are divided into section by denomination. Within each section can be found the various series of notes for that denomination. The series are arranged chronologically and will vary slightly from section to section, as some notes were issued in one series and not in another. An index page is provided at the beginning of each section.

To familiarize yourself with the various currency terms, the following illustration might be helpful:

To price a note correctly, it is necessary that it be accurately identified and graded. The illustrations will aid in identification, and a grading guide has been provided. In the case of some notes, particularly very old ones, the value depends upon minor details. In all such cases these details have been clearly noted.

Listings include the following information:

Date. This is the "series date," as it appears on the note, and may bear no relation whatsoever to the year in which the note was actually issued. The date of actual issue is not of importance to collectors. If the series date on the note carries a suffix letter, such as 1935A, it will be so indicated in the listing.

Seal. The color of the Treasury Seal will be noted, along with other information if relevant. The following abbreviations are also used: Sm.—small, Lg.—large; w/r—with rays, w/s—with scallops.

Signatures. All U.S. notes carry two signatures, and the names of each signer are given for every note listed. If different signature combinations exist for your note, be sure you refer to the correct signature combination. The listings will show you whether there is just one set of signatures for that note or more than one.

Type. In a small minority of cases, notes were issued in more than one type. For example, a slight change was made in the paper or printing. All recorded types are identified in the listings.

Issuing Bank. This information is provided for Federal Reserve Notes and Federal Reserve Bank Notes only. Check the Federal Reserve seal on your note to identify the issuing bank. In some instances there is a difference in value depending on where the note originated. Space prevents us from listing the numerous local banks issuing National Bank Notes.

A.B.P. The first price column is the A.B.P. or Average Buying Price. This is the approximate sum being paid by dealers for a specimen in the lowest listed grade of condition. The lowest listed grade of condition is the column next to the A.B.P. If the next column is headed "Good," the A.B.P. is for a specimen in Good condition. In all cases the A.B.P. includes the face value of the note. This is an important consideration insofar as U.S. notes, regardless of their age or physical condition, can still be spent as legal tender.

Current Selling Prices. The current selling prices are given in two or three different grades of condition, as indicated at the top of each price column. Different groups of notes are priced in different condition grades, owing to market availability. Some are virtually unobtainable in Uncirculated condition, so it would be pointless to give such a price. Others are of no premium value in less than V.F., hence V.F. is the lowest grade shown.

ONE DOLLAR NOTES

ORDER OF ISSUE

ONE DOLLAR NOTES (1862) UNITED STATES NOTES
(ALSO KNOWN AS LEGAL TENDER NOTES)

(Large Size)   **NOTE NO. 1**

Face Design: Portrait of Salmon Portland Chase
(1808–73), Secretary of the Treasury under Lincoln, red
Treasury Seal, signatures of Chittenden and Spinner, lower
right.

Back Design: Large circle center with legal tender obligation.

SERIES	SIGNATURES	SEAL	A.B.P.	GOOD	V. FINE	UNC.
1862	Chittenden-Spinner					
□Type I, National Bank Note, American Bank						
Note without monogram		Red	50.00	90.00	350.00	700.00
□Type II, National Bank Note, American Bank						
Note with monogram ABNCO		Red	50.00	75.00	300.00	725.00
□Type III, National Bank Note, National Bank						
Note without monogram		Red	40.00	65.00	280.00	645.00
□Type IV, National Bank Note, National Bank						
Note with monogram ABNCO		Red	40.00	65.00	270.00	750.00

ONE DOLLAR NOTES (1869) UNITED STATES NOTES
(ALSO KNOWN AS LEGAL TENDER NOTES)
(Large Size) **NOTE NO. 2**

Face Design: Portrait of President Washington in the center, large red seal to the right. Scene of Columbus in sight of land to left; also called "Rainbow Note" because of the many colors used in printing. Black ink for main design, red seal and serial numbers, green background for the serial number, green shading in upper-half and blue tint in paper left of portrait to deter counterfeiting.

Back Design: Green, ONE DOLLAR and ONE over "1" center, letters U.S. interwoven to left. Legal tender obligation to right of center.

SERIES	SIGNATURES	SEAL	A.B.P.	GOOD	V. FINE	UNC.
☐1869	Allison-Spinner	Red	60.00	110.00	300.00	1000.00

ONE DOLLAR NOTES (1874-1917)
UNITED STATES NOTES
(ALSO KNOWN AS LEGAL TENDER NOTES)
(Large Size)   NOTE NO. 3

Back Design: Large green "X" with UNITED STATES OF AMERICA in the center. Legal tender obligation and counterfeiting warning to right.

Face Design: No blue or green shading and tinting.

SERIES	SIGNATURES	SEAL	A.B.P.	GOOD	V. FINE	UNC.
☐ 1874	Allison-Spinner	Sm. Red	30.00	50.00	110.00	450.00
☐ 1875	Allison-New	Sm. Red	30.00	45.00	90.00	375.00
☐ 1875	Same Series A	Sm. Red	30.00	75.00	180.00	675.00
☐ 1875	Same Series B	Sm. Red	30.00	75.00	180.00	635.00
☐ 1875	Same Series C	Sm. Red	30.00	75.00	215.00	795.00
☐ 1875	Same Series D	Sm. Red	50.00	110.00	320.00	795.00
☐ 1875	Same Series E	Sm. Red	70.00	150.00	320.00	1100.00
☐ 1875	Allison-Wyman	Sm. Red	25.00	45.00	70.00	295.00
☐ 1878	Allison-Gilfillan	Sm. Red	25.00	45.00	90.00	375.00
☐ 1878	Allison-Gilfillan	Sm. Maroon	150.00	—	—	925.00
☐ 1880	Scofield-Gilfillan	Lg. Brown	20.00	50.00	90.00	295.00
☐ 1880	Bruce-Gilfillan	Lg. Brown	20.00	45.00	70.00	295.00
☐ 1880	Bruce-Wyman	Lg. Brown	20.00	45.00	60.00	295.00
☐ 1880	Rosecrans-Huston	Lg. Red	45.00	110.00	400.00	2000.00
☐ 1880	Rosecrans-Huston	Lg. Brown	45.00	110.00	450.00	2000.00
☐ 1880	Rosecrans-Nebeker	Lg. Brown	45.00	110.00	450.00	2000.00
☐ 1880	Rosecrans-Nebeker	Sm. Red	18.00	35.00	65.00	275.00
☐ 1880	Tillman-Morgan	Sm. Red	18.00	35.00	65.00	275.00
☐ 1917	Tehee-Burke	Sm. Red	18.00	24.00	40.00	150.00

Sm.—Small Seal, Lg.—Large Seal
*This note with signatures of Burke and Elliott is an error issue. The regular procedure was to have the signature of the Register of the Treasury on the left, and that of the Treasurer to the right. The signatures were transposed in this instance.

SERIES	SIGNATURES	SEAL	A.B.P.	GOOD	V. FINE	UNC.
☐1917	Elliott-Burke	Sm. Red	18.00	22.00	40.00	150.00
☐1917	Burke-Elliott*	Sm. Red	20.00	42.00	120.00	400.00
☐1917	Elliott-White	Sm. Red	18.00	21.00	40.00	135.00
☐1917	Speelman-White	Sm. Red	18.00	20.00	40.00	135.00

ONE DOLLAR NOTES (1923) UNITED STATES NOTES
(ALSO KNOWN AS LEGAL TENDER NOTES)
(Large Size)   **NOTE NO. 4**

Face Design: Portrait of President Washington in center. Red seal to left, red "1" to the right, red serial numbers.

Back Design: UNITED STATES OF AMERICA and ONE DOLLAR in center. Figures "1" to right and left. This was the last issue of Large Size ONE DOLLAR United States Notes. The last series of Large Size Notes was kept in use until 1929 when the first issue of Small Size Notes was released.

SERIES	SIGNATURES	SEAL	A.B.P.	GOOD	V. FINE	UNC.
☐1923	Speelman-White	Red	18.00	25.00	65.00	240.00

ONE DOLLAR NOTES (1928) UNITED STATES NOTES
(ALSO KNOWN AS LEGAL TENDER NOTES)
(Small Size)   **NOTE NO. 5**

Face Design: Red seal to left—red serial numbers, large ONE to right. This is the only issue of the $1 United States Note, Small Size. At the present time only the $100 United States Note is current.

Back Design: Large ONE in center with ONE DOLLAR overprint, back printed in green.

SERIES	SIGNATURES	SEAL	A.B.P.	GOOD	V. FINE	UNC.
☐ 1928	Woods-Woodin	Red	9.00	14.00	25.00	80.00

ONE DOLLAR NOTES (1863-1875)
NATIONAL BANK NOTES
FIRST CHARTER PERIOD (Large Size)   **NOTE NO. 6**

Face Design: Name of National Bank top center, maidens at altar below.

Back Design: Landing of Pilgrims center, State Seal of state issuing bank to left, eagle and flag.

SERIES	SIGNATURES	SEAL	A.B.P.	GOOD	V. FINE	UNC.
☐ Original*	Colby-Spinner	Red w/r	40.00	65.00	225.00	750.00
☐ Original*	Jeffries-Spinner	Red w/r	120.00	400.00	1200.00	2600.00
☐ Original*	Allison-Spinner	Red w/r	30.00	60.00	225.00	750.00
☐ 1875	Allison-New	Red w/s	30.00	60.00	225.00	700.00
☐ 1875	Allison-Wyman	Red w/s	30.00	60.00	225.00	700.00
☐ 1875	Allison-Gilfillan	Red w/s	30.00	60.00	225.00	700.00
☐ 1875	Scofield-Gilfillan	Red w/s	30.00	60.00	230.00	700.00

w/r—with Rays, w/s—with Scallops
*Early notes of the First Charter Period did not have the series imprinted on them. They are known by the date on the bill which was usually the date of charter or organization, or as the Original Series. These notes had a seal with rays or small notches. In 1875 the series was imprinted in red, and the seal was changed to have scallops around the border. The charter number was added to later issues of notes of the original series and to all notes of the 1875 series.

ONE DOLLAR NOTES (1886) SILVER CERTIFICATES
(Large Size)   **NOTE NO. 7**

SERIES	SIGNATURES	SEAL	A.B.P.	GOOD	V. FINE	UNC.
☐1886	Rosecrans-Jordan	Sm. Red	43.00	75.00	200.00	725.00
☐1886	Rosecrans-Hyatt	Sm. Red	43.00	75.00	200.00	850.00
☐1886	Rosecrans-Hyatt	Lg. Red	43.00	75.00	200.00	725.00
☐1886	Rosecrans-Huston	Lg. Red	43.00	75.00	195.00	775.00
☐1886	Rosecrans-Huston	Lg. Brown	43.00	65.00	225.00	750.00
☐1886	Rosecrans-Nebeker	Lg. Brown	44.00	65.00	225.00	775.00
☐1886	Rosecrans-Nebeker	Sm. Red	45.00	66.00	240.00	850.00

ONE DOLLAR NOTES (1891) SILVER CERTIFICATES
(Large Size)   **NOTE NO. 8**
Back Design
Face Design:
Same as Note
No. 7.

SERIES	SIGNATURES	SEAL	A.B.P.	GOOD	V. FINE	UNC.
☐1891	Rosecrans-Nebeker	Sm. Red	36.00	60.00	180.00	660.00
☐1891	Tillman-Morgan	Sm. Red	45.00	71.00	185.00	640.00

ONE DOLLAR NOTES (1896) SILVER CERTIFICATES
(Large Size)

NOTE NO. 9

Face Design: History instructing youth. To the right, panoramic view of the Capitol and Washington Monument. Constitution on tablet, names of famous Americans on top and side borders.

Back Design: Portrait of Martha Washington to left and President Washington to right with large numeral "1" in center.

There is a story that when this note was issued people objected to it because they said No. "1" (ONE) shouldn't stand between George and Martha Washington. The set consists of $1, $2, and $5 denominations. They all have very beautiful engravings, and they are truly the most beautiful notes ever issued by our government. They were first released in 1896 and replaced by a new issue in 1899. They were short-lived because of objections to the unclad female on the $5 Note.

SERIES	SIGNATURES	SEAL	A.B.P.	GOOD	V. FINE	UNC.
☐1896	Tillman-Morgan	Red	18.00	60.00	280.00	750.00
☐1896	Bruce-Roberts	Red	18.00	60.00	250.00	750.00

ONE DOLLAR NOTES (1899) SILVER CERTIFICATES
(Large Size)   **NOTE NO. 10**

Face Design: Eagle on flag and Capitol background over portraits of Presidents Lincoln and Grant.

Back Design

SERIES	SIGNATURES	SEAL	A.B.P.	GOOD	V. FINE	UNC.
	SERIES OF 1899 (above upper right serial number)					
☐1899	Lyons-Roberts	Blue	15.00	40.00	75.00	180.00
	SERIES OF 1899 (below upper right serial number)					
☐1899	Lyons-Roberts	Blue	15.00	25.00	45.00	165.00
☐1899	Lyons-Treat	Blue	15.00	25.00	50.00	175.00
☐1899	Vernon-Treat	Blue	15.00	25.00	50.00	175.00
☐1899	Vernon-McClung	Blue	15.00	25.00	50.00	175.00
	SERIES OF 1899 (vertical to right of blue seal)					
☐1899	Napier-McClung	Blue	15.00	25.00	45.00	170.00
☐1899	Napier-Thompson	Blue	20.00	40.00	100.00	475.00
☐1899	Parker-Burke	Blue	15.00	25.00	45.00	140.00
☐1899	Teehee-Burke	Blue	15.00	25.00	45.00	140.00
☐1899	Elliott-Burke	Blue	15.00	22.00	50.00	160.00
☐1899	Elliott-White	Blue	15.00	22.00	50.00	160.00

SERIES	SIGNATURES	SEAL	A.B.P.	GOOD	V. FINE	UNC.
☐1899	Speelman-White	Blue	15.00	22.00	50.00	175.00

ONE DOLLAR NOTES (1923) SILVER CERTIFICATES
(Large Size)   **NOTE NO. 11**

Face Design: Portrait of President Washington in center, blue seal left, blue 1 DOLLAR right, blue numbers.

Back Design: Same as note No. 4.

SERIES	SIGNATURES	SEAL	A.B.P.	GOOD	V. FINE	UNC.
☐1923	Speelman-White	Blue	8.00	16.00	22.00	50.00
☐1923	Woods-White	Blue	8.00	18.00	24.00	62.00
☐1923	Woods-Tate	Blue	12.00	25.00	45.00	250.00

ONE DOLLAR NOTES (1928) SILVER CERTIFICATES
(Small Size)   **NOTE NO. 12**

Face Design: Portrait of President Washington, blue seal to
the left, ONE to right, blue seal and numbers. ONE SILVER DOL-
LAR under portrait.

Back Design

First issue of Series 1928. U.S. paper money was reduced
in 1928 from the old Large Size to the size presently in use.
This was mostly an economy measure. Unlike Large Size
Notes, the Small Notes have a letter designation after the
date to denote a minor change in design or change of one
or both signatures.

SERIES	SIGNATURES	SEAL	A.B.P.	GOOD	V. FINE	UNC.
☐1928	Tate-Mellon	Blue	2.00	6.00	9.00	18.00
☐1928A	Woods-Mellon	Blue	2.00	4.00	7.00	17.00
☐1928B	Woods-Mills	Blue	2.00	5.00	9.00	19.00
☐1928C	Woods-Woodin	Blue	15.00	32.00	91.00	410.00
☐1928D	Julian-Woodin	Blue	15.00	30.00	80.00	310.00
☐1928E	Julian-Morgenthau	Blue	65.00	125.00	350.00	1100.00

ONE DOLLAR NOTES (1934) SILVER CERTIFICATES
(Small Size)   **NOTE NO. 13**

Face Design: Portrait of President Washington, blue "1" to left. ONE and blue seal to right. ONE DOLLAR IN SILVER under portrait.
Back Design: Same as note No. 12.

SERIES	SIGNATURES	SEAL	A.B.P.	GOOD	V. FINE	UNC.
☐1934	Julian-Morgenthau	Blue	1.75	3.00	8.00	32.00

ONE DOLLAR NOTES (1935) SILVER CERTIFICATES
(Small Size)   **NOTE NO. 14**

Face Design: Portrait of President Washington in center. Gray "1" to left, blue seal right, and blue numbers. ONE DOLLAR IN SILVER under portrait.

The following notes are without IN GOD WE TRUST on back.

SERIES	SIGNATURES	SEAL	A.B.P.	GOOD	V. FINE	UNC.
☐1935	Julian-Morgenthau	Blue	1.50	4.00	5.00	12.00
☐1935A	Julian-Morgenthau	Blue	1.50	2.50	4.00	5.00
☐1935A	Julian-Morgenthau	Brown	2.50	5.00	8.50	23.00

This note was a special issue for use in war zones in the Pacific area during World War II. Brown serial numbers and HAWAII stamped on front and back.

ONE DOLLAR NOTES (1935) SILVER CERTIFICATES
(Small Size)   **NOTE NO. 14**

SERIES SIGNATURES	SEAL	A.B.P.	GOOD	V. FINE	UNC.
☐1935A Julian-Morgenthau	Yellow	3.00	8.00	22.00	83.00

The above note was a special issue for use in war zones in the North African and European areas during World War II. Blue serial numbers and yellow seal.

| ☐1935A Julian-Morgenthau | Blue | 6.00 | 15.00 | 40.00 | 210.00 |

Red "R" between the Treasury Seal and signature of Morgenthau. This was an experimental issue to test wearing qualities of differently treated paper.

| ☐1935A Julian-Morgenthau | Blue | 5.00 | 14.00 | 34.00 | 200.00 |

Above note with red "S" between Treasury Seal and signature of Morgenthau. Experimental issue "R" was for regular paper, "S" for special paper.

☐1935B Julian-Vinson	Blue	1.50	2.10	5.00	6.50
☐1935C Julian-Snyder	Blue	1.50	2.10	5.00	6.50
☐1935D Clark-Snyder	Blue	1.50	2.00	3.00	4.50

Wide design on back. This and all notes of 1935 prior to this have the wide design. See Fig I.

| ☐1935D Clark-Snyder | Blue | 1.50 | 2.10 | 3.00 | 5.00 |

Narrow design on back. This and all $1 Notes following have narrow design. See Fig. II.

ONE DOLLAR NOTES (1935) SILVER CERTIFICATES
(Small Size)   **NOTE NO. 14**

SERIES SIGNATURES	SEAL	A.B.P.	GOOD	V. FINE	UNC.
☐1935E Priest-Humphrey	Blue	1.50	2.00	2.75	4.00
☐1935F Priest-Anderson	Blue	1.50	2.00	3.00	6.00
☐1935G Smith-Dillon	Blue	1.50	2.00	3.00	4.50

IN GOD WE TRUST added. All notes following have the motto.

	SEAL	A.B.P.	GOOD	V. FINE	UNC.
☐1935G Smith-Dillon	Blue	1.50	2.00	3.00	5.50
☐1935H Granahan-Dillon	Blue	1.50	2.00	3.00	6.00

ONE DOLLAR NOTES (1957) SILVER CERTIFICATES
(Small Size)   **NOTE NO. 14**

The following three notes are the last issue of the $1
Silver Certificates. The reason for the change in series from
1935H to 1957 was due to printing improvements. The 1935
Series, up until the issue of Clark and Snyder, was printed
in sheets of twelve subjects to a sheet. During the term of
Clark and Snyder notes were printed eighteen subjects to a
sheet. Starting with Series 1957, new high-speed rotary
presses were installed and notes were printed thirty-two
subjects to a sheet.

SERIES SIGNATURES	SEAL	A.B.P.	GOOD	V. FINE	UNC.
☐1957 Priest-Anderson	Blue	1.25	1.50	2.10	3.00
☐1957A Smith-Dillon	Blue	1.25	1.50	2.10	2.75
☐1957B Granahan-Dillon	Blue	1.25	1.50	2.10	3.00

The redemption of Silver Certificates by the U.S. Treasury
Department ended on June 24, 1968. These notes are
now worth only their face value, plus the numismatic
value to collectors. Notes in used condition are not
regarded as collectors' items.

ONE DOLLAR NOTES (1890)
TREASURY OR COIN NOTES

(Large Size)   **NOTE NO. 15**

Face Design: Portrait of Stanton, Secretary of War during the Civil War.

Back Design: Green large ornate ONE. Entire back is beautifully engraved.

SERIES	SIGNATURES	SEAL	A.B.P.	GOOD	V. FINE	UNC.
☐1890	Rosecrans-Huston	Brown	45.00	80.00	550.00	1365.00
☐1890	Rosecrans-Nebeker	Brown	45.00	80.00	540.00	1400.00
☐1890	Rosecrans-Nebeker	Red	45.00	80.00	530.00	1325.00

ONE DOLLAR NOTES (1891)
TREASURY OR COIN NOTES

(Large Size)

Face Design: Is similar to note No. 15.

Back Design: More unengraved area, numerous ONES and "1"s.

SERIES	SIGNATURES	SEAL	A.B.P.	GOOD	V. FINE	UNC.
☐1891	Rosecrans-Nebeker	Red	30.00	55.00	125.00	450.00
☐1891	Tillman-Morgan	Red	30.00	55.00	125.00	400.00
☐1891	Bruce-Roberts	Red	30.00	55.00	125.00	400.00

ONE DOLLAR NOTES (1918)
FEDERAL RESERVE BANK NOTES

(Large Size)   NOTE NO. 17

Face Design: Portrait of President Washington, signature to left of center. Bank and city center, blue seal to right. Signatures of government officials above. Signatures of bank officials below. Federal Reserve district letter and numbers in four corners.

Back Design: Flying eagle and flag in center. All are Series 1918 and have blue seals and blue numbers.

BANK & CITY	GOV'T SIGNATURES	BANK SIGNATURES	A.B.P.	GOOD	V. FINE	UNC.
☐ Boston	Teehee-Burke	Bullen-Morss	10.00	18.00	50.00	155.00
☐ Boston	Teehee-Burke	Willet-Morss	20.00	30.00	60.00	360.00
☐ Boston	Elliot-Burke	Willet-Morss	8.00	15.00	45.00	175.00

BANK & CITY	GOV'T SIGNATURES	BANK SIGNATURES	A.B.P.	GOOD	V. FINE	UNC.
☐ New York	Teehee-Burke	Sailer-Strong	10.00	18.00	50.00	175.00
☐ New York	Teehee-Burke	Hendricks-Strong	10.00	18.00	50.00	175.00
☐ New York	Elliott-Burke	Hendricks-Strong	10.00	18.00	50.00	175.00
☐ Philadelphia	Teehee-Burke	Hardt-Passmore	10.00	18.00	50.00	175.00
☐ Philadelphia	Teehee-Burke	Dyer-Passmore	10.00	18.00	50.00	175.00
☐ Philadelphia	Elliott-Burke	Dyer-Passmore	10.00	18.00	50.00	175.00
☐ Philadelphia	Elliott-Burke	Dyer-Norris	10.00	18.00	50.00	175.00
☐ Cleveland	Teehee-Burke	Baxter-Fancher	10.00	18.00	50.00	175.00
☐ Cleveland	Teehee-Burke	Davis-Fancher	10.00	18.00	50.00	175.00
☐ Cleveland	Elliott-Burke	Davis-Fancher	10.00	18.00	50.00	175.00
☐ Richmond	Teehee-Burke	Keesee-Seay	10.00	18.00	50.00	175.00
☐ Richmond	Elliott-Burke	Keesee-Seay	10.00	18.00	50.00	175.00
☐ Atlanta	Teehee-Burke	Pike-McCord	10.00	18.00	50.00	175.00
☐ Atlanta	Teehee-Burke	Bell-McCord	10.00	18.00	50.00	175.00
☐ Atlanta	Teehee-Burke	Bell-Wellborn	10.00	18.00	50.00	175.00
☐ Atlanta	Elliott-Burke	Bell-Wellborn	10.00	18.00	50.00	175.00
☐ Chicago	Teehee-Burke	McCloud-McDougal	10.00	18.00	50.00	175.00
☐ Chicago	Teehee-Burke	Cramer-McDougal	10.00	18.00	50.00	175.00
☐ Chicago	Elliott-Burke	Cramer-McDougal	10.00	18.00	50.00	175.00
☐ St. Louis	Teehee-Burke	Attebery-Wells	10.00	18.00	50.00	175.00
☐ St. Louis	Teehee-Burke	Attebery-Biggs	10.00	18.00	50.00	175.00

BANK & CITY	GOV'T SIGNATURES	BANK SIGNATURES	A.B.P.	GOOD	V. FINE	UNC.
☐ St. Louis	Elliott-Burke	Attebery-Biggs	10.00	18.00	50.00	175.00
☐ St. Louis	Elliott-Burke	White-Biggs	10.00	18.00	50.00	175.00
☐ Minneapolis	Teehee-Burke	Cook-Wold	12.00	21.00	60.00	250.00
☐ Minneapolis	Teehee-Burke	Cook-Young	100.00	200.00	450.00	1050.00
☐ Minneapolis	Elliott-Burke	Cook-Young	11.00	25.00	60.00	250.00
☐ Kansas City	Teehee-Burke	Anderson-Miller	10.00	18.00	45.00	175.00
☐ Kansas City	Elliott-Burke	Anderson-Miller	10.00	18.00	45.00	175.00
☐ Kansas City	Elliott-Burke	Helm-Miller	10.00	18.00	45.00	175.00
☐ Dallas	Teehee-Burke	Talley-VanZandt	10.00	18.00	45.00	175.00
☐ Dallas	Elliott-Burke	Talley-VanZandt	15.00	42.00	100.00	250.00
☐ Dallas	Elliott-Burke	Lawder-VanZandt	10.00	18.00	50.00	175.00
☐ San Francisco	Teehee-Burke	Clerk-Lynch	10.00	18.00	50.00	175.00
☐ San Francisco	Teehee-Burke	Clerk-Calkins	10.00	18.00	50.00	175.00
☐ San Francisco	Elliott-Burke	Clerk-Calkins	10.00	18.00	50.00	175.00
☐ San Francisco	Elliott-Burke	Ambrose-Calkins	10.00	18.00	50.00	175.00

ONE DOLLAR NOTES (1963)
FEDERAL RESERVE NOTES

(Small Size)

NOTE NO. 18

Face Design: Portrait of President Washington in center, black Federal Reserve seal with city and district letter to left, green Treasury Seal to right. Green serial numbers, Federal Reserve numbers in four corners.

Back Design: Same as all $1 Notes from 1935.

SERIES OF 1963, GRANAHAN-DILLON, GREEN SEAL

DISTRICT	A.B.P.	UNC.	DISTRICT	A.B.P.	UNC.
☐1A Boston	1.25	3.25	☐7G Chicago	1.25	3.25
☐2B New York	1.25	3.25	☐8H St. Louis	1.25	3.25
☐3C Philadelphia	1.25	3.25	☐9I Minneapolis	1.25	3.25
☐4D Cleveland	1.25	3.25	☐10J Kansas City	1.25	3.25
☐5E Richmond	1.25	3.25	☐11K Dallas	1.25	3.25
☐6F Atlanta	1.25	3.25	☐12L San Francisco	1.25	3.25

The Dallas note of this series as shown, with the letter "K" in the black seal and the number "11" in the four corners, does not have any more significance or value than any other notes with their respective district letter and corresponding number.

A false rumor was circulated several years ago that the "K" was for Kennedy, the "11" was for November (the month in which he was assassinated), and that the note was issued by the Dallas Bank to commemorate the occasion. The entire story is apocryphal.

This note is in no way associated with the late President Kennedy. The notes were authorized by the Act of June 4, 1963. This was five months before Kennedy was assassinated. The Federal Reserve district for Dallas is K-11.

SERIES OF 1963A, GRANAHAN-FOWLER, GREEN SEAL

DISTRICT	A.B.P.	UNC.	DISTRICT	A.B.P.	UNC.
☐1A Boston	1.25	3.50	☐7G Chicago	1.25	3.50
☐2B New York	1.25	3.50	☐8H St. Louis	1.25	3.50
☐3C Philadelphia	1.25	3.50	☐9I Minneapolis	1.25	3.50
☐4D Cleveland	1.25	3.50	☐10J Kansas City	1.25	3.50
☐5E Richmond	1.25	3.50	☐11K Dallas	1.25	3.50
☐6F Atlanta	1.25	3.50	☐12L San Francisco	1.25	3.50

ONE DOLLAR NOTES (1963-B) FEDERAL RESERVE (WITH SIGNATURE OF JOSEPH W. BARR)

(Small Size)   **NOTE NO. 18**

Joseph W. Barr served as Secretary of the Treasury from December 20, 1968, to January 20, 1969, filling the unexpired term of Henry H. Fowler. His signature appears on the $1 Federal Reserve Notes of the Series of 1963-B only.

During the one-month term of Joseph W. Barr, about 471 million notes were printed with his signature. These notes were for the following Federal Reserve Banks.

	REGULAR NUMBERS	A.B.P.	UNC.	STAR NUMBERS	A.B.P.	UNC.
☐2B New York	123,040,000	1.50	4.50	3,680,000	1.50	4.50
☐5E Richmond	93,600,000	1.50	4.50	3,040,000	1.50	4.50
☐7G Chicago	91,040,000	1.50	4.50	2,400,000	1.50	4.50
☐10J Kansas City	44,800,000	1.50	4.50	None Printed	1.50	4.50
☐12L San Francisco	106,400,000	1.50	4.50	3,040,000	1.50	4.50

ONE DOLLAR NOTES (1969)
FEDERAL RESERVE NOTES
(WORDING IN GREEN, TREASURY SEAL
CHANGED FROM LATIN TO ENGLISH)

FORMER DESIGN:
The former design had
the Latin inscription:
*"Thesaur. Amer.
Septent. Sigil.,"*
which has several
translations. It was
the Seal of the North
American Treasury.

NEW DESIGN:
This new design
drops the Latin and
states *"The Department
of The Treasury, 1789."*
First used on the $100
Note of the
Series 1966.

ONE DOLLAR NOTES (1969)
FEDERAL RESERVE NOTES

(Small Size)

NOTE NO. 18A

SERIES OF 1969, ELSTON-KENNEDY, GREEN SEAL

Boston	2.60	Cleveland	2.60	Chicago	2.60	Kansas City	2.60
New York	2.60	Richmond	2.60	St. Louis	2.60	Dallas	2.60
Philadelphia	2.60	Atlanta	2.60	Minneapolis	2.60	San Francisco	2.60

SERIES OF 1969A, KABIS-KENNEDY, GREEN SEAL

Boston	2.60	Cleveland	2.60	Chicago	2.60	Kansas City	2.60
New York	2.60	Richmond	2.60	St. Louis	2.60	Dallas	2.60
Philadelphia	2.60	Atlanta	2.60	Minneapolis	2.60	San Francisco	2.60

SERIES OF 1969B, KABIS-CONNALLY, GREEN SEAL

Boston	2.60	Cleveland	2.60	Chicago	2.60	Kansas City	2.60
New York	2.60	Richmond	2.60	St. Louis	2.60	Dallas	2.60
Philadelphia	2.60	Atlanta	2.60	Minneapolis	2.60	San Francisco	2.60

SERIES OF 1969C, BANUELOS-CONNALLY, GREEN SEAL

Boston	2.60	Cleveland	2.60	Chicago	2.60	Kansas City	2.60
New York	2.60	Richmond	2.60	St. Louis	2.60	Dallas	2.60
Philadelphia	2.60	Atlanta	2.60	Minneapolis	2.60	San Francisco	2.60

SERIES OF 1969D, BANUELOS-CONNALLY, GREEN SEAL

Boston	2.60	Cleveland	2.60	Chicago	2.60	Kansas City	2.60
New York	2.60	Richmond	2.60	St. Louis	2.60	Dallas	2.60
Philadelphia	2.60	Atlanta	2.60	Minneapolis	2.60	San Francisco	2.60

SERIES OF 1974, NEFF-SIMON, GREEN SEAL

Boston	2.10	Cleveland	2.10	Chicago	2.10	Kansas City	2.10
New York	2.10	Richmond	2.10	St. Louis	2.10	Dallas	2.10
Philadelphia	2.10	Atlanta	2.10	Minneapolis	2.10	San Francisco	2.10

SERIES OF 1977, MORTON-BLUMENTHAL, GREEN SEAL

Boston	2.10	Cleveland	2.10	Chicago	2.10	Kansas City	2.10
New York	2.10	Richmond	2.10	St. Louis	2.10	Dallas	2.10
Philadelphia	2.10	Atlanta	2.10	Minneapolis	2.10	San Francisco	2.10

SERIES OF 1977A, MORTON-MILLER, GREEN SEAL

Boston	2.10	Cleveland	2.10	Chicago	2.10	Kansas City	2.10
New York	2.10	Richmond	2.10	St. Louis	2.10	Dallas	2.10
Philadelphia	2.10	Atlanta	2.10	Minneapolis	2.10	San Francisco	2.10

SERIES OF 1981, BUCHANAN-REGAN, GREEN SEAL

Boston	2.10	Cleveland	2.10	Chicago	2.10	Kansas City	2.10
New York	2.10	Richmond	2.10	St. Louis	2.10	Dallas	2.10
Philadelphia	2.10	Atlanta	2.10	Minneapolis	2.10	San Francisco	2.10

SERIES OF 1981A, ORTEGA-REGAN, GREEN SEAL

Boston	2.10	Cleveland	2.10	Chicago	2.10	Kansas City	2.10
New York	2.10	Richmond	2.10	St. Louis	2.10	Dallas	2.10
Philadelphia	2.10	Atlanta	2.10	Minneapolis	2.10	San Francisco	2.10

SERIES OF 1981-A, ORTEGA-REGAN-REVERSE #129 LEFT

Boston	7.00	Cleveland	7.00	Chicago	7.00	Kansas City	7.00
New York	7.00	Richmond	7.00	St. Louis	7.00	Dallas	7.00
Philadelphia	7.00	Atlanta	7.00	Minneapolis	7.00	San Francisco	7.00

SERIES OF 1985, ORTEGA-BAKER, GREEN SEAL

Boston	2.10	Cleveland	2.10	Chicago	2.10	Kansas City	2.10
New York	2.10	Richmond	2.10	St. Louis	2.10	Dallas	2.10
Philadelphia	2.10	Atlanta	2.10	Minneapolis	2.10	San Francisco	2.10

SERIES OF 1985, ORTEGA-BAKER-REVERSE #129 LEFT

Boston	7.00	Cleveland	7.00	Chicago	7.00	Kansas City	7.00
New York	7.00	Richmond	7.00	St. Louis	7.00	Dallas	7.00
Philadelphia	7.00	Atlanta	7.00	Minneapolis	7.00	San Francisco	7.00

SERIES OF 1988, ORTEGA-BAKER, GREEN SEAL

Boston	1.90	Cleveland	1.90	Chicago	1.90	Kansas City	1.90
New York	1.90	Richmond	1.90	St. Louis	1.90	Dallas	1.90
Philadelphia	1.90	Atlanta	1.90	Minneapolis	1.90	San Francisco	1.90

SERIES OF 1988-A, VILLAIPANDO-BRADY

Boston	1.50	Cleveland	1.50	Chicago	1.50	Kansas City	1.50
New York	1.50	Richmond	1.50	St. Louis	1.50	Dallas	1.50
Philadelphia	1.50	Atlanta	1.50	Minneapolis	1.50	San Francisco	1.50

SERIES OF 1993, WITHROW-BENTSEN, GREEN SEAL

Boston	1.25	Cleveland	1.25	Chicago	1.25	Kansas City	1.25
New York	1.25	Richmond	1.25	St. Louis	1.25	Dallas	1.25
Philadelphia	1.25	Atlanta	1.25	Minneapolis	1.25	San Francisco	1.25

SERIES OF 1995, WITHROW-BENTSEN, GREEN SEAL

Boston	1.00	Cleveland	1.00	Chicago	1.00	Kansas City	1.00
New York	1.00	Richmond	1.00	St. Louis	1.00	Dallas	1.00
Philadelphia	1.00	Atlanta	1.00	Minneapolis	1.00	San Francisco	1.00

TWO DOLLAR NOTES

ORDER OF ISSUE

TWO DOLLAR NOTES (1862) UNITED STATES NOTES
(ALSO KNOWN AS LEGAL TENDER NOTES)
(Large Size)   **NOTE NO. 19**

Face Design: Portrait of Alexander Hamilton (1754–1804),
cloverleaf "2"s in upper corners, medallion with "II" in lower
left, medallion with "1, 2, 3" right of portrait.

Back Design: "2" in each corner, with "2" motif repeated in
scallop circles around obligation; back is printed green.

SERIES	SIGNATURES	SEAL	A.B.P.	GOOD	V. FINE	UNC.
☐1862	Chittenden-Spinner					
	Type I, American Banknote Company vertical in left border	Red	70.00	125.00	525.00	2050.00
☐1862	Chittenden-Spinner					
	Type II, National Banknote Company vertical in left border	Red	70.00	125.00	500.00	2000.00

TWO DOLLAR NOTES (1869) UNITED STATES NOTES
(ALSO KNOWN AS LEGAL TENDER NOTES)
(Large Size)   **NOTE NO. 20**

Face Design: Portrait of President Jefferson to left, Capitol in center, large red seal to right.

Back Design: Roman "II" left, arabic "2" center, TWO right. This is the companion note to the $1 "Rainbow Note" (see note No. 2).

SERIES	SIGNATURES	SEAL	A.B.P.	GOOD	V. FINE	UNC.
☐1869	Allison-Spinner	Red	75.00	140.00	550.00	1850.00

TWO DOLLAR NOTES (1874) UNITED STATES NOTES (ALSO KNOWN AS LEGAL TENDER NOTES)

(Large Size)   **NOTE NO. 21**

Face Design: Portrait of President Jefferson; same as previous note No. 20.

Back Design: Completely revised.

SERIES	SIGNATURES	SEAL	A.B.P.	GOOD	V. FINE	UNC.
☐1874	Allison-Spinner	Red	45.00	70.00	400.00	800.00
☐1875	Allison-New	Red	40.00	80.00	380.00	850.00
☐Series A	Allison-New	Red	50.00	110.00	450.00	1000.00
☐Series B	Allison-New	Red	50.00	110.00	450.00	1000.00
☐1875	Allison-Wyman	Red	28.00	80.00	350.00	850.00
☐1878	Allison-Gilfillan	Red	28.00	80.00	325.00	750.00
☐1878	Scofield-Gilfillan	Red	850.00	1000.00	2500.00	5000.00
☐1880	Scofield-Gilfillan	Brown	18.00	30.00	130.00	480.00
☐1880	Bruce-Gilfillan	Brown	18.00	30.00	110.00	470.00
☐1880	Bruce-Wyman	Brown	18.00	30.00	110.00	470.00
☐1880	Rosecrans-Huston	Red	50.00	100.00	600.00	2750.00
☐1880	Rosecrans-Huston	Brown	50.00	100.00	600.00	2750.00
☐1880	Rosecrans-Nebeker	Red	18.00	30.00	90.00	290.00
☐1880	Tillman-Morgan	Red	18.00	32.00	90.00	325.00

SERIES	SIGNATURES	SEAL	A.B.P.	GOOD	V. FINE	UNC.
☐1917	Teehee-Burke	Red	15.00	30.00	55.00	175.00
☐1917	Elliott-Burke	Red	15.00	30.00	55.00	175.00
☐1917	Elliott-White	Red	15.00	30.00	55.00	175.00
☐1917	Speelman-White	Red	15.00	30.00	55.00	175.00

TWO DOLLAR NOTES (1928) UNITED STATES NOTES
(ALSO KNOWN AS LEGAL TENDER NOTES)

(Small Size)

NOTE NO. 22

Face Design: Portrait of President Jefferson, red seal left, TWO right, red serial numbers.

Back Design: Jefferson Home—Monticello.

SERIES	SIGNATURES	SEAL	A.B.P.	GOOD	V. FINE	UNC.
☐1928	Tate-Mellon	Red	4.00	9.00	14.00	42.00
☐1928A	Woods-Mellon	Red	6.00	15.00	35.00	190.00
☐1928B	Woods-Mills	Red	25.00	50.00	90.00	650.00
☐1928C	Julian-Morgenthau	Red	3.00	6.00	13.00	70.00
☐1928D	Julian-Morgenthau	Red	3.00	5.00	10.00	18.00
☐1928E	Julian-Vinson	Red	3.00	6.00	16.00	45.00
☐1928F	Julian-Snyder	Red	3.00	4.00	9.00	20.00
☐1928G	Clark-Snyder	Red	3.00	4.00	8.00	15.00

TWO DOLLAR NOTES (1953) UNITED STATES NOTES
(ALSO KNOWN AS LEGAL TENDER NOTES)
(Small Size) **NOTE NO. 23**

Face Design: Portrait of President Jefferson, gray "2" to left, red seal to right over TWO.
Back Design: Same as note No. 22.

SERIES	SIGNATURES	SEAL	A.B.P.	GOOD	V. FINE	UNC.
☐1953	Priest-Humphrey	Red	2.00	3.00	4.50	9.00
☐1953A	Priest-Anderson	Red	2.00	3.00	4.50	7.50
☐1953B	Smith-Dillon	Red	2.00	3.00	4.00	7.00
☐1953C	Granahan-Dillon	Red	2.00	3.00	4.00	8.00

Back Design: IN GOD WE TRUST on back.
Face Design: Same as previous note.

SERIES	SIGNATURES	SEAL	A.B.P.	GOOD	V. FINE	UNC.
☐1963	Granahan-Dillon	Red	2.00	3.00	5.00	7.00
☐1963A	Granahan-Fowler	Red	2.00	3.00	5.00	7.00

Production of $2 United States Notes was discontinued on August 10, 1966.

TWO DOLLAR NOTES (1875) NATIONAL BANK NOTES
FIRST CHARTER PERIOD (Large Size)   **NOTE NO. 24**

Face Design: This note is known as the "Lazy Two Note" due to the unusual "lying down" shape of the "2" shown on the face. Liberty with flag and red seal.

Back Design: Sir Walter Raleigh in England, 1585, exhibiting corn and smoking tobacco from America, State Seal, and eagle.

SERIES	SIGNATURES	SEAL	A.B.P.	GOOD	V. FINE	UNC.
☐Original	Colby-Spinner	Red	120.00	210.00	700.00	3200.00
☐Original	Jeffries-Spinner	Red	225.00	800.00	1300.00	4400.00
☐Original	Allison-Spinner	Red	120.00	220.00	750.00	3100.00
☐1875	Allison-New	Red	120.00	220.00	750.00	2500.00
☐1875	Allison-Wyman	Red	120.00	220.00	750.00	2500.00
☐1875	Allison-Gilfillan	Red	120.00	220.00	750.00	2500.00
☐1875	Scofield-Gilfillan	Red	120.00	220.00	750.00	2500.00

TWO DOLLAR NOTES (1886) SILVER CERTIFICATES

(Large Size) NOTE NO. 25

Face Design: General Hancock portrait left. Treasury Seal to the right of center.

Back Design: "2" left and right, very ornate engraving, obligation in center of note. Note is printed in green.

SERIES	SIGNATURES	SEAL	A.B.P.	GOOD	V. FINE	UNC.
☐1886	Rosecrans-Jordan	Red	60.00	110.00	525.00	1350.00
☐1886	Rosecrans-Hyatt	Sm.Red	60.00	110.00	525.00	1350.00
☐1886	Rosecrans-Hyatt	Lg.Red	60.00	110.00	525.00	1350.00
☐1886	Rosecrans-Huston	Red	60.00	110.00	525.00	1350.00
☐1886	Rosecrans-Huston	Brown	60.00	110.00	525.00	1350.00

TWO DOLLAR NOTES (1891) SILVER CERTIFICATES
(Large Size)   **NOTE NO. 26**

Face Design: Portrait of William Windom, Secretary of the
Treasury 1881–84 and 1889–91, red seal right.

Back Design: "2" left and right, scalloped design center
with obligation, printed in green.

SERIES	SIGNATURES	SEAL	A.B.P.	GOOD	V. FINE	UNC.
☐1891	Rosecrans-Nebeker	Red	60.00	100.00	400.00	2600.00
☐1891	Tillman-Morgan	Red	60.00	120.00	400.00	2100.00

TWO DOLLAR NOTES (1896) SILVER CERTIFICATES
(Large Size)   **NOTE NO. 27**

Face Design: Science presenting Steam and Electricity to Industry and Commerce.

Back Design: Portraits of Robert Fulton and Samuel F.B. Morse.

This is the second note of the popular Educational Series.

SERIES	SIGNATURES	SEAL	A.B.P.	GOOD	V. FINE	UNC.
☐1896	Tillman-Morgan	Red	100.00	170.00	700.00	2000.00
☐1896	Bruce-Roberts	Red	100.00	150.00	700.00	1900.00

TWO DOLLAR NOTES (1899) SILVER CERTIFICATES
(Large Size)
NOTE NO. 28

Face Design: Portrait of President Washington between figures of Trade and Agriculture, blue "2" left, blue seal right.

Back Design

SERIES	SIGNATURES	SEAL	A.B.P.	GOOD	V. FINE	UNC.
☐1899	Lyons-Roberts	Blue	18.00	30.00	120.00	400.00
☐1899	Lyons-Treat	Blue	18.00	30.00	120.00	400.00
☐1899	Vernon-Treat	Blue	18.00	30.00	120.00	400.00
☐1899	Vernon-McClung	Blue	18.00	30.00	120.00	400.00
☐1899	Napier-McClung	Blue	18.00	30.00	120.00	400.00
☐1899	Napier-Thompson	Blue	20.00	35.00	270.00	1050.00
☐1899	Parker-Burke	Blue	18.00	30.00	120.00	400.00
☐1899	Teehee-Burke	Blue	18.00	30.00	120.00	400.00
☐1899	Elliott-Burke	Blue	18.00	30.00	120.00	400.00
☐1899	Speelman-White	Blue	18.00	30.00	120.00	400.00

TWO DOLLAR NOTES (1890-1891)
TREASURY OR COIN NOTES

(Large Size)   **NOTE NO. 29**

Face Design: Portrait of General James McPherson.

Back Design: Large TWO center, over obligation. Large "2" on engraved background right. Intricate engraving, printed green.

SERIES	SIGNATURES	SEAL	A.B.P.	GOOD	V. FINE	UNC.
☐1890	Rosecrans-Huston	Brown	140.00	250.00	950.00	3700.00
☐1890	Rosecrans-Nebeker	Brown	140.00	250.00	950.00	3700.00
☐1890	Rosecrans-Nebeker	Red	140.00	250.00	950.00	3700.00

TWO DOLLAR NOTES (1890-1891)
TREASURY OR COIN NOTES

(Large Size)   **NOTE NO. 30**

Face Design: Similar to note No. 29.
Back Design: Revised.

SERIES	SIGNATURES	SEAL	A.B.P.	GOOD	V. FINE	UNC.
☐1891	Rosecrans-Nebeker	Red	54.00	90.00	350.00	850.00
☐1891	Tillman-Morgan	Red	54.00	90.00	350.00	850.00
☐1891	Bruce-Roberts	Red	54.00	90.00	350.00	850.00

TWO DOLLAR NOTES (1918)
FEDERAL RESERVE BANK NOTES

(Large Size)

NOTE NO. 31

Face Design: Portrait of President Jefferson to left, name of bank in center, blue seal to the right, blue numbers, Federal Reserve district letter and number in four corners.

Back Design: American battleship of World War I.

TWO DOLLAR NOTES (1918)
FEDERAL RESERVE BANK NOTES

(Large Size)   **NOTE NO. 31**

BANK & CITY	GOV'T SIGNATURES	BANK SIGNATURES	A.B.P.	GOOD	V. FINE	UNC.
☐ Boston	Teehee-Burke	Bullen-Morss	45.00	95.00	200.00	460.00
☐ Boston	Teehee-Burke	Willet-Morss	45.00	95.00	200.00	460.00
☐ Boston	Elliot-Burke	Willet-Morss	45.00	95.00	200.00	460.00
☐ New York	Teehee-Burke	Sailer-Strong	45.00	95.00	200.00	460.00
☐ New York	Teehee-Burke	Hendricks-Strong	45.00	95.00	200.00	460.00
☐ New York	Elliott-Burke	Hendricks-Strong	45.00	95.00	200.00	460.00
☐ Philadelphia	Teehee-Burke	Hardt-Passmore	45.00	95.00	200.00	460.00
☐ Philadelphia	Teehee-Burke	Dyer-Passmore	45.00	95.00	200.00	460.00
☐ Philadelphia	Elliott-Burke	Dyer-Passmore	45.00	95 00	200.00	460.00
☐ Philadelphia	Elliott-Burke	Dyer-Norris	45.00	95.00	200.00	460.00
☐ Cleveland	Teehee-Burke	Baxter-Francher	45.00	95.00	200.00	460.00
☐ Cleveland	Teehee-Burke	Davis-Francher	45.00	95.00	200.00	460.00
☐ Cleveland	Elliott-Burke	Davis-Francher	45.00	95.00	200.00	460.00
☐ Richmond	Teehee-Burke	Keesee-Seay	45.00	95.00	200.00	460.00
☐ Richmond	Elliott-Burke	Keesee-Seay	45.00	95.00	200.00	460.00
☐ Atlanta	Teehee-Burke	Pike-McCord	45.00	95.00	200.00	460.00
☐ Atlanta	Teehee-Burke	Bell-McCord	45.00	95.00	200.00	460.00
☐ Atlanta	Elliott-Burke	Bell-Wellborn	45.00	95.00	200.00	460.00
☐ Chicago	Teehee-Burke	McCloud-McDougal	45.00	95.00	200.00	460.00

BANK & CITY	GOV'T SIGNATURES	BANK SIGNATURES	A.B.P.	GOOD	V. FINE	UNC.
☐ Chicago	Teehee-Burke	Cramer-McDougal				
			45.00	95.00	200.00	460.00
☐ Chicago	Elliott-Burke	Cramer-McDougal				
			45.00	95.00	200.00	460.00
☐ St. Louis	Teehee-Burke	Attebery-Wells				
			45.00	95.00	200.00	460.00
☐ St. Louis	Teehee-Burke	Attebery-Biggs				
			45.00	95.00	200.00	460.00
☐ St. Louis	Elliott-Burke	Attebery-Biggs				
			45.00	95.00	200.00	460.00
☐ St. Louis	Elliott-Burke	White-Biggs				
			45.00	95.00	275.00	600.00
☐ Minneapolis	Teehee-Burke	Cook-Wold				
			45.00	95.00	275.00	600.00
☐ Minneapolis	Elliott-Burke	Cook-Young				
			45.00	95.00	200.00	460.00
☐ Kansas City	Teehee-Burke	Anderson-Miller				
			45.00	95.00	200.00	460.00
☐ Kansas City	Elliott-Burke	Helm-Miller				
			45.00	95.00	200.00	460.00
☐ Dallas	Teehee-Burke	Talley-VanZandt				
			45.00	95.00	200.00	460.00
☐ Dallas	Elliott-Burke	Talley-VanZandt				
			45.00	95.00	200.00	460.00
☐ San Francisco	Teehee-Burke	Clerk-Lynch				
			45.00	95.00	200.00	460.00
☐ San Francisco	Elliott-Burke	Clerk-Calkins				
			45.00	95.00	200.00	460.00
☐ San Francisco	Elliott-Burke	Ambrose-Calkins				
			45.00	95.00	200.00	460.00

TWO DOLLAR NOTES (1976)
FEDERAL RESERVE NOTES

(Small Size)   NOTE NO. 31A

Face Design: Portrait of President Jefferson.

Back Design: Signing of the Declaration of Independence.

SERIES OF 1976, NEFF-SIMON, GREEN SEAL

DISTRICT	A.B.P.	UNC.	DISTRICT	A.B.P.	UNC.
☐1A Boston	2.50	4.50	☐7G Chicago	2.50	4.50
☐2B New York	2.50	4.50	☐8H St. Louis	2.50	4.50
☐3C Philadelphia	2.50	4.50	☐9I Minneapolis	2.50	4.50
☐4D Cleveland	2.50	4.50	☐10J Kansas City	2.50	4.50
☐5E Richmond	2.50	4.50	☐11K Dallas	2.50	4.50
☐6F Atlanta	2.50	4.50	☐12L San Francisco	2.50	4.50

FIVE DOLLAR NOTES

FIVE DOLLAR NOTES (1861) DEMAND NOTES

(Large Size)   **NOTE NO. 32**

Face Design: Left, Statue of America by Crawford atop United States Capitol. Center, numeral "5" in green. Right, portrait of Alexander Hamilton, statesman, first Secretary of the Treasury.

Back Design: Numerous small "5s" in ovals. This note has no Treasury Seal. The signatures are those of Treasury Department employees who signed for officials.

CITY	A.B.P.	GOOD	V. GOOD
☐Boston (I)	275.00	1500.00	2600.00
☐New York (I)	275.00	1500.00	2600.00
☐Philadelphia (I)	275.00	1500.00	2600.00
☐Cincinnati (I)	500.00	8000.00	16,500.00
☐St. Louis (I)	500.00	8000.00	16,500.00
☐Boston (II)	275.00	350.00	550.00
☐New York (II)	275.00	350.00	550.00
☐Philadelphia (II)	275.00	350.00	550.00
☐Cincinnati (II)	300.00	6000.00	12,000.00
☐St. Louis (II)	300.00	6000.00	12,000.00

FIVE DOLLAR NOTES (1875-1907)
UNITED STATES NOTES
(ALSO KNOWN AS LEGAL TENDER NOTES)
(Large Size)   **NOTE NO. 35**

Back Design: Note No. 33. First Obligation.

Back Design: Note No. 33A. Second Obligation

SERIES	SIGNATURES	SEAL	A.B.P.	GOOD	V. FINE	UNC.
☐1862	Crittenden-Spinner*	Red	40.00	85.00	375.00	750.00
☐1862	Crittenden-Spinner**	Red	40.00	80.00	375.00	750.00
☐1863	Crittenden-Spinner**	Red	40.00	85.00	375.00	750.00

*First Obligation
**Second Obligation

FIVE DOLLAR NOTES (1869) UNITED STATES NOTES
(ALSO KNOWN AS LEGAL TENDER NOTES)
(Large Size)   **NOTE NO. 34**

Face Design: Portrait of President Jackson on left. Pioneer and family in center.

Back Design: Color, green. This is a companion note to the $1 and $2 Notes of 1869 "Rainbow Notes."

SERIES	SIGNATURES	SEAL	A.B.P.	GOOD	V. FINE	UNC.
☐1869	Allison-Spinner	Red	42.00	100.00	300.00	725.00

FIVE DOLLAR NOTES (1875-1907)
UNITED STATES NOTES
(ALSO KNOWN AS LEGAL TENDER NOTES)
(Large Size)   **NOTE NO. 35**

Back Design: Revised.
Face Design: Similar to previous note.

SERIES	SIGNATURES	SEAL	A.B.P.	GOOD	V. FINE	UNC.
☐1875	Allison-New	Red	17.00	50.00	125.00	550.00
☐1875A	Allison-New	Red	18.00	50.00	120.00	700.00
☐1875B	Allison-New	Red	18.00	50.00	120.00	700.00
☐1875	Allison-Wyman	Red	18.00	50.00	225.00	850.00
☐1878	Allison-Gilfillan	Red	25.00	60.00	235.00	850.00
☐1880	Scofield-Gilfillan	Brown	18.00	100.00	275.00	875.00
☐1880	Bruce-Gilfillan	Brown	15.00	40.00	200.00	750.00
☐1880	Bruce-Wyman	Brown	15.00	40.00	200.00	800.00
☐1880	Bruce-Wyman	Red	15.00	45.00	220.00	1350.00
☐1880	Rosecrans-Jordan	Red	15.00	42.00	200.00	900.00
☐1880	Rosecrans-Hyatt	Red	15.00	42.00	200.00	875.00
☐1880	Rosecrans-Huston	Red	22.00	50.00	215.00	900.00
☐1880	Rosecrans-Huston	Brown	18.00	50.00	220.00	950.00
☐1880	Rosecrans-Nebeker	Brown	20.00	50.00	220.00	900.00
☐1880	Rosecrans-Nebeker	Red	12.00	42.00	220.00	350.00
☐1880	Tillman-Morgan	Red	11.00	32.00	80.00	325.00
☐1880	Bruce-Roberts	Red	11.00	32.00	80.00	325.00
☐1880	Lyons-Roberts	Red	11.00	32.00	80.00	325.00
☐1907	Vernon-Treat	Red	11.00	30.00	65.00	225.00
☐1907	Vernon-McClung	Red	11.00	24.00	65.00	225.00
☐1907	Napier-McClung	Red	11.00	24.00	65.00	225.00
☐1907	Napier-Thompson	Red	40.00	90.00	280.00	675.00
☐1907	Parker-Burke	Red	10.00	24.00	65.00	215.00
☐1907	Teehee-Burke	Red	10.00	24.00	65.00	215.00
☐1907	Elliott-Burke	Red	10.00	24.00	65.00	215.00

SERIES	SIGNATURES	SEAL	A.B.P.	GOOD	V. FINE	UNC.
☐1907	Elliott-White	Red	14.00	24.00	60.00	215.00
☐1907	Speelman-White	Red	14.00	24.00	60.00	215.00
☐1907	Woods-White	Red	14.00	24.00	60.00	250.00

FIVE DOLLAR NOTES (1928) UNITED STATES NOTES
(ALSO KNOWN AS LEGAL TENDER NOTES)

(Small Size) **NOTE NO. 36**

Face Design: Portrait of President Lincoln center. Red seal to left, red serial numbers.

Back Design: Lincoln Memorial in Washington, D.C.

SERIES	SIGNATURES	SEAL	A.B.P	GOOD	V. FINE	UNC.
☐1928	Woods-Mellon	Red	6.00	7.00	11.00	32.00
☐1928A	Woods-Mills	Red	6.00	7.00	13.00	55.00
☐1928B	Julian-Morgenthau	Red	6.00	7.00	11.00	22.00
☐1928C	Julian-Morgenthau	Red	6.00	7.00	11.00	22.00
☐1928D	Julian-Vinson	Red	6.00	7.00	18.00	145.00
☐1928E	Julian-Snyder	Red	6.00	7.00	11.00	23.00
☐1928F	Clark-Snyder	Red	6.00	7.00	11.00	23.00

FIVE DOLLAR NOTES (1953-1963)
UNITED STATES NOTES

(Small Size)   **NOTE NO. 37**

Face Design: Similar to previous note. Portrait of President Lincoln center. Red seal is moved to the right, red numbers.
Back Design: Similar to previous note.

SERIES	SIGNATURES	SEAL	A.B.P.	GOOD	V. FINE	UNC.
☐1953	Priest-Humphrey	Red	6.00	7.50	9.00	18.00
☐1953A	Priest-Anderson	Red	6.00	7.50	11.00	18.00
☐1953B	Smith-Dillon	Red	6.00	7.50	9.00	13.00
☐1953C	Granahan-Dillon	Red	6.00	7.50	9.00	18.00

FIVE DOLLAR NOTES (1953-1963)
UNITED STATES NOTES
(ALSO KNOWN AS LEGAL TENDER NOTES)

(Small Size)   **NOTE NO. 37A**

Back Design: The following notes have IN GOD WE TRUST on the back.
Face Design: Similar to previous note.

SERIES	SIGNATURES	SEAL	A.B.P.	GOOD	V. FINE	UNC.
☐1963	Granahan-Dillon	Red	6.00	7.50	11.00	16.00

Production of $5 United States Notes ended in 1967.

FIVE DOLLAR NOTES (1863-1875)
NATIONAL BANK NOTES
FIRST CHARTER PERIOD (Large Size)   **NOTE NO. 38**

Face Design: The Columbus Note. The face shows Columbus in sight of land and Columbus with an Indian princess.

Back Design: Christopher Columbus landing at San Salvador, 1492. Also the State Seal left, and American eagle right.

SERIES	SIGNATURES	SEAL	A.B.P.	GOOD	V. FINE	UNC.
☐Original	Chittenden-Spinner	Red	45.00	80.00	250.00	1300.00
☐Original	Colby-Spinner	Red	45.00	80.00	250.00	1250.00
☐Original	Jeffries-Spinner	Red	180.00	500.00	1600.00	3600.00
☐Original	Allison-Spinner	Red	45.00	75.00	250.00	1300.00
☐1875	Allison-New	Red	45.00	75.00	250.00	1200.00
☐1875	Allison-Wyman	Red	45.00	75.00	250.00	1200.00
☐1875	Allison-Gilfillan	Red	45.00	75.00	250.00	1200.00
☐1875	Scofield-Gilfillan	Red	45.00	75.00	250.00	1200.00
☐1875	Bruce-Gilfillan	Red	45.00	75.00	250.00	1200.00
☐1875	Bruce-Wyman	Red	45.00	75.00	250.00	1200.00
☐1875	Bruce-Jordan	Red		EXTREMELY RARE		
☐1875	Rosecrans-Huston	Red	45.00	75.00	250.00	1200.00
☐1875	Rosecrans-Jordan	Red	45.00	75.00	250.00	1200.00

FIVE DOLLAR NOTES (1882) NATIONAL BANK NOTES
SECOND CHARTER PERIOD (Large Size)   **NOTE NO. 39**

First Issue (Brown seal and brown backs)
Face Design: Portrait of President Garfield left. Name of bank
and city center, brown seal to right. Brown charter number.

Back Design: Brown border design similar to previous note.
Center oval now has the bank's charter number in green.
The top signatures are those of the Treasury officials.
Bottom signatures, usually handwritten or probably rubber-
stamped, are bank officials.

SERIES	SIGNATURES	SEAL	A.B.P.	GOOD	V. FINE	UNC.
☐1882	Bruce-Gilfillan	Brown	25.00	65.00	160.00	675.00
☐1882	Bruce-Wyman	Brown	25.00	65.00	160.00	675.00
☐1882	Bruce-Jordan	Brown	25.00	65.00	160.00	675.00
☐1882	Rosecrans-Jordan	Brown	25.00	65.00	160.00	675.00
☐1882	Rosecrans-Hyatt	Brown	25.00	65.00	160.00	675.00
☐1882	Rosecrans-Huston	Brown	25.00	65.00	160.00	675.00
☐1882	Rosecrans-Nebeker	Brown	25.00	65.00	160.00	675.00
☐1882	Rosecrans-Morgan	Brown	70.00	165.00	400.00	1100.00
☐1882	Tillman-Morgan	Brown	25.00	65.00	160.00	675.00
☐1882	Tillman-Roberts	Brown	25.00	65.00	160.00	675.00
☐1882	Bruce-Roberts	Brown	25.00	65.00	160.00	675.00
☐1882	Lyons-Roberts	Brown	25.00	65.00	160.00	675.00
☐1882	Lyons-Treat	(Unknown in any collection)				
☐1882	Vernon-Treat	Brown	25.00	70.00	160.00	675.00

FIVE DOLLAR NOTES (1882) NATIONAL BANK NOTES
SECOND CHARTER PERIOD (Large Size) **NOTE NO. 40**

Face Design: Similar to preceding portrait of President Garfield.

Back Design: Back is now green with date "1882–1908" in center.

SERIES	SIGNATURES	SEAL	A.B.P.	GOOD	V. FINE	UNC.
☐1882	Rosecrans-Huston	Blue	30.00	50.00	120.00	575.00
☐1882	Rosecrans-Nebeker	Blue	30.00	50.00	120.00	575.00
☐1882	Rosecrans-Morgan	Blue	100.00	200.00	800.00	1850.00
☐1882	Tillman-Morgan	Blue	30.00	50.00	120.00	575.00
☐1882	Tillman-Roberts	Blue	30.00	50.00	120.00	575.00
☐1882	Bruce-Roberts	Blue	30.00	50.00	120.00	575.00
☐1882	Lyons-Roberts	Blue	30.00	50.00	120.00	575.00
☐1882	Vernon-Treat	Blue	30.00	50.00	120.00	575.00
☐1882	Vernon-McClung	Blue				RARE
☐1882	Napier-McClung	Blue				RARE

FIVE DOLLAR NOTES (1882) NATIONAL BANK NOTES
SECOND CHARTER PERIOD, Third Issue (Large Size) **NOTE NO. 41**

Face Design: Same as note No. 39. Blue seal.

Back Design: Similar to note No. 40, FIVE DOLLARS replaces "1882–1908."

SERIES	SIGNATURES	SEAL	A.B.P.	GOOD	V. FINE	UNC.
☐1882	Tillman-Morgan	Blue	48.00	80.00	320.00	1275.00
☐1882	Tillman-Roberts	Blue	48.00	80.00	320.00	1275.00
☐1882	Bruce-Roberts	Blue	48.00	80.00	320.00	1275.00
☐1882	Lyons-Roberts	Blue	48.00	80.00	320.00	1275.00
☐1882	Vernon-Treat	Blue	48.00	80.00	320.00	1275.00
☐1882	Napier-McClung	Blue	48.00	80.00	320.00	1275.00
☐1882	Teehee-Burke	Blue		EXTREMELY RARE		

FIVE DOLLAR NOTES (1902) NATIONAL BANK NOTES
THIRD CHARTER PERIOD (Large Size)   **NOTE NO. 42**

First Issue (Red seal and charter numbers.**)**

Face Design: Portrait of President Harrison left, name of bank and city center, Treasury Seal to right, red seal and charter number.

Back Design: Landing of pilgrims.

SERIES	SIGNATURES	SEAL	A.B.P.	GOOD	V. FINE	UNC.
☐1902	Lyons-Roberts	Red	48.00	60.00	165.00	800.00
☐1902	Lyons-Treat	Red	48.00	60.00	165.00	800.00
☐1902	Vernon-Treat	Red	48.00	60.00	165.00	800.00

FIVE DOLLAR NOTES (1902) NATIONAL BANK NOTES
THIRD CHARTER PERIOD (Large Size)   **NOTE NO. 42A**
SECOND ISSUE

SERIES	SIGNATURES	SEAL	A.B.P.	GOOD	V. FINE	UNC.
☐1902	Lyons-Roberts	Blue	9.00	21.00	45.00	295.00
☐1902	Lyons-Treat	Blue	9.00	21.00	45.00	295.00
☐1902	Vernon-Treat	Blue	9.00	21.00	45.00	295.00
☐1902	Vernon-McClung	Blue	9.00	21.00	45.00	295.00
☐1902	Napier-McClung	Blue	9.00	21.00	45.00	295.00
☐1902	Napier-Thompson	Blue	15.00	32.00	65.00	475.00
☐1902	Napier-Burke	Blue	9.00	21.00	45.00	295.00
☐1902	Parker-Burke	Blue	9.00	21.00	45.00	295.00
☐1902	Teehee-Burke	Blue	9.00	21.00	80.00	325.00

FIVE DOLLAR NOTES (1902) NATIONAL BANK NOTES
THIRD CHARTER PERIOD (Large Size)   **NOTE NO. 42B**
Third Issue (Blue seal and numbers.)

The following notes do not have date of "1902–1908" on the back.

SERIES	SIGNATURES	SEAL	A.B.P.	GOOD	V. FINE	UNC.
☐1902	Lyons-Roberts	Blue	8.50	18.00	47.00	235.00
☐1902	Lyons-Treat	Blue	8.50	18.00	47.00	235.00
☐1902	Vernon-Treat	Blue	8.50	18.00	47.00	235.00
☐1902	Vernon-McClung	Blue	8.50	18.00	47.00	235.00
☐1902	Napier-McClung	Blue	8.50	18.00	47.00	235.00
☐1902	Napier-Thompson	Blue	8.50	18.00	60.00	250.00
☐1902	Napier-Burke	Blue	8.50	18.00	47.00	235.00
☐1902	Parker-Burke	Blue	8.50	18.00	47.00	235.00
☐1902	Teehee-Burke	Blue	8.50	18.00	47.00	235.00
☐1902	Elliott-Burke	Blue	8.50	18.00	47.00	235.00
☐1902	Elliott-White	Blue	8.50	18.00	47.00	235.00
☐1902	Speelman-White	Blue	8.50	18.00	47.00	235.00
☐1902	Woods-White	Blue	8.50	18.00	47.00	235.00
☐1902	Woods-Tate	Blue	8.50	18.00	47.00	235.00
☐1902	Jones-Woods	Blue	25.00	85.00	180.00	420.00

FIVE DOLLAR NOTES (1929) NATIONAL BANK NOTES
(Small Size)   **NOTE NO. 43**

TYPE I

TYPE II

Face Design: Portrait of President Lincoln in center, name of bank to left, brown seal to the right. Type I—charter number in black. Type II—similar; charter number added in brown.

Back Design: Lincoln Memorial.

SERIES	SIGNATURES	SEAL	A.B.P.	GOOD	V. FINE	UNC.
☐1929	Type I Jones-Woods	Brown	6.50	10.00	18.00	65.00
☐1929	Type II Jones-Woods	Brown	6.50	12.00	25.00	70.00

FIVE DOLLAR NOTES (1870)
NATIONAL GOLD BANK NOTES

(Large Size)   **NOTE NO. 44**

Face Design: Vignettes of Columbus sighting land. Presentation of an Indian princess. Red seal. Signatures, Allison-Spinner.

Back Design: California State Seal left, gold coins center, American eagle right.

DATE	BANK	CITY	A.B.P.	GOOD	V. GOOD
☐1870 First National Gold Bank		San Francisco	360.00	600.00	1400.00
☐1872 National Gold Bank and Trust Co.		San Francisco	360.00	600.00	1400.00
☐1872 National Gold Bank of D.O. Mills and Co.		Sacramento	480.00	800.00	1650.00
☐1873 First National Gold Bank		Santa Barbara	480.00	800.00	1650.00
☐1873 First National Gold Bank		Stockton	480.00	800.00	2100.00
☐1874 Farmers National Gold Bank		San Jose	480.00	800.00	2100.00

FIVE DOLLAR NOTES (1886-1891)
SILVER CERTIFICATES

(Large Size)

NOTE NO. 45

Face Design: Portrait of President Grant.

Back Design: Five silver dollars.

SERIES	SIGNATURES	SEAL	A.B.P.	GOOD	V. FINE	UNC.
☐1886	Rosecrans-Jordan	Red	120.00	200.00	900.00	3200.00
☐1886	Rosecrans-Hyatt	Sm. Red	120.00	200.00	800.00	2400.00
☐1886	Rosecrans-Hyatt	Lg. Red	120.00	200.00	870.00	3000.00
☐1886	Rosecrans-Huston	Lg. Red	120.00	200.00	870.00	2800.00
☐1886	Rosecrans-Huston	Brown	120.00	200.00	800.00	2800.00
☐1886	Rosecrans-Nebeker	Brown	120.00	200.00	900.00	2600.00
☐1886	Rosecrans-Nebeker	Sm. Red	150.00	250.00	1300.00	4200.00

FIVE DOLLAR NOTES (1891) SILVER CERTIFICATES
(Large Size)   NOTE NO. 46

Face Design: Similar to previous note.

Back Design: Revised.

SERIES	SIGNATURES	SEAL	A.B.P.	GOOD	V. FINE	UNC.
☐1891	Rosecrans-Nebeker	Red	60.00	100.00	600.00	2850.00
☐1891	Tillman-Morgan	Red	60.00	100.00	600.00	2750.00

FIVE DOLLAR NOTES (1896) SILVER CERTIFICATES
(Large Size)

NOTE NO. 47

Face Design: Portraits of General Grant and General Sheridan.

Back Design: Five females representing Electricity as the dominant force in the world.

This was the last note of the popular Education Series.

SERIES	SIGNATURES	SEAL	A.B.P.	GOOD	V. FINE	UNC.
☐1896	Tillman-Morgan	Red	150.00	260.00	1000.00	3900.00
☐1896	Bruce-Roberts	Red	150.00	260.00	1000.00	3900.00
☐1896	Lyons-Roberts	Red	150.00	260.00	1000.00	3900.00

FIVE DOLLAR NOTES (1899) SILVER CERTIFICATES
(Large Size)   **NOTE NO. 48**

Face Design: Portrait of Indian chief.

Back Design: Green "V" and "5."

SERIES	SIGNATURES	SEAL	A.B.P.	GOOD	V. FINE	UNC.
☐1899	Lyons-Roberts	Blue	48.00	95.00	365.00	1300.00
☐1899	Lyons-Treat	Blue	48.00	95.00	365.00	1250.00
☐1899	Vernon-Treat	Blue	48.00	95.00	365.00	1250.00
☐1899	Vernon-McClung	Blue	48.00	95.00	365.00	1250.00
☐1899	Napier-McClung	Blue	48.00	95.00	365.00	1250.00
☐1899	Napier-Thompson	Blue	48.00	95.00	400.00	2300.00
☐1899	Parker-Burke	Blue	48.00	95.00	365.00	1250.00
☐1899	Teehee-Burke	Blue	48.00	95.00	365.00	1250.00
☐1899	Elliott-Burke	Blue	48.00	95.00	365.00	1250.00
☐1899	Elliott-White	Blue	48.00	95.00	365.00	1250.00
☐1899	Speelman-White	Blue	48.00	95.00	365.00	1250.00

FIVE DOLLAR NOTES (1923) SILVER CERTIFICATES
(Large Size)   **NOTE NO. 49**

Face Design: Portrait of President Lincoln in oval, nickname "Porthole Note," blue seal left, blue "5" right.

Back Design: Obverse of Great Seal of the United States.

SERIES	SIGNATURES	SEAL	A.B.P.	GOOD	V. FINE	UNC.
☐1923	Speelman-White	Blue	48.00	80.00	400.00	1250.00

FIVE DOLLAR NOTES (1934) SILVER CERTIFICATES
(Small Size)   **NOTE NO. 50**

First Issue (Small size of $5 Silver Certificates 1934.)
Face Design: Portrait of President Lincoln, blue "5" to left, blue seal to right.

Back Design: All Small Size $5 Notes have the same back design.

SERIES	SIGNATURES	SEAL	A.B.P.	GOOD	V. FINE	UNC.
☐1934	Julian-Morgenthau	Blue	6.00	7.00	9.00	22.00
☐1934A	Julian-Morgenthau	Blue	6.00	7.00	9.00	20.00
☐1934A	Julian-Morgenthau	Yellow	6.50	8.00	16.00	70.00

This note, with yellow Treasury Seal, was a Special Issue during World War II for military use in combat areas of North Africa and Europe.

SERIES	SIGNATURES	SEAL	A.B.P.	GOOD	V. FINE	UNC.
☐1934B	Julian-Vinson	Blue	6.00	7.50	9.00	36.00
☐1934C	Julian-Synder	Blue	6.00	7.50	9.00	22.00
☐1934C	Clark-Snyder	Blue	6.00	7.50	10.00	20.00

FIVE DOLLAR NOTES (1953) SILVER CERTIFICATES
(Small Size)   **NOTE NO. 51**

Face Design: The following notes are similar to the previous note. The face design has been revised. Gray "5" replaces blue "5" to left of Lincoln. Blue seal is slightly smaller.

Back Design: Same as previous note.

SERIES	SIGNATURES	SEAL	A.B.P.	GOOD	V. FINE	UNC.
☐1953	Priest-Humphrey	Blue	4.00	7.00	8.00	16.00
☐1953A	Priest-Anderson	Blue	4.00	7.00	8.00	15.00
☐1953B	Smith-Dillon	Blue	4.00	7.00	8.00	15.00

Production of $5 Silver Certificates ended in 1962.

FIVE DOLLAR NOTES (1890) TREASURY OR COIN NOTES
(Large Size)   **NOTE NO. 52**

Face Design: Portrait of General George Henry Thomas (1816–70), the "Rock of Chickamaugua."

Back Design: Note No. 52.

SERIES	SIGNATURES	SEAL	A.B.P.	GOOD	V. FINE	UNC.
☐1890	Rosecrans-Huston	Brown	90.00	150.00	575.00	2000.00
☐1890	Rosecrans-Nebeker	Brown	66.00	110.00	550.00	1900.00
☐1890	Rosecrans-Nebeker	Red	66.00	110.00	550.00	1900.00

Back Design: Note No. 53.
Face Design: Same as previous note.

SERIES	SIGNATURES	SEAL	A.B.P.	GOOD	V.FINE	UNC.
☐1891	Rosecrans-Nebeker	Red	54.00	90.00	200.00	750.00
☐1891	Tillman-Morgan	Red	54.00	90.00	200.00	950.00
☐1891	Bruce-Roberts	Red	54.00	90.00	200.00	950.00
☐1891	Lyons-Roberts	Red	54.00	90.00	200.00	950.00

FIVE DOLLAR NOTES (1914)
FEDERAL RESERVE NOTES

(Large Size)   **NOTE NO. 54**

Face Design: Portrait of President Lincoln center, Federal Reserve Seal left, Treasury Seal right.

Back Design: Scene of Columbus in sight of land left, landing of pilgrims right.

SERIES OF 1914, RED TREASURY SEAL AND RED NUMBERS

SERIES CITY	SIGNATURES	SEAL	A.B.P.	GOOD	V. FINE	UNC.
☐1914 Boston	Burke-McAdoo	Red	18.00	30.00	80.00	315.00
☐1914 New York	Burke-McAdoo	Red	18.00	30.00	80.00	315.00
☐1914 Philadelphia	Burke-McAdoo	Red	18.00	30.00	80.00	315.00
☐1914 Cleveland	Burke-McAdoo	Red	18.00	30.00	80.00	315.00
☐1914 Richmond	Burke-McAdoo	Red	18.00	30.00	80.00	315.00
☐1914 Atlanta	Burke-McAdoo	Red	18.00	30.00	80.00	315.00
☐1914 Chicago	Burke-McAdoo	Red	18.00	30.00	80.00	315.00
☐1914 St. Louis	Burke-McAdoo	Red	18.00	30.00	80.00	315.00
☐1914 Minneapolis	Burke-McAdoo	Red	18.00	30.00	80.00	315.00
☐1914 Kansas City	Burke-McAdoo	Red	18.00	30.00	80.00	315.00
☐1914 Dallas	Burke-McAdoo	Red	18.00	30.00	80.00	315.00
☐1914 San Francisco	Burke-McAdoo	Red	18.00	30.00	80.00	315.00

FIVE DOLLAR NOTES (1914)
FEDERAL RESERVE NOTES

NOTE NO. 54A

SERIES OF 1914, BLUE TREASURY SEAL AND BLUE NUMBERS

SERIES CITY	SIGNATURES	SEAL	A.B.P.	GOOD	V. FINE	UNC.
☐1914 Boston	Burke-McAdoo	Blue	8.00	12.00	33.00	95.00
☐1914 Boston	Burke-Glass	Blue	8.00	12.00	33.00	95.00
☐1914 Boston	Burke-Huston	Blue	8.00	12.00	33.00	95.00
☐1914 Boston	White-Mellon	Blue	8.00	12.00	33.00	95.00
☐1914 New York	Burke-McAdoo	Blue	8.00	12.00	33.00	95.00
☐1914 New York	Burke-Glass	Blue	8.00	12.00	33.00	95.00
☐1914 New York	Burke-Huston	Blue	8.00	12.00	33.00	95.00
☐1914 New York	White-Mellon	Blue	8.00	12.00	33.00	95.00
☐1914 Philadelphia	Burke-McAdoo	Blue	8.00	12.00	33.00	95.00
☐1914 Philadelphia	Burke-Glass	Blue	8.00	12.00	33.00	95.00
☐1914 Philadelphia	Burke-Huston	Blue	8.00	12.00	33.00	95.00

SERIES CITY	SIGNATURES	SEAL	A.B.P.	GOOD	V. FINE	UNC.
☐1914 Philadelphia	White-Mellon	Blue	8.00	12.00	33.00	95.00
☐1914 Cleveland	Burke-McAdoo	Blue	8.00	12.00	33.00	95.00
☐1914 Cleveland	Burke-Glass	Blue	8.00	12.00	33.00	95.00
☐1914 Cleveland	Burke-Huston	Blue	8.00	12.00	33.00	95.00
☐1914 Cleveland	White-Mellon	Blue	8.00	12.00	33.00	95.00
☐1914 Richmond	Burke-McAdoo	Blue	8.00	12.00	33.00	95.00
☐1914 Richmond	Burke-Glass	Blue	8.00	12.00	33.00	95.00
☐1914 Richmond	Burke-Huston	Blue	8.00	12.00	33.00	95.00
☐1914 Richmond	White-Mellon	Blue	8.00	12.00	33.00	95.00
☐1914 Atlanta	Burke-McAdoo	Blue	8.00	12.00	33.00	95.00
☐1914 Atlanta	Burke-Glass	Blue	8.00	12.00	33.00	95.00
☐1914 Atlanta	Burke-Huston	Blue	8.00	12.00	33.00	95.00
☐1914 Atlanta	White-Mellon	Blue	8.00	12.00	33.00	95.00
☐1914 Chicago	Burke-McAdoo	Blue	8.00	12.00	33.00	95.00
☐1914 Chicago	Burke-Glass	Blue	8.00	12.00	33.00	95.00
☐1914 Chicago	Burke-Huston	Blue	8.00	12.00	33.00	95.00
☐1914 Chicago	White-Mellon	Blue	8.00	12.00	33.00	95.00
☐1914 St. Louis	Burke-McAdoo	Blue	8.00	12.00	33.00	95.00
☐1914 St. Louis	Burke-Glass	Blue	8.00	14.00	33.00	95.00
☐1914 St. Louis	Burke-Huston	Blue	8.00	12.00	33.00	95.00
☐1914 St. Louis	White-Mellon	Blue	8.00	12.00	33.00	95.00
☐1914 Minneapolis	Burke-McAdoo	Blue	8.00	14.00	35.00	95.00
☐1914 Minneapolis	Burke-Glass	Blue	8.00	14.00	35.00	95.00
☐1914 Minneapolis	Burke-Huston	Blue	8.00	12.00	33.00	95.00
☐1914 Minneapolis	White-Mellon	Blue	8.00	12.00	33.00	95.00
☐1914 Kansas City	Burke-McAdoo	Blue	8.00	12.00	33.00	95.00
☐1914 Kansas City	Burke-Glass	Blue	8.00	14.00	33.00	95.00
☐1914 Kansas City	Burke-Huston	Blue	8.00	12.00	33.00	95.00
☐1914 Kansas City	White-Mellon	Blue	8.00	12.00	33.00	95.00
☐1914 Dallas	Burke-McAdoo	Blue	8.00	13.00	35.00	95.00
☐1914 Dallas	Burke-Glass	Blue	8.00	15.00	36.00	95.00
☐1914 Dallas	Burke-Huston	Blue	8.00	12.00	33.00	95.00
☐1914 Dallas	White-Mellon	Blue	8.00	12.00	33.00	95.00
☐1914 San Francisco	Burke-McAdoo	Blue	8.00	12.00	33.00	95.00
☐1914 San Francisco	Burke-Glass	Blue	8.00	14.00	35.00	95.00
☐1914 San Francisco	Burke-Huston	Blue	8.00	12.00	33.00	95.00
☐1914 San Francisco	White-Mellon	Blue	8.00	12.00	33.00	95.00

FIVE DOLLAR NOTES (1928)
FEDERAL RESERVE NOTES

(Small Size)

NOTE NO. 55

Face Design: Portrait of President Lincoln center, black Federal Reserve Seal with numeral for district in center. City of issuing bank in seal circle. Green Treasury Seal to right.
Back Design: Similar to note No. 50; Lincoln Memorial in Washington, D.C.

SERIES OF 1928,
SIGNATURES OF TATE AND MELLON, GREEN SEAL

BANK	A.B.P.	GOOD	V.FINE	UNC.	BANK	A.B.P.	GOOD	V.FINE	UNC.
☐ Boston	6.50	8.00	12.00	65.00	☐ Chicago	6.50	8.00	12.00	65.00
☐ New York	6.50	8.00	12.00	65.00	☐ St. Louis	6.50	8.00	12.00	65.00
☐ Philadelphia	6.50	8.00	12.00	65.00	☐ Minneapolis	6.50	8.00	12.00	65.00
☐ Cleveland	6.50	8.00	12.00	65.00	☐ Kansas City	6.50	8.00	12.00	65.00
☐ Richmond	6.50	8.00	12.00	65.00	☐ Dallas	6.50	8.00	12.00	65.00
☐ Atlanta	6.50	8.00	12.00	65.00	☐ San Francisco	6.50	8.00	12.00	65.00

SERIES OF 1928A,
SIGNATURES OF WOODS-MELLON, GREEN SEAL

BANK	A.B.P.	GOOD	V.FINE	UNC.	BANK	A.B.P.	GOOD	V.FINE	UNC.
☐ Boston	6.50	8.00	12.00	45.00	☐ Chicago	6.50	8.00	12.00	45.00
☐ New York	6.50	8.00	12.00	45.00	☐ St. Louis	6.50	8.00	12.00	45.00
☐ Philadelphia	6.50	8.00	12.00	45.00	☐ Minneapolis	6.50	8.00	12.00	45.00
☐ Cleveland	6.50	8.00	12.00	45.00	☐ Kansas City	6.50	8.00	12.00	45.00
☐ Richmond	6.50	8.00	12.00	45.00	☐ Dallas	6.50	8.00	12.00	45.00
☐ Atlanta	6.50	8.00	12.00	45.00	☐ San Francisco	6.50	8.00	12.00	45.00

SERIES OF 1928B,
SIGNATURES OF WOODS-MELLON, GREEN SEAL

The black Federal Reserve Seal now has a letter for district in place of the numeral.

BANK	A.B.P.	GOOD	V. FINE	UNC.	BANK	A.B.P.	GOOD	V.FINE	UNC.
☐Boston	6.50	9.00	20.00	55.00	☐Chicago	6.50	9.00	20.00	55.00
☐New York	6.50	9.00	20.00	55.00	☐St. Louis	6.50	9.00	20.00	55.00
☐Philadelphia	6.50	9.00	20.00	55.00	☐Minneapolis	6.50	9.00	20.00	55.00
☐Cleveland	6.50	9.00	20.00	55.00	☐Kansas City	6.50	9.00	20.00	55.00
☐Richmond	6.50	9.00	20.00	55.00	☐Dallas	6.50	9.00	20.00	55.00
☐Atlanta	6.50	9.00	20.00	55.00	☐San Francisco	6.50	9.00	20.00	55.00

FIVE DOLLAR NOTES (1928)
FEDERAL RESERVE NOTES
SERIES OF 1928C, *
SIGNATURES OF WOODS-WOODIN, GREEN SEAL

BANK	A.B.P.	GOOD	V. FINE	UNC.	BANK	A.B.P.	GOOD	V.FINE	UNC.
☐Cleveland	38.00	80.00	190.00	800.00	☐ San				
☐Atlanta	38.00	80.00	190.00	400.00	Francisco	38.00	80.00	190.00	800.00

*This series not issued by other banks.

SERIES OF 1928D, *
SIGNATURES OF WOODS-MILLS, GREEN SEAL

BANK	A.B.P.	GOOD	V. FINE	UNC.
☐Atlanta	48.00	100.00	200.00	800.00

*This series not issued by other banks.

SERIES OF 1934, JULIAN-MORGENTHAU, GREEN SEAL

"Redeemable in Gold" was removed from obligation over Federal Reserve Seal. Also, the green Treasury Seal on this note is known in a light and dark color. The light seal is worth about 10–20 percent more in most cases.

BANK	A.B.P.	V. FINE	UNC.	BANK	A.B.P.	V.FINE	UNC.
☐Boston	6.00	10.00	25.00	☐St. Louis	6.00	10.00	25.00
☐New York	6.00	10.00	25.00	☐Minneapolis	6.00	10.00	25.00
☐Philadelphia	6.00	10.00	25.00	☐Kansas City	6.00	10.00	25.00
☐Cleveland	6.00	10.00	25.00	☐Dallas	6.00	10.00	25.00
☐Richmond	6.00	10.00	25.00	☐San Francisco	6.00	10.00	25.00
☐Atlanta	6.00	10.00	25.00	☐San Francisco*	17.00	45.00	200.00
☐Chicago	6.00	10.00	25.00				

*This note has brown Treasury Seal and is surprinted HAWAII. For use in Pacific area of operations during World War II.

(Small Size)

Note—1934A (Julian-Morgenthau) is surprinted HAWAII. It was used in the Pacific area during World War II.

SERIES OF 1934A, JULIAN-MORGENTHAU, GREEN SEAL

BANK	A.B.P.	V.FINE	UNC.	BANK	A.B.P.	V.FINE	UNC.
☐Boston	6.00	10.00	25.00	☐Atlanta	6.00	10 00	25.00
☐New York	6.00	10.00	25.00	☐Chicago	6.00	10 00	25.00
☐Philadelphia	6.00	10.00	25.00	☐St. Louis	6.00	10.00	25.00
☐Cleveland	6.00	10.00	25.00	☐San Francisco	6.00	10.00	25.00
☐Richmond	6.00	10.00	25.00	☐San Francisco*	15.00	35.00	140.00

*This note has brown Treasury Seal and is surprinted HAWAII. For use in Pacific area of operations during World War II.

FIVE DOLLAR NOTES (1934)
FEDERAL RESERVE NOTES

(Small Size)

Face Design: Same as note No. 55.
Back Design: Same as note No. 50.

SERIES OF 1934B,
SIGNATURES OF JULIAN-VINSON, GREEN SEAL

BANK	A.B.P.	V.FINE	UNC.	BANK	A.B.P.	V.FINE	UNC.
☐Boston	6.00	11.00	26.00	☐Chicago	6.00	11 00	26.00
☐New York	6.00	11.00	26.00	☐St. Louis	6.00	11 00	26.00
☐Philadelphia	6.00	11.00	26.00	☐Minneapolis	6.00	11.00	26.00
☐Cleveland	6.00	11.00	26.00	☐Kansas City	6.00	11.00	26.00
☐Richmond	6.00	11.00	26.00	☐Dallas		NOT ISSUED	
☐Atlanta	6.00	11.00	26.00	☐San Francisco	6.00	11.00	26.00

SERIES OF 1934C,
SIGNATURES OF JULIAN-SNYDER, GREEN SEAL

BANK	A.B.P.	V.FINE	UNC.	BANK	A.B.P.	V.FINE	UNC.
☐Boston	6.00	9.00	23.00	☐Chicago	6.00	9.00	23.00
☐New York	6.00	9.00	23.00	☐St. Louis	6.00	9.00	23.00

BANK	A.B.P.	V.FINE	UNC.	BANK	A.B.P.	V.FINE	UNC.
☐Philadelphia	6.00	9.00	23.00	☐Minneapolis	6.00	9.00	23.00
☐Cleveland	6.00	9.00	23.00	☐Kansas City	6.00	9.00	23.00
☐Richmond	6.00	9.00	23.00	☐Dallas	6.00	9.00	23.00
☐Atlanta	6.00	9.00	23.00	☐San Francisco	6.00	9.00	23.00

SERIES OF 1934D,
SIGNATURES OF CLARK-SNYDER, GREEN SEAL

BANK	A.B.P.	V.FINE	UNC.	BANK	A.B.P.	V.FINE	UNC.
☐Boston	5.50	8.00	20.00	☐Chicago	5.50	8.00	20.00
☐New York	5.50	8.00	20.00	☐St. Louis	5.50	8.00	20.00
☐Philadelphia	5.50	8.00	20.00	☐Minneapolis	5.50	8.00	20.00
☐Cleveland	5.50	8.00	20.00	☐Kansas City	5.50	8.00	20.00
☐Richmond	5.50	8.00	20.00	☐Dallas	5.50	8.00	20.00
☐Atlanta	5.50	8.00	20.00	☐San Francisco	5.50	8.00	20.00

FIVE DOLLAR NOTES (1950)
FEDERAL RESERVE NOTES
BLACK FEDERAL RESERVE SEAL AND
GREEN TREASURY SEALS ARE NOW SMALLER

(Small Size)　　　　　　　　　　　　　　　　NOTE NO. 57

Face Design: Similar to note No. 55.
Back Design: Similar to note No. 50.

FIVE DOLLAR NOTES (1950-1963)
FEDERAL RESERVE NOTES

(Small Size)　　　　　　　　　　　　　　　　NOTE NO. 57

SERIES OF 1950,
SIGNATURES OF CLARK-SNYDER, GREEN SEAL

BANK	A.B.P.	V.FINE	UNC.	BANK	A.B.P.	V.FINE	UNC.
☐Boston	5.50	7.50	21.00	☐Chicago	5.50	7.50	21.00
☐New York	5.50	7.50	21.00	☐St. Louis	5.50	7.50	21.00
☐Philadelphia	5.50	7.50	21.00	☐Minneapolis	5.50	7.50	21.00
☐Cleveland	5.50	7.50	21.00	☐Kansas City	5.50	7.50	21.00
☐Richmond	5.50	7.50	21.00	☐Dallas	5.50	7.50	21.00
☐Atlanta	5.50	7.50	21.00	☐San Francisco	5.50	7.50	21.00

SERIES OF 1950A, PRIEST-HUMPHREY, GREEN SEAL

	UNC.		UNC.		UNC.		UNC.
Boston	18.00	Cleveland	18.00	Chicago	18.00	Kansas City	18.00
New York	18.00	Richmond	18.00	St. Louis	18.00	Dallas	18.00
Philadelphia	18.00	Atlanta	18.00	Minneapolis	18.00	San Francisco	18.00

SERIES OF 1950B, PRIEST-ANDERSON, GREEN SEAL

Boston	18.00	Cleveland	18.00	Chicago	18.00	Kansas City	18.00

	UNC.		UNC.		UNC.		UNC.
New York	18.00	Richmond	18.00	St. Louis	18.00	Dallas	18.00
Philadelphia	18.00	Atlanta	18.00	Minneapolis	18.00	San Francisco	18.00

SERIES OF 1950C, SMITH-DILLON, GREEN SEAL

Boston	16.00	Cleveland	16.00	Chicago	16.00	Kansas City	16.00
New York	16.00	Richmond	16.00	St. Louis	16.00	Dallas	16.00
Philadelphia	16.00	Atlanta	16.00	Minneapolis	16.00	San Francisco	16.00

SERIES OF 1950D, GRANAHAN-DILLON, GREEN SEAL

Boston	17.00	Cleveland	17.00	Chicago	17.00	Kansas City	17.00
New York	17.00	Richmond	17.00	St. Louis	17.00	Dallas	17.00
Philadelphia	17.00	Atlanta	17.00	Minneapolis	17.00	San Francisco	17.00

SERIES OF 1950E, GRANAHAN-FOWLER, GREEN SEAL

New York	30.00	Chicago	30.00	San Francisco	30.00

This note was issued by only three banks.

FIVE DOLLAR NOTES (1963)
FEDERAL RESERVE NOTES
("IN GOD WE TRUST" IS ADDED ON THE BACK)

(Small Size) **NOTE NO. 57A**

SERIES OF 1963, GRANAHAN-DILLON, GREEN SEAL

	UNC.		UNC.		UNC.		UNC.
Boston	15.00	Cleveland	15.00	Chicago	15.00	Kansas City	15.00
New York	15.00	Richmond	—	St. Louis	15.00	Dallas	15.00
Philadelphia	15.00	Atlanta	15.00	Minneapolis	—	San Francisco	15.00

SERIES OF 1963A, GRANAHAN-FOWLER, GREEN SEAL

Boston	14.00	Cleveland	14.00	Chicago	14.00	Kansas City	14.00
New York	14.00	Richmond	—	St. Louis	14.00	Dallas	14.00
Philadelphia	14.00	Atlanta	14.00	Minneapolis	14.00	San Francisco	14.00

FIVE DOLLAR NOTES (1969)
FEDERAL RESERVE NOTES
(WORDING IN GREEN TREASURY SEAL
CHANGED FROM LATIN TO ENGLISH)

(Small Size) **NOTE NO. 57B**

SERIES OF 1969, ELSTON-KENNEDY, GREEN SEAL

Boston	12.00	Cleveland	12.00	Chicago	12.00	Kansas City	12.00
New York	12.00	Richmond	12.00	St. Louis	12.00	Dallas	12.00
Philadelphia	12.00	Atlanta	12.00	Minneapolis	12.00	San Francisco	12.00

SERIES OF 1969A, KABIS-CONNALLY, GREEN SEAL

Boston	11.00	Cleveland	11.00	Chicago	11.00	Kansas City	11.00
New York	11.00	Richmond	11.00	St. Louis	11.00	Dallas	11.00
Philadelphia	11.00	Atlanta	11.00	Minneapolis	11.00	San Francisco	11.00

FIVE DOLLAR NOTES (1969)
FEDERAL RESERVE NOTES
(WORDING IN GREEN TREASURY SEAL
CHANGED FROM LATIN TO ENGLISH)

(Small Size)   **NOTE NO. 57B**

SERIES OF 1969B, BANUELOS-CONNALLY, GREEN SEAL

	UNC.		UNC.		UNC.		UNC.
Boston	10.00	Cleveland	10.00	Chicago	10.00	Kansas City	10.00
New York	10.00	Richmond	10.00	St. Louis	10.00	Dallas	10.00
Philadelphia	10.00	Atlanta	10.00	Minneapolis	10.00	San Francisco	10.00

SERIES OF 1969C, BANUELOS-SHULTZ, GREEN SEAL

Boston	10.00	Cleveland	10.00	Chicago	10.00	Kansas City	10.00
New York	10.00	Richmond	10.00	St. Louis	10.00	Dallas	10.00
Philadelphia	10.00	Atlanta	10.00	Minneapolis	10.00	San Francisco	10.00

SERIES OF 1974, NEFF-SIMON, GREEN SEAL

Boston	9.50	Cleveland	9.50	Chicago	9.50	Kansas City	9.50
New York	9.50	Richmond	9.50	St. Louis	9.50	Dallas	9.50
Philadelphia	9.50	Atlanta	9.50	Minneapolis	9.50	San Francisco	9.50

SERIES OF 1977, MORTON-BLUMENTHAL, GREEN SEAL

Boston	8.00	Cleveland	8.00	Chicago	8.00	Kansas City	8.00
New York	8.00	Richmond	8.00	St. Louis	8.00	Dallas	8.00
Philadelphia	8.00	Atlanta	8.00	Minneapolis	8.00	San Francisco	8.00

SERIES OF 1977A, MORTON-MILLER, GREEN SEAL

Boston	8.00	Cleveland	8.00	Chicago	8.00	Kansas City	8.00
New York	8.00	Richmond	8.00	St. Louis	8.00	Dallas	8.00
Philadelphia	8.00	Atlanta	8.00	Minneapolis	8.00	San Francisco	8.00

SERIES OF 1981, BUCHANAN-REGAN, GREEN SEAL

Boston	7.00	Cleveland	7.00	Chicago	7.00	Kansas City	7.00
New York	7.00	Richmond	7.00	St. Louis	7.00	Dallas	7.00
Philadelphia	7.00	Atlanta	7.00	Minneapolis	7.00	San Francisco	7.00

SERIES OF 1981A, ORTEGA-REGAN, GREEN SEAL

Boston	7.00	Cleveland	7.00	Chicago	7.00	Kansas City	7.00
New York	7.00	Richmond	7.00	St. Louis	7.00	Dallas	7.00
Philadelphia	7.00	Atlanta	7.00	Minneapolis	7.00	San Francisco	7.00

SERIES OF 1985, ORTEGA-BAKER, GREEN SEAL

Boston	7.00	Cleveland	7.00	Chicago	7.00	Kansas City	7.00
New York	7.00	Richmond	7.00	St. Louis	7.00	Dallas	7.00
Philadelphia	7.00	Atlanta	7.00	Minneapolis	7.00	San Francisco	7.00

SERIES OF 1988, ORTEGA-BAKER, GREEN SEAL

Boston	6.50	Cleveland	6.50	Chicago	6.50	Kansas City	6.50
New York	6.50	Richmond	6.50	St. Louis	6.50	Dallas	6.50
Philadelphia	6.50	Atlanta	6.50	Minneapolis	6.50	San Francisco	6.50

SERIES OF 1988A, VILLALPANDO-BRADY, GREEN SEAL

	UNC.		UNC.		UNC.		UNC.
Boston	6.00	Cleveland	6.00	Chicago	6.00	Kansas City	6.00
New York	6.00	Richmond	6.00	St. Louis	6.00	Dallas	6.00
Philadelphia	6.00	Atlanta	6.00	Minneapolis	6.00	San Francisco	6.00

SERIES OF 1993, WITHROW-BENTSEN, GREEN SEAL

	UNC.		UNC.		UNC.		UNC.
Boston	5.50	Cleveland	5.50	Chicago	5.50	Kansas City	5.50
New York	5.50	Richmond	5.50	St. Louis	5.50	Dallas	5.50
Philadelphia	5.50	Atlanta	5.50	Minneapolis	5.50	San Francisco	5.50

SERIES OF 1995, WITHROW-BENTSEN, GREEN SEAL

	UNC.		UNC.		UNC.		UNC.
Boston	5.00	Cleveland	5.00	Chicago	5.00	Kansas City	5.00
New York	5.00	Richmond	5.00	St. Louis	5.00	Dallas	5.00
Philadelphia	5.00	Atlanta	5.00	Minneapolis	5.00	San Francisco	5.00

FIVE DOLLAR NOTES (1918)
FEDERAL RESERVE BANK NOTES
(ALL WITH BLUE SEAL AND BLUE SERIAL NUMBERS)
(Large Size)

NOTE NO. 58

Face Design: Portrait of President Lincoln with Reserve City in center.

Back Design: Same as note No. 54.

BANK & CITY	SERIES	GOV'T SIGNATURES	BANK SIGNATURES	A.B.P.	GOOD	V. FINE	UNC.
☐Boston	1918	Teehee-Burke	Bullen-Morse	250.00	600.00	1000.00	2000.00
☐New York	1918	Teehee-Burke	Hendricks-Strong	24.00	40.00	90.00	425.00
☐Philadelphia	1918	Teehee-Burke	Hardt-Passmore	24.00	40.00	90.00	425.00
☐Philadelphia	1918	Teehee-Burke	Dyer-Passmore	24.00	40.00	90.00	425.00
☐Cleveland	1918	Teehee-Burke	Dyer-Fancher	24.00	40.00	90.00	425.00
☐Cleveland	1918	Teehee-Burke	Davis-Fancher	24.00	40.00	90.00	425.00
☐Cleveland	1918	Elliott-Burke	Davis-Fancher	24.00	40.00	90.00	425.00
☐Atlanta	1915	Teehee-Burke	Bell-Wellborn	24.00	40.00	110.00	525.00
☐Atlanta	1915	Teehee-Burke	Pike-McCord	24.00	40.00	110.00	525.00

☐Atlanta	1918 Teehee-Burke Pike-McCord				
		24.00	40.00	90.00	425.00
☐Atlanta	1918 Teehee-Burke Bell-Wellborn				
		24.00	40.00	90.00	425.00
☐Atlanta	1918 Elliott-Burke Bell-Wellborn				
		24.00	40.00	90.00	425.00
☐Chicago	1915 Teehee-Burke McLallen-McDougal				
		24.00	40.00	110.00	525.00
☐Chicago	1918 Teehee-Burke McCloud-McDougal				
		20.00	38.00	90.00	425.00
☐Chicago	1918 Teehee-Burke Cramer-McDougal				
		20.00	38.00	90.00	425.00
☐St. Louis	1918 Teehee-Burke Attebery-Wells				
		20.00	38.00	90.00	375.00
☐St. Louis	1918 Teehee-Burke Attebery-Biggs				
		20.00	38.00	90.00	375.00
☐St. Louis	1918 Elliott-BurkeWhite-Biggs				
		20.00	38.00	90.00	425.00
☐Minneapolis	1918 Teehee-Burke Cook-Wold				
		20.00	38.00	90.00	425.00
☐Kansas City	1915 Teehee-Burke Anderson-Miller				
		24.00	40.00	110.00	525.00
☐Kansas City	1915 Teehee-Burke Cross-Miller				
		24.00	40.00	110.00	525.00
☐Kansas City	1915 Teehee-Burke Helm-Miller				
		24.00	40.00	110.00	525.00
☐Kansas City	1918 Teehee-Burke Anderson-Miller				
		24.00	38.00	90.00	425.00
☐Kansas City	1918 Elliott-BurkeHelm-Miller				
		24.00	38.00	90.00	425.00
☐Dallas	1915 Teehee-Burke Hoopes-VanZandt				
		24.00	40.00	125.00	525.00
☐Dallas	1915 Teehee-Burke Talley-VanZandt				
		24.00	40.00	110.00	525.00
☐Dallas	1918 Teehee-Burke Talley-VanZandt				
		24.00	38.00	90.00	425.00
☐San Francisco	1915 Teehee-Burke Clerk-Lynch				
		24.00	40.00	125.00	525.00
☐San Francisco	1918 Teehee-Burke Clerk-Lynch				
		24.00	38.00	90.00	425.00

FIVE DOLLAR NOTES (1929)
FEDERAL RESERVE BANK NOTES

(Small Size)

NOTE NO. 59

Face Design: Portrait of President Lincoln.
SERIES 1929, BROWN SEAL

BANK & CITY	SIGNATURES	A.B.P.	GOOD	V.FINE	UNC.
☐ Boston	Jones-Woods	6.50	10.00	16.00	95.00
☐ New York	Jones-Woods	6.50	10.00	15.00	80.00
☐ Philadelphia	Jones-Woods	6.50	10.00	16.00	80.00
☐ Cleveland	Jones-Woods	6.50	10.00	16.00	80.00
☐ Richmond	Jones-Woods	6.50	10.00	14.00	120.00
☐ Atlanta	Jones-Woods	6.50	10.00	14.00	70.00
☐ Chicago	Jones-Woods	6.50	10.00	14.00	70.00
☐ St. Louis	Jones-Woods	6.50	10.00	150.00	350.00
☐ Minneapolis	Jones-Woods	6.50	10.00	40.00	135.00
☐ Kansas City	Jones-Woods	6.50	10.00	15.00	75.00
☐ Dallas	Jones-Woods	75.00	180.00	750.00	2100.00
☐ San Francisco	Jones-Woods	75.00	350.00	725.00	2000.00

TEN DOLLAR NOTES

ORDER OF ISSUE

TEN DOLLAR NOTES (1861) DEMAND NOTES
NO TREASURY SEAL

(Large Size)   **NOTE NO. 60**

Face Design: Portrait of President Lincoln left, female figure with sword and shield.

Back Design: Ornate designs of TEN.

PAYABLE AT	A.B.P.	GOOD	V. GOOD
☐ Boston (I)	960.00	1600.00	7600.00
☐ New York (I)	960.00	1600.00	7600.00
☐ Philadelphia (I)	960.00	1600.00	7600.00
☐ Cincinnati (I)	700.00	2500.00	RARE
☐ St. Louis (I)	1500.00	2500.00	RARE
☐ Boston (II)	300.00	600.00	1250.00
☐ New York (II)	300.00	550.00	1250.00
☐ Philadelphia (II)	300.00	550.00	1250.00
☐ Cincinnati (II)	4200.00	7800.00	18,000.00
☐ St. Louis (II)	4500.00	8200.00	25,000.00

TEN DOLLAR NOTES (1862-1863)
UNITED STATES NOTES
(ALSO KNOWN AS LEGAL TENDER NOTES)

(Large Size)   **NOTE NO. 61**

Back Design
Face Design: Similar to previous note.

SERIES	SIGNATURES	SEAL	A.B.P.	GOOD	V.FINE	UNC.
☐1862	Chittenden-Spinner*	Red	100.00	175.00	750.00	2000.00
☐1862	Chittenden-Spinner**	Red	100.00	175.00	750.00	2000.00
☐1863	Chittenden-Spinner**	Red	100.00	175.00	750.00	2000.00

* First Obligation: Similar to note No. 33.
** Second Obligation: Shown above.

TEN DOLLAR NOTES (1869) UNITED STATES NOTES
(Large Size)   **NOTE NO. 62**

Face Design: Portrait of Daniel Webster left, presentation of
Indian princess right. (This note is nicknamed "Jackass Note,"
because the EAGLE between the signatures resembles a
donkey when it is held upside down.)

SERIES	SIGNATURES	SEAL	A.B.P.	GOOD	V.FINE	UNC.
☐1869	Allison-Spinner	Red	80.00	175.00	650.00	1800.00

TEN DOLLAR NOTES (1875-1880)
UNITED STATES NOTES

(Large Size)   **NOTE NO. 63**

Face Design: Similar to previous note.

Back Design: Revised.

SERIES	SIGNATURES	SEAL	A.B.P.	GOOD	V.FINE	UNC.
☐1875	Allison-New	Red	70.00	125.00	550.00	2100.00
☐Same as above, Series A		Red	60.00	100.00	500.00	2000.00
☐1878	Allison-Gilfillan	Red	60.00	100.00	500.00	2000.00
☐1880	Scofield-Gilfillan	Brown	50.00	90.00	400.00	1150.00
☐1880	Bruce-Gilfillan	Brown	50.00	85.00	300.00	950.00
☐1880	Bruce-Wyman	Brown	50.00	85.00	300.00	950.00
☐1880	Bruce-Wyman	Red Plain	50.00	85.00	400.00	1000.00
☐1880	Rosecrans-Jordan	Red Plain	50.00	85.00	500.00	1050.00
☐1880	Rosecrans-Hyatt	Red Plain	50.00	85.00	500.00	1050.00
☐1880	Rosecrans-Hyatt	Red Spikes	50.00	85.00	500.00	1000.00
☐1880	Rosecrans-Huston	Red Spikes	50.00	85.00	450.00	1050.00
☐1880	Rosecrans-Huston	Brown	50.00	85.00	900.00	2500.00
☐1880	Rosecrans-Nebeker	Brown	40.00	70.00	400.00	1050.00
☐1880	Rosecrans-Nebeker	Red	40.00	70.00	400.00	750.00
☐1880	Tillman-Morgan	Red	40.00	70.00	325.00	750.00

SERIES	SIGNATURES	SEAL	A.B.P.	GOOD	V.FINE	UNC.
☐1880 Bruce-Roberts		Red	40.00	65.00	350.00	750.00
☐1880 Lyons-Roberts		Red	40.00	65.00	325.00	750.00

TEN DOLLAR NOTES (1901) UNITED STATES NOTES
(Large Size)   **NOTE NO. 64**

Face Design: American bison (buffalo) center, portrait of Lewis left, portrait of Clark right.

Back Design: Female allegorical figure in arch.

SERIES	SIGNATURES	SEAL	A.B.P.	GOOD	V.FINE	UNC.
☐1901	Lyons-Roberts	Red	75.00	130.00	475.00	1350.00
☐1901	Lyons-Treat	Red	75.00	130.00	475.00	1350.00
☐1901	Vernon-Treat	Red	75.00	130.00	475.00	1350.00
☐1901	Vernon-McClung	Red	75.00	130.00	475.00	1350.00
☐1901	Napier-McClung	Red	75.00	130.00	475.00	1350.00
☐1901	Parker-Burke	Red	75.00	130.00	475.00	1350.00
☐1901	Teehee-Burke	Red	75.00	130.00	475.00	1350.00
☐1901	Elliott-White	Red	75.00	130.00	475.00	1350.00
☐1901	Speelman-White	Red	75.00	130.00	475.00	1350.00

TEN DOLLAR NOTES (1923) UNITED STATES NOTES
(Large Size)   **NOTE NO. 65**

Face Design: Portrait of President Jackson center, red seal left, red "X" to right.

Back Design

SERIES	SIGNATURES	SEAL	A.B.P.	GOOD	V.FINE	UNC.
☐1923	Speelman-White	Red	70.00	200.00	800.00	3200.00

TEN DOLLAR NOTES (1863-1875)
NATIONAL BANK NOTES
FIRST CHARTER PERIOD (Large Size)   **NOTE NO. 66**

Face Design: Benjamin Franklin and kite left, name of bank and city center. Effigy of Liberty and eagle right.

Back Design: Border green, center black. DeSoto on horseback at Mississippi River.

SERIES	SIGNATURES	SEAL	A.B.P.	GOOD	V.FINE	UNC.
☐Original	Chittenden-Spinner	Red	60.00	100.00	360.00	2400.00
☐Original	Colby-Spinner	Red	60.00	100.00	400.00	2400.00
☐Original	Jeffries-Spinner	Red	360.00	500.00	2000.00	RARE
☐Original	Allison-Spinner	Red	60.00	100.00	400.00	2400.00
☐1875	Allison-New	Red	60.00	100.00	400.00	1800.00
☐1875	Allison-Wyman	Red	60.00	100.00	400.00	1800.00
☐1875	Allison-Gilfillan	Red	60.00	100.00	400.00	1800.00
☐1875	Scofield-Gilfillan	Red	60.00	100.00	400.00	1800.00
☐1875	Bruce-Gilfillan	Red	60.00	100.00	400.00	1800.00
☐1875	Bruce-Wyman	Red	60.00	100.00	400.00	1800.00
☐1875	Rosecrans-Huston	Red	60.00	100.00	400.00	1800.00
☐1875	Rosecrans-Nebeker	Red	60.00	100.00	400.00	1800.00

TEN DOLLAR NOTES (1882) NATIONAL BANK NOTES
SECOND CHARTER PERIOD (Large Size)　　　　NOTE NO. 68

First Issue (Brown seal and brown backs)
Face Design: Similar to note No. 66.
Back Design: Similar to note No. 39, but border in brown with green Charter Number.

SERIES	SIGNATURES	SEAL	A.B.P.	GOOD	V.FINE	UNC.
☐1882	Bruce-Gilfillan	Brown	39.00	65.00	210.00	750.00
☐1882	Bruce-Wyman	Brown	39.00	65.00	210.00	750.00
☐1882	Bruce-Jordan	Brown	39.00	65.00	210.00	750.00
☐1882	Rosecrans-Jordan	Brown	39.00	65.00	210.00	750.00
☐1882	Rosecrans-Hyatt	Brown	39.00	65.00	210.00	750.00
☐1882	Rosecrans-Huston	Brown	39.00	65.00	210.00	750.00
☐1882	Rosecrans-Nebeker	Brown	39.00	65.00	210.00	750.00
☐1882	Rosecrans-Morgan	Brown	150.00	250.00	750.00	1100.00
☐1882	Tillman-Morgan	Brown	39.00	65.00	210.00	750.00
☐1882	Tillman-Roberts	Brown	39.00	65.00	210.00	750.00

SERIES	SIGNATURES	SEAL	A.B.P.	GOOD	V.FINE	UNC.
☐1882	Bruce-Roberts	Brown	40.00	65.00	210.00	750.00
☐1882	Lyons-Roberts	Brown	40.00	65.00	210.00	750.00
☐1882	Lyons-Treat	Brown	40.00	65.00	210.00	750.00
☐1882	Vernon-Treat	Brown	40.00	65.00	210.00	750.00

Second Issue (Blue seal, green back with date "1882–1908")
Face Design: Similar to note No. 66.
Back Design: Similar to note No. 40.
(Large Size)

NOTE NO. 69

SERIES	SIGNATURES	SEAL	A.B.P.	GOOD	V.FINE	UNC.
☐1882	Rosecrans-Huston	Blue	36.00	50.00	210.00	750.00
☐1882	Rosecrans-Nebeker	Blue	36.00	50.00	210.00	750.00
☐1882	Rosecrans-Morgan	Blue	100.00	180.00	500.00	1150.00
☐1882	Tillman-Morgan	Blue	36.00	50.00	210.00	750.00
☐1882	Tillman-Roberts	Blue	36.00	50.00	210.00	750.00
☐1882	Bruce-Roberts	Blue	36.00	50.00	210.00	750.00
☐1882	Lyons-Roberts	Blue	36.00	50.00	210.00	750.00
☐1882	Vernon-Treat	Blue	36.00	50.00	210.00	750.00
☐1882	Vernon-McClung	Blue	36.00	50.00	210.00	750.00
☐1882	Napier-McClung	Blue	36.00	50.00	210.00	750.00

TEN DOLLAR NOTES (1882) NATIONAL BANK NOTES
NOTE NO. 70

Third Issue (Blue seal, green back with value in block letters)
Face Design: Similar to previous notes (*see* note No. 66).
Back Design: Similar to note No. 41.

SERIES	SIGNATURES	SEAL	A.B.P.	GOOD	V. FINE	UNC.
☐1882	Tillman-Roberts	Blue	32.00	85.00	325.00	2200.00
☐1882	Lyons-Roberts	Blue	32.00	100.00	310.00	2600.00
☐1882	Vernon-Treat	Blue	32.00	85.00	360.00	2200.00
☐1882	Napier-McClung	Blue	32.00	80.00	310.00	2200.00

These notes may exist with other signatures, but are very rare.

TEN DOLLAR NOTES (1902) NATIONAL BANK NOTES
THIRD CHARTER PERIOD (Large Size)   **NOTE NO. 71**

First Issue (Red seal and red Charter Numbers)
Face Design: Portrait of President McKinley left, name of bank and city in center.

SERIES	SIGNATURES	SEAL	A.B.P.	GOOD	V.FINE	UNC.
☐1902	Lyons-Roberts	Red	36.00	60.00	180.00	800.00
☐1902	Lyons-Treat	Red	36.00	60.00	180.00	800.00
☐1902	Vernon-Treat	Red	36.00	60.00	210.00	850.00

TEN DOLLAR NOTES (1902) NATIONAL BANK NOTES
THIRD CHARTER PERIOD (Large Size)   **NOTE NO. 71A**

Second Issue (Blue seal and numbers, "1902–1908" on the back)
Back Design: Same as note No. 69, date 1902–1908.
Face Design: Same as note No. 70.

SERIES	SIGNATURES	SEAL	A.B.P.	GOOD	V.FINE	UNC.
☐1902	Lyons-Roberts	Blue	14.00	23.00	60.00	325.00
☐1902	Lyons-Treat	Blue	14.00	23.00	60.00	325.00
☐1902	Vernon-Treat	Blue	14.00	23.00	60.00	325.00
☐1902	Vernon-McClung	Blue	14.00	23.00	60.00	325.00
☐1902	Napier-McClung	Blue	14.00	23.00	60.00	325.00

SERIES	SIGNATURES	SEAL	A.B.P.	GOOD	V.FINE	UNC.
☐1902	Napier-Thompson	Blue	15.00	30.00	75.00	650.00
☐1902	Napier-Burke	Blue	14.00	23.00	60.00	325.00
☐1902	Parker-Burke	Blue	14.00	23.00	60.00	325.00
☐1902	Teehee-Burke	Blue	15.00	25.00	65.00	325.00

Third Issue (Blue seal and numbers, without date on back.)

SERIES	SIGNATURES	SEAL	A.B.P.	GOOD	V.FINE	UNC.
☐1902	Lyons-Roberts	Blue	13.00	20.00	60.00	235.00
☐1902	Lyons-Treat	Blue	13.00	20.00	60.00	235.00
☐1902	Vernon-Treat	Blue	13.00	20.00	60.00	235.00
☐1902	Vernon-McClung	Blue	13.00	20.00	60.00	235.00
☐1902	Napier-McClung	Blue	13.00	20.00	60.00	235.00
☐1902	Napier-Thompson	Blue	13.00	24.00	85.00	650.00
☐1902	Napier-Burke	Blue	13.00	20.00	60.00	235.00
☐1902	Parker-Burke	Blue	13.00	20.00	60.00	235.00
☐1902	Teehee-Burke	Blue	13.00	20.00	60.00	235.00
☐1902	Elliott-Burke	Blue	13.00	20.00	60.00	235.00
☐1902	Elliott-White	Blue	13.00	20.00	60.00	235.00
☐1902	Speelman-White	Blue	13.00	20.00	60.00	235.00
☐1902	Woods-White	Blue	13.00	20.00	60.00	235.00
☐1902	Woods-Tate	Blue	13.00	20.00	60.00	235.00
☐1902	Jones-Woods	Blue	40.00	82.00	280.00	1100.00

TEN DOLLAR NOTES (1929) NATIONAL BANK NOTES
(Small Size) **NOTE NO. 72**

Face Design, Type I: Portrait of Hamilton center, name of bank left, brown seal right, Charter Number black.

Face Design, Type II: Charter Number added in brown.

Back Design: United States Treasury Building.

SERIES SIGNATURES	SEAL	A.B.P.	GOOD	V.FINE	UNC.
☐1929, Type I Jones-Woods	Brown	11.00	14.00	24.00	70.00
☐1929, Type II Jones-Woods	Brown	11.00	14.00	24.00	78.00

TEN DOLLAR NOTES (1870-1875)
NATIONAL GOLD BANK NOTES

(Large Size)   **NOTE NO. 67**

Face Design: Similar to note No. 66.

Back Design: State Seal left, gold coins center, American eagle right.

The following have signatures of Allison-Spinner and a red Treasury Seal.

DATE	BANK	CITY	A.B.P.	GOOD	V. GOOD
☐1870	First National Gold Bank	San Francisco	380.00	650.00	2400.00
☐1872	National Gold Bank and Trust Co.	San Francisco	380.00	650.00	2400.00
☐1872	National Gold Bank of D.O. Mills and Co.	Sacramento	540.00	900.00	2800.00
☐1873	First National Gold Bank	Santa Barbara	600.00	1000.00	2800.00
☐1873	First National Gold Bank	Stockton	540.00	900.00	3000.00
☐1874	Farmers Nat'l Gold Bank	San Jose	540.00	900.00	3000.00
☐1874	First National Gold Bank	Petaluma	540.00	900.00	3000.00
☐1875	First National Gold Bank	Oakland	540.00	900.00	3000.00

TEN DOLLAR NOTES (1880) SILVER CERTIFICATES
(Large Size) **NOTE NO. 73**

Face Design: Portrait of Robert Morris left.

Back Design: Printed in black ink, SILVER in large letters.

SERIES	SIGNATURES	SEAL	A.B.P.	GOOD	V.FINE	UNC.
☐1880	Scofield-Gilfillan	Brown	150.00	300.00	1035.00	3200.00
☐1880	Bruce-Gilfillan	Brown	150.00	300.00	1035.00	3100.00
☐1880	Bruce-Wyman	Brown	150.00	300.00	1035.00	3100.00
☐1880	Bruce-Wyman	Red	150.00	300.00	1035.00	2700.00

TEN DOLLAR NOTES (1886) SILVER CERTIFICATES
(Large Size)   **NOTE NO. 74**

SERIES	SIGNATURES	SEAL	A.B.P.	GOOD	V.FINE	UNC.
☐1886	Rosencrans-Jordan	Sm. Red	240.00	420.00	1100.00	3200.00
☐1886	Rosecrans-Hyatt	Sm. Red	240.00	420.00	1100.00	3200.00
☐1886	Rosecrans-Hyatt	Lg. Red	240.00	420.00	1100.00	3200.00
☐1886	Rosecrans-Huston	Lg. Red	240.00	420.00	1100.00	3200.00
☐1886	Rosecrans-Huston	Lg. Brown	240.00	420.00	1100.00	3200.00
☐1886	Rosecrans-Nebeker	Lg. Brown	240.00	420.00	1100.00	3250.00
☐1886	Rosecrans-Nebeker	Sm. Red	240.00	420.00	1100.00	3250.00

TEN DOLLAR NOTES (1891-1908)
SILVER CERTIFICATES
(Large Size)   **NOTE NO. 75**

Face Design:
Same as
note No. 74.
Back Design

SERIES	SIGNATURES	SEAL	A.B.P.	GOOD	V.FINE	UNC.
☐1891	Rosecrans-Nebeker	Red	66.00	110.00	500.00	2000.00
☐1891	Tillman-Morgan	Red	66.00	110.00	500.00	2000.00
☐1891	Bruce-Roberts	Red	66.00	110.00	500.00	2000.00
☐1891	Lyons-Roberts	Red	66.00	110.00	500.00	2000.00
☐1891	Vernon-Treat	Blue	60.00	100.00	500.00	1850.00
☐1891	Vernon-McClung	Blue	60.00	100.00	500.00	1850.00
☐1891	Parker-Burke	Blue	60.00	100.00	500.00	1850.00

TEN DOLLAR NOTES (1933) SILVER CERTIFICATES
(Small Size)   **NOTE NO. 76**

Face Design: Portrait of Alexander Hamilton center. Blue
seal to left, blue numbers.

Back Design: Green United States Treasury Building.

SERIES	SIGNATURES	SEAL	A.B.P.	GOOD	V.FINE	UNC.
☐1933	Julian-Woodin	Blue	510.00	850.00	2400.00	7000.00

TEN DOLLAR NOTES (1934) SILVER CERTIFICATES
(Small Size)   **NOTE NO. 77**

Face Design: Blue "10" to left of portrait, Treasury Seal is
now to right.
Back Design: Similar to previous issue.

TEN DOLLAR NOTES (1934) SILVER CERTIFICATES
(Small Size)   NOTE NO. 77

SERIES	SIGNATURES	SEAL	A.B.P.	GOOD	V.FINE	UNC.
☐ 1934	Julian-Morgenthau	Blue	12.00	14.00	22.00	72.00
☐ 1934	Julian-Morgenthau*	Yellow	175.00	415.00	1200.00	7000.00
☐ 1934A	Julian-Morgenthau	Blue	12.00	16.00	22.00	65.00
☐ 1934A	Julian-Morgenthau*	Yellow	13.00	18.00	22.00	165.00
☐ 1934B	Julian-Vinson	Blue	12.00	25.00	87.00	1250.00
☐ 1934C	Julian-Snyder	Blue	12.00	15.00	26.00	70.00
☐ 1934D	Clark-Snyder	Blue	12.00	15.00	26.00	65.00

* Silver Certificates with a yellow seal were a special issue for use in combat areas of North Africa and Europe during World War II.

TEN DOLLAR NOTES (1953) SILVER CERTIFICATES
(Small Size)   NOTE NO. 78

Face Design: Gray "10" to left of portrait. Treasury Seal is smaller.
Back Design: Back similar to previous note.

SERIES	SIGNATURES	SEAL	A.B.P.	GOOD	V.FINE	UNC.
☐ 1953	Priest-Humphrey	Blue	13.00	12.00	18.00	75.00
☐ 1953A	Priest-Anderson	Blue	35.00	15.00	21.00	180.00
☐ 1953B	Smith-Dillon	Blue	13.00	14.00	18.00	75.00

Regarding note No. 78, there were 720,000 issued. This was the last issue of $10 Silver Certificates. These were not issued with IN GOD WE TRUST on the back. Production ended in 1962.

TEN DOLLAR (1879) REFUNDING CERTIFICATES
NOTE NO. 78A

Face Design: Portrait of Benjamin Franklin.

Back Design: Large TEN, ornate cornucopia border.

SERIES	SIGNATURES	SEAL	A.B.P.	GOOD	V.FINE	UNC.
☐1879	Scofield-Gilfillan					
PAY TO ORDER		Red	135.00		VERY RARE	
☐1879	Scofield-Gilfillan					
PAY TO BEARER		Red	135.00	225.00	1000.00	2200.00

TEN DOLLAR NOTES (1907) GOLD CERTIFICATES
(Large Size)   **NOTE NO. 79**

Face Design: Portrait of Hillegas center, yellow x left, yellow seal right, yellow numbers.

Back Design: The backs are a bright yellow color.

SERIES	SIGNATURES	SEAL	A.B.P.	GOOD	V.FINE	UNC.
☐1907	Vernon-Treat	Gold	14.00	24.00	110.00	425.00
☐1907	Vernon-McClung	Gold	14.00	24.00	110.00	425.00
☐1907	Napier-McClung	Gold	14.00	24.00	110.00	425.00
☐1907	Napier-Thompson	Gold	28.00	48.00	150.00	1100.00
☐1907	Parker-Burke	Gold	14.00	24.00	110.00	425.00
☐1907	Teehee-Burke	Gold	14.00	24.00	110.00	425.00
☐1922	Speelman-White	Gold	14.00	24.00	110.00	425.00

TEN DOLLAR NOTES (1928) GOLD CERTIFICATES
(Small Size) **NOTE NO. 80**

Face Design: Portrait of Alexander Hamilton center, yellow
seal to left, yellow numbers.

Back Design: Printed in green ink.

SERIES	SIGNATURES	SEAL	A.B.P.	GOOD	V.FINE	UNC.
☐1928	Woods-Mellon	Gold	14.00	20.00	45.00	250.00

TEN DOLLAR NOTES (1890) TREASURY OR COIN NOTES
(Large Size)   **NOTE NO. 81**

Face Design: Portrait of General Philip Sheridan.

Back Design:
Very ornate
large TEN.

SERIES	SIGNATURES	SEAL	A.B.P.	GOOD	V.FINE	UNC.
☐1890	Rosecrans-Huston	Lg. Brown	85.00	180.00	850.00	2650.00
☐1890	Rosecrans-Nebeker	Lg. Brown	85.00	190.00	850.00	2650.00
☐1890	Rosecrans-Nebeker	Sm. Red	85.00	180.00	850.00	2650.00

TEN DOLLAR NOTES (1891) TREASURY OR COIN NOTES
(Large Size)   **NOTE NO. 81A**

Face Design:
Same as No. 81.
Back Design:
Ornate small
TEN.

SERIES	SIGNATURES	SEAL	A.B.P.	GOOD	V.FINE	UNC.
☐1891	Rosecrans-Nebeker	Sm. Red	40.00	100.00	500.00	1550.00
☐1891	Tillman-Morgan	Sm. Red	39.00	90.00	500.00	1550.00
☐1891	Bruce-Roberts	Sm. Red	39.00	90.00	500.00	1550.00

TEN DOLLAR NOTES (1914)
FEDERAL RESERVE NOTES

(Large Size)   **NOTE NO. 82**

Face Design: Portrait of President Jackson center, Federal Reserve Seal left, Treasury Seal right.

Back Design: Scenes of farming and industry.

The following have signatures of Burke-McAdoo, red seals and red serial numbers.

SERIES	CITY	SEAL	A.B.P.	GOOD	V.FINE	UNC.
☐1914	Boston	Red	19.00	34.00	95.00	450.00
☐1914	New York	Red	19.00	34.00	95.00	450.00
☐1914	Philadelphia	Red	20.00	32.00	100.00	450.00
☐1914	Cleveland	Red	20.00	32.00	100.00	450.00
☐1914	Richmond	Red	20.00	32.00	100.00	450.00
☐1914	Atlanta	Red	20.00	32.00	100.00	450.00
☐1914	Chicago	Red	20.00	32.00	100.00	450.00
☐1914	St. Louis	Red	20.00	32.00	100.00	450.00
☐1914	Minneapolis	Red	20.00	32.00	100.00	450.00
☐1914	Kansas City	Red	20.00	32.00	100.00	450.00
☐1914	Dallas	Red	20.00	32.00	100.00	450.00
☐1914	San Francisco	Red	20.00	32.00	100.00	450.00

TEN DOLLAR NOTES (1914)
FEDERAL RESERVE NOTES

(Large Size)

NOTE NO. 82A

BANK & CITY	SIGNATURES	SEAL	A.B.P.	V.FINE	UNC.
☐ Boston	Burke-McAdoo	Blue	22.00	38.00	120.00
☐ Boston	Burke-Glass	Blue	22.00	38.00	120.00
☐ Boston	Burke-Huston	Blue	22.00	38.00	120.00
☐ Boston	White-Mellon	Blue	22.00	38.00	120.00
☐ New York	Burke-McAdoo	Blue	22.00	38.00	120.00
☐ New York	Burke-Glass	Blue	22.00	38.00	120.00
☐ New York	Burke-Huston	Blue	22.00	38.00	120.00
☐ New York	White-Mellon	Blue	22.00	38.00	120.00
☐ Philadelphia	Burke-McAdoo	Blue	22.00	38.00	120.00
☐ Philadelphia	Burke-Glass	Blue	22.00	38.00	120.00
☐ Philadelphia	Burke-Huston	Blue	22.00	38.00	120.00
☐ Philadelphia	White-Mellon	Blue	22.00	38.00	120.00
☐ Cleveland	Burke-McAdoo	Blue	22.00	38.00	120.00
☐ Cleveland	Burke-Glass	Blue	22.00	38.00	120.00
☐ Cleveland	Burke-Huston	Blue	22.00	38.00	120.00
☐ Cleveland	White-Mellon	Blue	22.00	38.00	120.00
☐ Richmond	Burke-McAdoo	Blue	22.00	38.00	120.00
☐ Richmond	Burke-Glass	Blue	22.00	38.00	120.00
☐ Richmond	Burke-Huston	Blue	22.00	38.00	120.00
☐ Richmond	White-Mellon	Blue	22.00	38.00	120.00
☐ Atlanta	Burke-McAdoo	Blue	22.00	38.00	120.00
☐ Atlanta	Burke-Glass	Blue	22.00	38.00	120.00
☐ Atlanta	Burke-Huston	Blue	22.00	38.00	120.00
☐ Atlanta	White-Mellon	Blue	22.00	38.00	120.00
☐ Chicago	Burke-McAdoo	Blue	22.00	38.00	120.00
☐ Chicago	Burke-Glass	Blue	21.00	35.00	120.00
☐ Chicago	Burke-Huston	Blue	21.00	35.00	120.00
☐ Chicago	White-Mellon	Blue	21.00	35.00	120.00
☐ St. Louis	Burke-McAdoo	Blue	22.00	38.00	120.00
☐ St. Louis	Burke-Glass	Blue	22.00	38.00	120.00
☐ St. Louis	Burke-Huston	Blue	22.00	38.00	120.00
☐ St. Louis	White-Mellon	Blue	22.00	38.00	120.00
☐ Minneapolis	Burke-McAdoo	Blue	22.00	38.00	120.00
☐ Minneapolis	Burke-Glass	Blue	22.00	38.00	120.00
☐ Minneapolis	Burke-Huston	Blue	22.00	38.00	120.00
☐ Minneapolis	White-Mellon	Blue	22.00	38.00	120.00
☐ Kansas City	Burke-McAdoo	Blue	22.00	38.00	120.00
☐ Kansas City	Burke-Glass	Blue	22.00	38.00	120.00

BANK & CITY	SIGNATURES	SEAL	A.B.P.	V.FINE	UNC.
☐ Kansas City	Burke-Huston	Blue	20.00	38.00	120.00
☐ Kansas City	White-Mellon	Blue	20.00	38.00	120.00
☐ Dallas	Burke-McAdoo	Blue	20.00	38.00	120.00
☐ Dallas	Burke-Glass	Blue	20.00	38.00	120.00
☐ Dallas	Burke-Huston	Blue	20.00	38.00	120.00
☐ Dallas	White-Mellon	Blue	20.00	38.00	120.00
☐ San Francisco	Burke-McAdoo	Blue	20.00	38.00	120.00
☐ San Francisco	Burke-Glass	Blue	20.00	42.00	150.00
☐ San Francisco	Burke-Huston	Blue	20.00	38.00	120.00
☐ San Francisco	White Mellon	Blue	20.00	38.00	120.00

TEN DOLLAR NOTES (1928-1928A)
FEDERAL RESERVE NOTES

(Small Size)

NOTE NO. 83

Face Design: Portrait of Alexander Hamilton center, black Federal Reserve Seal left, with number over green Treasury Seal to the right.

Back Design: United States Treasury Building.

SERIES OF 1928, SIGNATURES OF TATE-MELLON, GREEN SEAL

BANK & CITY	A.B.P.	V.FINE	UNC.	BANK & CITY	A.B.P.	V.FINE	UNC.
☐ Boston	12.00	22.00	45.00	☐ Chicago	15.00	24.00	70.00
☐ New York	12.00	22.00	45.00	☐ St. Louis	15.00	24.00	70.00
☐ Philadelphia	12.00	22.00	45.00	☐ Minneapolis	15.00	24.00	70.00
☐ Cleveland	12.00	22.00	45.00	☐ Kansas City	15.00	24.00	70.00

BANK & CITY	A.B.P.	V.FINE	UNC.	BANK & CITY	A.B.P.	V.FINE	UNC.
☐ Richmond	12.00	24.00	70.00	☐ Dallas	12.00	24.00	70.00
☐ Atlanta	12.00	24.00	70.00	☐ San Francisco	12.00	24.00	70.00

SERIES OF 1928A,
SIGNATURES OF WOODS-MELLON, GREEN SEAL

BANK & CITY	A.B.P.	V.FINE	UNC.	BANK & CITY	A.B.P.	V.FINE	UNC.
☐ Boston	12.00	18.00	65.00	☐ Chicago	12.00	18.00	65.00
☐ New York	12.00	18.00	65.00	☐ St. Louis	12.00	18.00	65.00
☐ Philadelphia	12.00	18.00	65.00	☐ Minneapolis	12.00	18.00	65.00
☐ Cleveland	12.00	18.00	65.00	☐ Kansas City	12.00	18.00	65.00
☐ Richmond	12.00	18.00	65.00	☐ Dallas	12.00	18.00	65.00
☐ Atlanta	12.00	18.00	65.00	☐ San Francisco	12.00	18.00	65.00

TEN DOLLAR NOTES (1928B-1928C)
FEDERAL RESERVE NOTES

(Small Issue)   **NOTE NO. 83A**

Face Design: Alexander Hamilton; black Federal Reserve
Seal left, has letter instead of number.
Back Design: Same as note No. 83.

SERIES OF 1928B,
SIGNATURES OF WOODS-MELLON, GREEN SEAL

BANK & CITY	A.B.P.	V.FINE	UNC.	BANK & CITY	A.B.P.	V.FINE	UNC.
☐ Boston	12.00	18.00	52.00	☐ Chicago	12.00	16.00	44.00
☐ New York	12.00	16.00	44.00	☐ St. Louis	12.00	16.00	44.00
☐ Philadelphia	12.00	16.00	44.00	☐ Minneapolis	12.00	18.00	52.00
☐ Cleveland	12.00	16.00	44.00	☐ Kansas City	12.00	16.00	44.00
☐ Richmond	12.00	18.00	52.00	☐ Dallas	12.00	16.00	44.00
☐ Atlanta	12.00	16.00	44.00	☐ San Francisco	12.00	18.00	52.00

SERIES OF 1928C,
SIGNATURES OF WOOD-MILLS, GREEN SEAL

BANK & CITY	A.B.P.	V.FINE	UNC.	BANK & CITY	A.B.P.	V.FINE	UNC.
☐ New York	18.00	30.00	100.00	☐ Atlanta	18.00	30.00	100.00
☐ Cleveland	18.00	30.00	100.00	☐ Chicago	18.00	30.00	100.00
☐ Richmond	18.00	30.00	100.00				

TEN DOLLAR NOTES (1934)
FEDERAL RESERVE NOTES

(Small Size)   **NOTE NO. 83B**

SERIES OF 1934,
SIGNATURES OF JULIAN-MORGENTHAU, GREEN SEAL

BANK & CITY	A.B.P.	V.FINE	UNC.	BANK & CITY	A.B.P.	V.FINE	UNC.
☐ Boston	12.00	15.00	30.00	☐ Chicago	10.00	16.00	32.00
☐ New York	12.00	15.00	30.00	☐ St. Louis	10.00	16.00	32.00
☐ Philadelphia	12.00	15.00	30.00	☐ Minneapolis	10.00	16.00	32.00
☐ Cleveland	12.00	15.00	30.00	☐ Kansas City	10.00	16.00	32.00
☐ Richmond	12.00	15.00	30.00	☐ Dallas	10.00	16.00	32.00
☐ Atlanta	12.00	15.00	30.00	☐ San Francisco	10.00	16.00	32.00

The green Treasury Seal on this note is known in a light and dark color. The light seal is worth about 10–20 percent more in most cases. REDEEMABLE IN GOLD removed from obligation over Federal Reserve Seal.

TEN DOLLAR NOTES (1934)
FEDERAL RESERVE NOTES

(Small Size)   **NOTE NO. 83B**

SERIES OF 1934A,
SIGNATURES OF JULIAN-MORGENTHAU, GREEN SEAL

BANK & CITY	A.B.P.	V.FINE	UNC.	BANK & CITY	A.B.P.	V.FINE	UNC.
☐ Boston	12.00	15.00	25.00	☐ Chicago	9.00	15.50	28.00
☐ New York	12.00	15.00	25.00	☐ St. Louis	9.00	15.50	28.00
☐ Philadelphia	12.00	15.00	25.00	☐ Minneapolis	9.00	15.50	28.00
☐ Cleveland	12.00	15.00	25.00	☐ Kansas City	9.00	15.50	28.00
☐ Richmond	12.00	15.00	25.00	☐ Dallas	9.00	15.50	28.00
☐ Atlanta	12.00	15.00	25.00	☐ San Francisco*	9.00	15.50	28.00

* San Francisco, 1934A, with brown seal and overprinted HAWAII on face and back. Special issue for use in combat areas during World War II. Value in V. FINE $35, value in UNC. $250.

SERIES OF 1934B,
SIGNATURES OF JULIAN-VINSON, GREEN SEAL

BANK & CITY	A.B.P.	V.FINE	UNC.	BANK & CITY	A.B.P.	V.FINE	UNC.
☐ Boston	12.00	16.00	28.00	☐ Chicago	10.00	16.50	30.00
☐ New York	12.00	16.00	28.00	☐ St. Louis	10.00	16.50	30.00
☐ Philadelphia	12.00	16.00	28.00	☐ Minneapolis	10.00	16.50	30.00
☐ Cleveland	12.00	16.00	28.00	☐ Kansas City	10.00	16.50	30.00
☐ Richmond	12.00	16.00	28.00	☐ Dallas	10.00	16.50	30.00
☐ Atlanta	12.00	16.00	28.00	☐ San Francisco	10.00	16.50	30.00

SERIES OF 1934C,
SIGNATURES OF JULIAN-SNYDER, GREEN SEAL

BANK & CITY	A.B.P.	V.FINE	UNC.	BANK & CITY	A.B.P.	V.FINE	UNC.
☐Boston	12.00	15.00	25.00	☐Chicago	12.00	15.00	25.00
☐New York	12.00	15.00	25.00	☐St. Louis	12.00	15.00	25.00
☐Philadelphia	12.00	15.00	25.00	☐Minneapolis	12.00	15.00	25.00
☐Cleveland	12.00	15.00	25.00	☐Kansas City	12.00	15.00	25.00
☐Richmond	12.00	15.00	25.00	☐Dallas	12.00	15.00	25.00
☐Atlanta	12.00	15.00	25.00	☐San Francisco	12.00	15.00	25.00

SERIES OF 1934D,
SIGNATURES OF CLARK-SNYDER, GREEN SEAL

BANK & CITY	A.B.P.	V.FINE	UNC.	BANK & CITY	A.B.P.	V.FINE	UNC.
☐Boston	12.00	15.00	25.00	☐Chicago	12.00	15.00	25.00
☐New York	12.00	15.00	25.00	☐St. Louis	12.00	15.00	25.00
☐Philadelphia	12.00	15.00	25.00	☐Minneapolis	12.00	15.00	25.00
☐Cleveland	12.00	15.00	25.00	☐Kansas City	12.00	15.00	25.00
☐Richmond	12.00	15.00	25.00	☐Dallas	12.00	15.00	25.00
☐Atlanta	12.00	15.00	25.00	☐San Francisco	12.00	15.00	25.00

TEN DOLLAR NOTES (1950)
FEDERAL RESERVE NOTES

(Small Size)   NOTE NO. 83C

SERIES OF 1950, CLARK-SNYDER SIGNATURES, GREEN SEAL

	UNC.
Issued for all Federal Reserve Banks	28.00

TEN DOLLAR NOTES (1950)
FEDERAL RESERVE NOTES

(Small Size)   NOTE NO. 83C

SERIES OF 1950A,
SIGNATURES OF PRIEST-HUMPHREY, GREEN SEAL

	UNC.
Issued for all Federal Reserve Banks	22.00

SERIES OF 1950B,
SIGNATURES OF PRIEST-ANDERSON, GREEN SEAL

	UNC.
Issued for all Federal Reserve Banks	23.00

SERIES OF 1950C,
SIGNATURES OF SMITH-DILLON, GREEN SEAL

	UNC.
Issued for all Federal Reserve Banks	21.00

SERIES OF 1950D,
SIGNATURES OF GRANAHAN-DILLON, GREEN SEAL

	UNC.
Issued for all Federal Reserve Banks	21.00

SERIES OF 1950E,
SIGNATURES OF GRANAHAN-FOWLER, GREEN SEAL

BANK	UNC.	BANK	UNC.
☐New York	22.00	☐San Francisco	22.00
☐Chicago	22.00	ONLY DISTRICTS USED	

TEN DOLLAR NOTES (1963)
FEDERAL RESERVE NOTES
("IN GOD WE TRUST" ADDED ON BACK)
(Small Size) **NOTE NO. 83D**

SERIES OF 1963,
SIGNATURES OF GRANAHAN-DILLON, GREEN SEAL
Issued for all banks except Minneapolis   20.00

SERIES OF 1963A,
SIGNATURES OF GRANAHAN-FOWLER, GREEN SEAL
Issued for all Federal Reserve Banks   20.00

TEN DOLLAR NOTES (1969)
FEDERAL RESERVE NOTES
(WORDING IN GREEN TREASURY SEAL
CHANGED FROM LATIN TO ENGLISH)
(Small Size) **NOTE NO. 83E**

SERIES OF 1969, SIGNATURES OF ELSTON-KENNEDY
Issued for all Federal Reserve Banks   21.00

SERIES OF 1969A, SIGNATURES OF KABIS-CONNALLY
Issued for all Federal Reserve Banks   21.00

SERIES OF 1969B, SIGNATURES OF BANUELOS-CONNALLY
Issued for all Federal Reserve Banks   18.00

SERIES OF 1969C, SIGNATURES OF BANUELOS-SHULTZ
Issued for all Federal Reserve Banks   18.00

SERIES OF 1974, SIGNATURES OF NEFF-SIMON
Issued for all Federal Reserve Banks   16.00

SERIES OF 1977, SIGNATURES OF MORTON-BLUMENTHAL
Issued for all Federal Reserve Banks   16.00

SERIES OF 1977A, SIGNATURES OF MORTON-MILLER
Issued for all Federal Reserve Banks   16.00

SERIES OF 1981,
SIGNATURES OF BUCHANAN-REGAN, GREEN SEAL
Issued for all Federal Reserve Banks   14.00

SERIES OF 1981A,
SIGNATURES OF ORTEGA-REGAN, GREEN SEAL
Issued for all Federal Reserve Banks   14.00

SERIES OF 1985,
SIGNATURES OF ORTEGA-BAKER, GREEN SEAL

	UNC.
Issued for all Federal Reserve Banks	14.00

SERIES OF 1988A,
SIGNATURES OF VILLALPANDO-BRADY, GREEN SEAL

BANK	UNC.	BANK	UNC.
☐ Boston	13.00	☐ Chicago	13.00
☐ New York	13.00	☐ St. Louis	13.00
☐ Philadelphia	13.00	☐ Minneapolis	13.00
☐ Cleveland	13.00	☐ Kansas City	13.00
☐ Richmond	13.00	☐ Dallas	13.00
☐ Atlanta	13.00	☐ San Francisco	13.00

SERIES OF 1990,
SIGNATURES OF VILLALPANDO-BRADY, GREEN SEAL

BANK	UNC.	BANK	UNC.
☐ Boston	12.00	☐ Chicago	12.00
☐ New York	12.00	☐ St. Louis	12.00
☐ Philadelphia	12.00	☐ Minneapolis	12.00
☐ Cleveland	12.00	☐ Kansas City	12.00
☐ Richmond	12.00	☐ Dallas	12.00
☐ Atlanta	12.00	☐ San Francisco	12.00

SERIES OF 1993,
SIGNATURES OF WITHROW-BENTSEN, GREEN SEAL

BANK	UNC.	BANK	UNC.
☐ Boston	11.00	☐ Chicago	11.00
☐ New York	11.00	☐ St. Louis	11.00
☐ Philadelphia	11.00	☐ Minneapolis	11.00
☐ Cleveland	11.00	☐ Kansas City	11.00
☐ Richmond	11.00	☐ Dallas	11.00
☐ Atlanta	11.00	☐ San Francisco	11.00

SERIES OF 1995,
SIGNATURES OF WITHROW-BENTSEN, GREEN SEAL

BANK	UNC.	BANK	UNC.
☐ Boston	10.00	☐ Chicago	10.00
☐ New York	10.00	☐ St. Louis	10.00
☐ Philadelphia	10.00	☐ Minneapolis	10.00
☐ Cleveland	10.00	☐ Kansas City	10.00
☐ Richmond	10.00	☐ Dallas	10.00
☐ Atlanta	10.00	☐ San Francisco	10.00

TEN DOLLAR NOTES (1915-1918)
FEDERAL RESERVE BANK NOTES

(Large Size)   **NOTE NO. 84**

Face Design: Portrait of President Jackson to left, bank and city in center, blue seal to the right.

Back Design: Similar to note No. 82.

BANK & CITY	SERIES	GOV'T SIGNATURES	BANK SIGNATURES	A.B.P.	GOOD	V.FINE	UNC.
☐New York	1918	Teehee-Burke	Hendricks-Strong				
				60.00	100.00	500.00	2100.00
☐Atlanta	1915	Teehee-Burke	Bell-Wellborn				
				60.00	100.00	500.00	1700.00
☐Atlanta	1918	Elliott-Burke	Bell-Wellborn				
				60.00	100.00	500.00	1700.00
☐Chicago	1915	Teehee-Burke	McLallen-McDougal				
				60.00	100.00	500.00	1700.00
☐Chicago	1918	Teehee-Burke	McCloud-McDougal				
				60.00	100.00	500.00	1700.00
☐St. Louis	1918	Teehee-Burke	Attebery-Wells				
				60.00	110.00	525.00	1700.00
☐Kansas City	1915	Teehee-Burke	Anderson-Miller				
				60.00	110.00	525.00	1700.00

BANK & CITY	SERIES	GOV'T SIGNATURES	BANK SIGNATURES	A.B.P.	GOOD	V.FINE	UNC.
☐Kansas City	1915	Teehee-Burke	Cross-Miller				
				60.00	110.00	525.00	1700.00
☐Kansas City	1915	Teehee-Burke	Helm-Miller				
				60.00	110.00	525.00	1700.00
☐Dallas	1915	Teehee-Burke	Hoopes-Van Zandt				
				60.00	110.00	525.00	1700.00
☐Dallas	1915	Teehee-Burke	Gilbert-Van Zandt				
				60.00	110.00	710.00	2200.00
☐Dallas	1915	Teehee-Burke	Talley-Van Zandt				
				60.00	110.00	525.00	1700.00

TEN DOLLAR NOTES (1929)
FEDERAL RESERVE BANK NOTES

(Small Size)   **NOTE NO. 85**

Face Design: Portrait of Alexander Hamilton.

Back Design: Same as all small size $10 notes.

SIGNATURES OF JONES-WOODS, BROWN SEAL

BANK	SEAL	A.B.P.	GOOD	V.FINE	UNC.
☐Boston	Brown	11.00	12.00	23.00	85.00
☐New York	Brown	11.00	12.00	22.00	75.00
☐Philadelphia	Brown	11.00	12.00	22.00	75.00
☐Cleveland	Brown	11.00	12.00	22.00	70.00

☐Richmond	Brown	11.00	12.00	22.00	98.00
☐Atlanta	Brown	11.00	12.00	22.00	98.00
☐Chicago	Brown	11.00	12.00	22.00	75.00
☐St. Louis	Brown	11.00	12.00	22.00	75.00
☐Minneapolis	Brown	11.00	12.00	22.00	90.00
☐Kansas City	Brown	11.00	12.00	21.00	75.00
☐Dallas	Brown	100.00	210.00	40.00	1100.00
☐San Francisco	Brown	11.00	12.00	24.00	115.00

TWENTY DOLLAR NOTES

ORDER OF ISSUE

TWENTY DOLLAR NOTES (1861) DEMAND NOTES
(Large Size)   **NOTE NO. 86**

Face Design: Liberty with sword and shield.

Back Design: Intricate design of numerals, "20." Demand Notes have no Treasury Seal.

SERIES	PAYABLE AT	A.B.P.	GOOD	V.GOOD
☐ 1861	Boston (I)	RARE	RARE	RARE
☐ 1861	New York (I)	2800.00	4800.00	10,000.00
☐ 1861	Philadelphia (I)	2800.00	4800.00	10,000.00
☐ 1861	Cincinnati (I)	RARE	RARE	RARE
☐ 1861	St. Louis (I)	(Unknown in any collection)		
☐ 1861	Boston (II)	RARE	RARE	RARE
☐ 1861	New York (II)	2800.00	4800.00	10,000.00
☐ 1861	Philadelphia (II)	2800.00	4800.00	10,000.00
☐ 1861	Cincinnati (II)	RARE	RARE	RARE
☐ 1861	St. Louis (II)	(Unknown in any collection)		

Counterfeits and expertly repaired specimens exist. Use caution in buying.

TWENTY DOLLAR NOTES (1862-1863)
UNITED STATES NOTES
(ALSO KNOWN AS LEGAL TENDER NOTES)
(Large Size)

NOTE NO. 86A

Face Design: Liberty with sword and shield.

Back Design: Second obligation. This note was also issued with first obligation on the back. See note Nos. 33 and 33A.

SERIES	SIGNATURES	SEAL	A.B.P.	GOOD	V.FINE	UNC.
☐1862	Chittenden-Spinner*	Red	240.00	425.00	1200.00	3200.00
☐1862	Chittenden-Spinner**	Red	240.00	425.00	1200.00	3200.00
☐1863	Chittenden-Spinner**	Red	240.00	425.00	1200.00	3200.00

* First Obligation: Similar to note No. 33.
** Second Obligation: Shown above.

TWENTY DOLLAR NOTES (1869)
UNITED STATES NOTES
(ALSO KNOWN AS LEGAL TENDER NOTES)
(Large Size)   **NOTE NOS. 87-87A**

SERIES	SIGNATURES	SEAL	A.B.P.	GOOD	V.FINE	UNC.
☐1869	Allison-Spinner	Red	125.00	210.00	1500.00	4600.00
87A Series Back Design: Revised						
☐1875	Allison-New	Red	42.00	95.00	750.00	2400.00
☐1878	Allison-Gilfillan	Red	42.00	85.00	700.00	2100.00
☐1880	Scofield-Gilfillan	Lg. Brown	42.00	85.00	600.00	1700.00
☐1880	Bruce-Gilfillan	Lg. Brown	42.00	95.00	600.00	1675.00
☐1880	Bruce-Wyman	Lg. Brown	42.00	86.00	600.00	1675.00
☐1880	Bruce-Wyman	Lg. Red	42.00	85.00	500.00	1675.00
☐1880	Rosecrans-Jordan	Lg. Red	42.00	85.00	500.00	1675.00
☐1880	Rosecrans-Hyatt	Red Plain	42.00	85.00	500.00	1675.00
☐1880	Rosecrans-Hyatt	Red Spikes	42.00	85.00	600.00	1800.00
☐1880	Rosecrans-Huston	Lg. Red	42.00	85.00	600.00	1800.00
☐1880	Rosecrans-Huston	Lg. Brown	42.00	85.00	500.00	1800.00
☐1880	Rosecrans-Nebeker	Lg. Brown	42.00	80.00	600.00	1000.00
☐1800	Rosecrans-Nebeker	Sm. Red	42.00	80.00	350.00	1000.00
☐1880	Tillman-Morgan	Sm. Red	35.00	70.00	350.00	1000.00
☐1880	Bruce-Roberts	Sm. Red	35.00	70.00	350.00	1050.00
☐1880	Lyons-Roberts	Sm. Red	35.00	70.00	350.00	1050.00
☐1880	Vernon-Treat	Sm. Red	35.00	70.00	325.00	875.00
☐1880	Vernon-McClung	Sm. Red	35.00	70.00	325.00	875.00
☐1880	Teehee-Burke	Sm. Red	35.00	70.00	325.00	875.00
☐1880	Elliott-White	Sm. Red	35.00	70.00	325.00	875.00

TWENTY DOLLAR NOTES (1863-1875)
NATIONAL BANK NOTES
FIRST CHARTER PERIOD (Large Size)

NOTE NO. 88

Face Design: Battle of Lexington left, name of bank in center. Columbia with flag right.

Back Design: Green border, black center picture of baptism of Pocahontas.

SERIES	SIGNATURES	SEAL	A.B.P.	GOOD	V.FINE	UNC.
☐ Original	Chittenden-Spinner	Red	100.00	200.00	1200.00	3900.00
☐ Original	Colby-Spinner	Red	100.00	210.00	1000.00	3800.00
☐ Original	Jeffries-Spinner	Red	150.00	600.00	2100.00	4600.00
☐ Original	Allison-Spinner	Red	85.00	240.00	1100.00	3700.00
☐ 1875	Allison-New	Red	85.00	200.00	1000.00	3500.00
☐ 1875	Allison-Wyman	Red	90.00	200.00	1000.00	3600.00
☐ 1875	Allison-Gilfillan	Red	85.00	200.00	1000.00	3500.00
☐ 1875	Scofield-Gilfillan	Red	85.00	200.00	1000.00	3500.00
☐ 1875	Bruce-Gilfillan	Red	85.00	200.00	1000.00	3500.00
☐ 1875	Bruce-Wyman	Red	100.00	240.00	1000.00	3850.00
☐ 1875	Rosecrans-Huston	Red	85.00	200.00	1100.00	3500.00
☐ 1875	Rosecrans-Nebeker	Red	100.00	450.00	1250.00	4300.00
☐ 1875	Tillman-Morgan	Red	100.00	450.00	1300.00	4400.00

TWENTY DOLLAR NOTES (1882)
NATIONAL BANK NOTES
SECOND CHARTER PERIOD (Large Size)   **NOTE NO. 88A**

First Issue (Brown seal and brown backs.)
Face Design: Similar to note No. 88.
Back Design: Similar to note No. 39, border is brown, green Charter Number in center.

SERIES	SIGNATURES	SEAL	A.B.P.	GOOD	V.FINE	UNC.
☐1882	Bruce-Gilfillan	Brown	45.00	75.00	350.00	1200.00
☐1882	Bruce-Wyman	Brown	45.00	75.00	350.00	1200.00
☐1882	Bruce-Jordan	Brown	45.00	75.00	350.00	1200.00
☐1882	Rosecrans-Jordan	Brown	45.00	75.00	350.00	1200.00
☐1882	Rosecrans-Hyatt	Brown	45.00	75.00	350.00	1200.00
☐1882	Rosecrans-Huston	Brown	45.00	75.00	350.00	1200.00
☐1882	Rosecrans-Nebeker	Brown	45.00	75.00	350.00	1000.00
☐1882	Rosecrans-Morgan	Brown	130.00	280.00	800.00	2100.00
☐1882	Tillman-Morgan	Brown	45.00	75.00	350.00	1100.00
☐1882	Tillman-Roberts	Brown	45.00	75.00	350.00	1100.00
☐1882	Bruce-Roberts	Brown	45.00	75.00	350.00	1100.00
☐1882	Lyons-Roberts	Brown	45.00	75.00	350.00	1100.00
☐1882	Lyons-Treat	Brown	45.00	75.00	350.00	1100.00
☐1882	Vernon-Treat	Brown	45.00	75.00	350.00	1100.00

SECOND CHARTER PERIOD, Second Issue   **NOTE NO. 88B**

Face Design: Similar to note No. 88.
Back Design: Similar to note No. 40.

SERIES	SIGNATURES	SEAL	A.B.P.	GOOD	V.FINE	UNC.
☐1882	Rosecrans-Huston	Blue	42.00	70.00	275.00	875.00
☐1882	Rosecrans-Nebeker	Blue	42.00	70.00	275.00	875.00
☐1882	Rosecrans-Morgan	Blue	120.00	300.00	800.00	1600.00
☐1882	Tillman-Morgan	Blue	42.00	70.00	275.00	875.00
☐1882	Tillman-Roberts	Blue	42.00	70.00	275.00	875.00
☐1882	Bruce-Roberts	Blue	42.00	70.00	275.00	875.00
☐1882	Lyons-Roberts	Blue	42.00	70.00	275.00	875.00
☐1882	Vernon-Treat	Blue	42.00	70.00	275.00	875.00
☐1882	Napier-McClung	Blue	42.00	70.00	275.00	875.00

SECOND CHARTER PERIOD, Third Issue. Large Size   **NOTE NO. 88C**

Face Design: Similar to note No. 88 with blue seal.
Back Design: Similar to note No. 41, green back, value in block letters.

SERIES	SIGNATURES	SEAL	A.B.P.	GOOD	V.FINE	UNC.
☐1882	Tillman-Morgan	Blue	48.00	80.00	450.00	1800.00
☐1882	Lyons-Roberts	Blue	48.00	80.00	500.00	2200.00
☐1882	Lyons-Treat	Blue	48.00	80.00	450.00	2200 00
☐1882	Vernon-Treat	Blue	48.00	80.00	450.00	1800.00
☐1882	Napier-McClung	Blue	48.00	80.00	450.00	1800.00
☐1882	Teehee-Burke	Blue	48..00	80.00	550.00	2300.00

TWENTY DOLLAR NOTES (1902)
NATIONAL BANK NOTES
THIRD CHARTER PERIOD, First Issue (Large Size)   **NOTE NO. 89**

Face Design: Portrait of McCulloch left, name of bank center, Treasury Seal right.

SERIES	SIGNATURES	SEAL	A.B.P.	GOOD	V.FINE	UNC.
☐1902	Lyons-Roberts	Red	30.00	75.00	250.00	1000.00
☐1902	Lyons-Treat	Red	30.00	75.00	250.00	1000.00
☐1902	Vernon-Treat	Red	30.00	75.00	270.00	1650.00

Second Issue (Date "1902–1908" added on back, Treasury Seal and serial numbers blue)

SERIES	SIGNATURES	SEAL	A.B.P.	GOOD	V.FINE	UNC.
☐1902	Lyons-Roberts	Blue	18.00	30.00	80.00	350.00
☐1902	Lyons-Treat	Blue	18.00	30.00	80.00	350.00
☐1902	Vernon-Treat	Blue	18.00	30.00	80.00	350.00
☐1902	Vernon-McClung	Blue	18.00	30.00	80.00	350.00
☐1902	Napier-McClung	Blue	18.00	30.00	80.00	350.00
☐1902	Napier-Thompson	Blue	18.00	34.00	90.00	600.00
☐1902	Napier-Burke	Blue	18.00	30.00	80.00	350.00
☐1902	Parker-Burke	Blue	22.00	30.00	80.00	350.00

Third Issue (Date "1902–1908" removed from back, seal and serial numbers blue)

SERIES	SIGNATURES	SEAL	A.B.P.	GOOD	V.FINE	UNC.
☐1902	Lyons-Roberts	Blue	22.00	30.00	70.00	290.00
☐1902	Lyons-Treat	Blue	22.00	30.00	70.00	290.00
☐1902	Vernon-Treat	Blue	22.00	30.00	70.00	290.00
☐1902	Vernon-McClung	Blue	22.00	30.00	70.00	290.00

SERIES	SIGNATURES	SEAL	A.B.P.	GOOD	V.FINE	UNC.
☐1902	Napier-McClung	Blue	20.00	32.00	70.00	290.00
☐1902	Napier-Thompson	Blue	20.00	32.00	75.00	300.00
☐1902	Napier-Burke	Blue	20.00	32.00	70.00	320.00
☐1902	Parker-Burke	Blue	20.00	32.00	70.00	320.00
☐1902	Teehee-Burke	Blue	20.00	32.00	70.00	320.00
☐1902	Elliott-Burke	Blue	20.00	32.00	70.00	320.00
☐1902	Elliott-White	Blue	20.00	32.00	70.00	320.00
☐1902	Speelman-White	Blue	20.00	32.00	70.00	320.00
☐1902	Woods-White	Blue	20.00	32.00	70.00	320.00
☐1902	Woods-Tate	Blue	22.00	42.00	160.00	500.00
☐1902	Jones-Woods	Blue	175.00	400.00	1100.00	5200.00

TWENTY DOLLAR NOTES (1929)
NATIONAL BANK NOTES

(Small Size)   **NOTE NO. 90**

Face Design, Type I: Portrait of President Jackson in center, name of bank to left, brown seal right. Charter number in black.

Face Design, Type II.

Back Design: The White House, similar to all $20 Small Notes.

SERIES	SIGNATURES	SEAL	A.B.P.	GOOD	V.FINE	UNC.
☐1929, Type I	Jones-Woods	Brown	14.00	22.00	40.00	120.00
☐1929, Type II	Jones-Woods	Brown	14.00	22.00	42.00	125.00

TWENTY DOLLAR NOTES (1880)
SILVER CERTIFICATES

(Large Size)

NOTE NO. 91

Face Design: Portrait of Stephen Decatur right. TWENTY SILVER DOLLARS in center.

Back Design: SILVER in large block letters.

SERIES	SIGNATURES	SEAL	A.B.P.	GOOD	V.FINE	UNC.
☐1880	Scofield-Gilfillan	Brown	90.00	500.00	1800.00	7500.00
☐1880	Bruce-Gilfillan	Brown	90.00	500.00	1800.00	7500.00
☐1880	Bruce-Wyman	Brown	90.00	500.00	1800.00	7500.00
☐1880	Bruce-Wyman	Sm. Red	400.00	1500.00	2400.00	8200.00

This note was also issued in the Series of 1878. They are very rare.

TWENTY DOLLAR NOTES (1886)
SILVER CERTIFICATES

(Large Size)   **NOTE NO. 92**

Face Design: Portrait of Daniel Manning center, Agriculture left, Industry right.

Back Design: Double-diamond design center.

SERIES	SIGNATURES	SEAL	A.B.P.	GOOD	V.FINE	UNC.
☐1886	Rosecrans-Hyatt	Lg. Red	300.00	650.00	3200.00	9500.00
☐1886	Rosecrans-Huston	Lg. Brown	300.00	650.00	3200.00	9500.00
☐1886	Rosecrans-Nebeker	Lg. Brown	300.00	650.00	3200.00	9500.00
☐1886	Rosecrans-Nebeker	Sm. Red	375.00	1000.00	3400.00	9700.00

TWENTY DOLLAR NOTES (1891)
SILVER CERTIFICATES
(NOT ISSUED IN SMALL SIZE NOTES)

(Large Size)   **NOTE NO. 93**

Face Design: Same as note No. 92.

Back Design: Revised.

SERIES	SIGNATURES	SEAL	A.B.P.	GOOD	V.FINE	UNC.
☐1891	Rosecrans-Nebeker	Red	75.00	130.00	670.00	2600.00
☐1891	Tillman-Morgan	Red	75.00	130.00	670.00	2600.00
☐1891	Bruce-Roberts	Red	75.00	130.00	670.00	2600.00
☐1891	Lyons-Roberts	Red	75.00	130.00	670.00	2600.00
☐1891	Parker-Burke	Blue	75.00	130.00	670.00	2600.00
☐1891	Teehee-Burke	Blue	75.00	130.00	670.00	2600.00

TWENTY DOLLAR NOTES (1882) GOLD CERTIFICATES
(Large Size)   **NOTE NO. 94**

Face Design: Portrait of President Garfield right, TWENTY DOLLARS IN GOLD COIN center.

Back Design: Large "20" left, eagle and arrows center, bright orange color.

SERIES	SIGNATURES	SEAL	A.B.P.	GOOD	V.FINE	UNC.
☐1882*	Bruce-Gilfillan	Brown		VERY RARE		
☐1882	Bruce-Gilfillan	Brown	660.00	1100.00	3500.00	7500.00
☐1882	Bruce-Wyman	Brown	480.00	800.00	2200.00	4000.00
☐1882	Rosecrans-Huston	Brown	270.00	450.00	2500.00	5000.00
☐1882	Lyons-Roberts	Red	54.00	90.00	650.00	2300.00

*This note has a countersigned signature.

TWENTY DOLLAR NOTES (1905) GOLD CERTIFICATES
(Large Size)
NOTE NO. 95

Face Design: Portrait of President Washington center, "XX" left, Treasury Seal right.

Back Design: Eagle and shield center, printed in bright orange color.

SERIES	SIGNATURES	SEAL	A.B.P.	GOOD	V.FINE	UNC.
☐1905	Lyons-Roberts	Red	210.00	350.00	1300.00	6800.00
☐1905	Lyons-Treat	Red	210.00	350.00	1300.00	6800.00
☐1906	Vernon-Treat	Gold	42.00	70.00	130.00	540.00
☐1906	Vernon-McClung	Gold	42.00	70.00	130.00	575.00
☐1906	Napier-McClung	Gold	42.00	70.00	130.00	575.00
☐1906	Napier-Thompson	Gold	60.00	100.00	200.00	750.00
☐1906	Parker-Burke	Gold	42.00	70.00	130.00	600.00
☐1906	Tehee-Burke	Gold	42.00	70.00	130.00	600.00
☐1922	Speelman-White	Gold	42.00	70.00	120.00	450.00

TWENTY DOLLAR NOTES (1928) GOLD CERTIFICATES
(Small Size)   **NOTE NO. 96**

Face Design: Portrait of President Jackson center, gold seal left, gold serial numbers.

Back Design: The White House, printed green, similar to all Small Size $20 Notes.

SERIES	SIGNATURES	SEAL	A.B.P.	V.FINE	UNC.
☐1928	Woods-Mellon	Gold	36.00	60.00	200.00

TWENTY DOLLAR NOTES (1890) TREASURY NOTES
(Large Size)   **NOTE NO. 97**

Face Design: Portrait of John Marshall, Supreme Court Chief Justice, left, "20" center.

Back Design

SERIES	SIGNATURES	SEAL	A.B.P.	GOOD	V.FINE	UNC.
☐1890	Rosecrans-Huston	Brown	250.00	500.00	3500.00	9700.00
☐1890	Rosecrans-Nebeker	Brown	250.00	500.00	3500.00	9700.00
☐1890	Rosecrans-Nebeker	Red	250.00	500.00	3500.00	9700.00

(Large Size) **NOTE NO. 97A**

Back Design

Face Design: Same as previous note.

SERIES	SIGNATURES	SEAL	A.B.P.	GOOD	V.FINE	UNC.
☐1891	Tillman-Morgan	Red	600.00	1000.00	4200.00	12000.00
☐1891	Bruce-Roberts	Red	600.00	1000.00	4200.00	12000.00

TWENTY DOLLAR NOTES (1914)
FEDERAL RESERVE NOTES

(Large Size) **NOTE NO. 98**
Face Design: Portrait of President Cleveland center, Federal Reserve Seal left, Treasury Seal right.

Back Design: Scenes of transportation. Locomotive left, steamship right.

SERIES OF 1914, SIGNATURES OF BURKE-McADOO, RED TREASURY SEAL

BANK	A.B.P.	V.FINE	UNC.	BANK	A.B.P.	V.FINE	UNC.
☐Boston	35.00	200.00	920.00	☐Chicago	35.00	250.00	975.00
☐New York	35.00	200.00	920.00	☐St. Louis	35.00	250.00	975.00
☐Philadelphia	35.00	200.00	920.00	☐Minneapolis	35.00	250.00	975.00
☐Cleveland	35.00	200.00	920.00	☐Kansas City	35.00	250.00	975.00
☐Richmond	35.00	200.00	920.00	☐Dallas	35.00	250.00	975.00
☐Atlanta	35.00	200.00	920.00	☐San Francisco	35.00	250.00	975.00

SERIES OF 1914, BLUE TREASURY SEAL AND BLUE SERIAL NUMBERS

This note was issued with signatures of Burke-McAdoo, Burke-Glass, Burke-Huston, and White-Mellon.

	A.B.P.	V.FINE	UNC.
Issued for all Federal Reserve Banks	30.00	60.00	175.00

TWENTY DOLLAR NOTES (1928)
FEDERAL RESERVE NOTES

(Small Size)   **NOTE NO. 99**

Face Design: Portrait of President Jackson center, black Federal Reserve Seal with numeral for district in center. City of issuing bank in seal circle. Green Treasury Seal right.

Back Design: Picture of the White House, similar to all Small Size $20 Notes.

SERIES OF 1928, SIGNATURES OF TATE-MELLON, GREEN SEAL

BANK	A.B.P.	V.FINE	UNC.	BANK	A.B.P.	V.FINE	UNC.
☐Boston	22.00	40.00	95.00	☐Chicago	22.00	40.00	95.00
☐New York	22.00	40.00	95.00	☐St. Louis	22.00	40.00	95.00
☐Philadelphia	22.00	40.00	95.00	☐Minneapolis	22.00	40.00	95.00
☐Cleveland	22.00	40.00	95.00	☐Kansas City	22.00	40.00	95.00
☐Richmond	22.00	40.00	95.00	☐Dallas	22.00	40.00	95.00
☐Atlanta	22.00	40.00	95.00	☐San Francisco	22.00	40.00	95.00

SERIES OF 1928A,
SIGNATURES OF WOODS-MELLON, GREEN SEAL

CITY	A.B.P.	V.FINE	UNC.	CITY	A.B.P.	V.FINE	UNC.
☐Boston	22.00	40.00	95.00	☐Chicago	22.00	40.00	95.00
☐New York	22.00	40.00	95.00	☐St. Louis	22.00	40.00	95.00
☐Philadelphia	22.00	40.00	95.00	☐Minneapolis		NOT ISSUED	
☐Cleveland	22.00	40.00	95.00	☐Kansas City	22.00	40.00	95.00
☐Richmond	22.00	40.00	95.00	☐Dallas	22.00	40.00	95.00
☐Atlanta	22.00	40.00	95.00	☐San Francisco		NOT ISSUED	

TWENTY DOLLAR NOTES (1928)
FEDERAL RESERVE NOTES
(Small Size)   NOTE NO. 100
SERIES OF 1928B,
SIGNATURES OF WOODS-MELLON, GREEN SEAL

The face and back design are similar to previous note. Numeral in Federal Reserve Seal is now changed to a letter.

BANK	A.B.P.	V.FINE	UNC.	BANK	A.B.P.	V.FINE	UNC.
☐Boston	22.00	29.00	75.00	☐Chicago	20.00	32.00	75.00
☐New York	22.00	29.00	75.00	☐St. Louis	20.00	32.00	75.00
☐Philadelphia	22.00	29.00	75.00	☐Minneapolis	20.00	32.00	75.00
☐Cleveland	22.00	29.00	75.00	☐Kansas City	20.00	32.00	75.00
☐Richmond	22.00	29.00	75.00	☐Dallas	20.00	32.00	75.00
☐Atlanta	22.00	29.00	75.00	☐San Francisco	20.00	32.00	75.00

SERIES OF 1928C, SIGNATURES OF WOODS-MILLS, GREEN SEAL

Only two banks issued this note.

BANK	A.B.P.	V.FINE	UNC.	BANK	A.B.P.	V.FINE	UNC.
☐Chicago	75.00	200.00	600.00	☐San Francisco	75.00	200.00	700.00

TWENTY DOLLAR NOTES (1934)
FEDERAL RESERVE NOTES
(Small Size)   NOTE NO. 100A
SIGNATURES OF JULIAN-MORGENTHAU, GREEN SEAL

Face and back design are similar to previous note. "Redeemable in Gold" removed from obligation over Federal Reserve Seal.

BANK	GOOD	V.FINE	UNC.	BANK	GOOD	V.FINE	UNC.
☐Boston	24.00	30.00	45.00	☐St. Louis	18.00	30.00	48.00
☐New York	24.00	30.00	45.00	☐Minneapolis	18.00	30.00	48.00
☐Philadelphia	24.00	30.00	45.00	☐Kansas City	18.00	30.00	48.00
☐Cleveland	24.00	30.00	45.00	☐Dallas	18.00	30.00	48.00
☐Richmond	24.00	30.00	45.00	☐San Francisco	18.00	30.00	48.00
☐Atlanta	24.00	30.00	45.00	☐San Francisco*			
☐Chicago	24.00	30.00	45.00	(HAWAII)	56.00	145.00	750.00

* The San Francisco Federal Reserve Note with brown seal and brown serial numbers, and overprinted HAWAII on face and back, was a special issue for the armed forces in the Pacific area during World War II.

TWENTY DOLLAR NOTES (1934A)
FEDERAL RESERVE NOTES

(Small Size)   **NOTE NO. 101**
SERIES OF 1934A, SIGNATURES OF JULIAN-MORGENTHAU

BANK	A.B.P.	V.FINE	UNC.	BANK	A.B.P.	V.FINE	UNC.
☐ Boston	21.00	30.00	45.00	☐ St. Louis	21.00	32.00	50.00
☐ New York	21.00	30.00	45.00	☐ Minneapolis	21.00	32.00	50.00
☐ Philadelphia	21.00	30.00	45.00	☐ Kansas City	21.00	32.00	50.00
☐ Cleveland	21.00	30.00	45.00	☐ Dallas	21.00	32.00	50.00
☐ Richmond	21.00	30.00	45.00	☐ San Francisco	21.00	32.00	50.00
☐ Atlanta	21.00	30.00	45.00	☐ San Francisco*			
☐ Chicago	21.00	30.00	45.00	(HAWAII)	26.00	50.00	335.00

* The San Francisco Federal Reserve Note with brown seal and brown serial numbers, and overprinted HAWAII on face and back, was a special issue for the armed forces in the Pacific area during World War II.

SERIES OF 1934B,
SIGNATURES OF JULIAN-VINSON, GREEN SEAL

BANK	A.B.P.	V.FINE	UNC.	BANK	A.B.P.	V.FINE	UNC.
☐ Boston	24.00	29.00	44.00	☐ Chicago	18.00	30.00	50.00
☐ New York	24.00	29.00	44.00	☐ St. Louis	18.00	30.00	50.00
☐ Philadelphia	24.00	29.00	44.00	☐ Minneapolis	18.00	30.00	50.00
☐ Cleveland	24.00	29.00	44.00	☐ Kansas City	18.00	30.00	50.00
☐ Richmond	24.00	29.00	44.00	☐ Dallas	18.00	30.00	50.00
☐ Atlanta	24.00	29.00	44.00	☐ San Francisco	18.00	30.00	50.00

SERIES OF 1934C,
SIGNATURES OF JULIAN-SNYDER, GREEN SEAL

Back Design: This has been modified with this series, balcony added to the White House.

BANK	A.B.P.	V.FINE	UNC.	BANK	A.B.P.	V.FINE	UNC.
☐ Boston	22.00	29.00	44.00	☐ Chicago	20.00	32.00	50.00
☐ New York	22.00	29.00	44.00	☐ St. Louis	20.00	32.00	50.00
☐ Philadelphia	22.00	29.00	44.00	☐ Minneapolis	20.00	32.00	50.00
☐ Cleveland	22.00	29.00	44.00	☐ Kansas City	20.00	32.00	50.00
☐ Richmond	22.00	29.00	44.00	☐ Dallas	20.00	32.00	50.00
☐ Atlanta	22.00	29.00	44.00	☐ San Francisco	20.00	32.00	50.00

SERIES OF 1934D,
SIGNATURES OF CLARK-SNYDER, GREEN SEAL

BANK	A.B.P.	V.FINE	UNC.	BANK	A.B.P.	V.FINE	UNC.
☐ Boston	22.00	28.00	42.00	☐ Chicago	18.00	30.00	45.00
☐ New York	22.00	28.00	42.00	☐ St. Louis	18.00	30.00	45.00
☐ Philadelphia	22.00	28.00	42.00	☐ Minneapolis	18.00	30.00	45.00
☐ Cleveland	22.00	28.00	42.00	☐ Kansas City	18.00	30.00	45.00
☐ Richmond	22.00	28.00	42.00	☐ Dallas	18.00	30.00	45.00
☐ Atlanta	22.00	28.00	42.00	☐ San Francisco	18.00	30.00	45.00

TWENTY DOLLAR NOTES (1950)
FEDERAL RESERVE NOTES

(Small Size)   **NOTE NO. 102**

SERIES OF 1950,
SIGNATURES OF CLARK-SNYDER, GREEN SEAL

The black Federal Seal and green Treasury Seal are slightly smaller.

BANK	A.B.P.	UNC.	BANK	A.B.P.	UNC.
☐ Boston	22.00	40.00	☐ Chicago	26.00	45.00
☐ New York	22.00	40.00	☐ St. Louis	26.00	45.00
☐ Philadelphia	22.00	40.00	☐ Minneapolis	26.00	45.00
☐ Cleveland	22.00	40.00	☐ Kansas City	26.00	45.00

BANK	A.B.P.	UNC.	BANK	A.B.P.	UNC.
☐Richmond	22.00	40.00	☐Dallas	26.00	45.00
☐Atlanta	22.00	40.00	☐San Francisco	26.00	45.00

SERIES OF 1950A,
SIGNATURES OF PRIEST-HUMPHREY, GREEN SEAL
Issued for all Federal Reserve Banks   35.00

SERIES OF 1950B,
SIGNATURES OF PRIEST-ANDERSON, GREEN SEAL
Issued for all Federal Reserve Banks   35.00

SERIES OF 1950C, SIGNATURES OF SMITH-DILLON, GREEN SEAL
Issued for all Federal Reserve Banks   34.00

SERIES OF 1950D,
SIGNATURES OF GRANAHAN-DILLON, GREEN SEAL
Issued for all Federal Reserve Banks   35.00

SERIES OF 1950E,
SIGNATURES OF GRANAHAN-FOWLER, GREEN SEAL
Issued only for New York, Chicago, and San Francisco   35.00

TWENTY DOLLAR NOTES (1963)
FEDERAL RESERVE NOTES
(Small Size)   **NOTE NO. 102A**

SERIES OF 1963,
SIGNATURES OF GRANAHAN-DILLON, GREEN SEAL
Issued for all banks except Minneapolis   34.00

SERIES OF 1963A,
SIGNATURES OF GRANAHAN-FOWLER, GREEN SEAL
Issued for all Federal Reserve Banks   35.00

SERIES OF 1969,
SIGNATURES OF ELSTON-KENNEDY, GREEN SEAL
Issued for all Federal Reserve Banks   35.00

SERIES OF 1969A,
SIGNATURES OF KABIS-CONNALLY, GREEN SEAL
Issued for all Federal Reserve Banks   34.00

SERIES OF 1969B, SIGNATURES OF BANUELOS-CONNALLY
Issued for all Federal Reserve Banks   32.00

SERIES OF 1969C,
SIGNATURES OF BANUELOS-SHULTZ, GREEN SEAL
Issued for all Federal Reserve Banks   32.00

SERIES OF 1974, SIGNATURES OF NEFF-SIMON, GREEN SEAL
Issued for all Federal Reserve Banks   33.00

SERIES OF 1977,
SIGNATURES OF MORTON-BLUMENTHAL, GREEN SEAL
Issued for all Federal Reserve Banks   28.00

SERIES OF 1977A,
SIGNATURES OF MORTON-MILLER, GREEN SEAL UNC.
Issued for all Federal Reserve Banks 29.00
SERIES OF 1981,
SIGNATURES OF BUCHANAN-REGAN, GREEN SEAL
Issued for all Federal Reserve Banks 27.00
SERIES OF 1981A,
SIGNATURES OF ORTEGA-REGAN, GREEN SEAL
Issued for all Federal Reserve Banks 25.00
SERIES OF 1985,
SIGNATURES OF ORTEGA-BAKER, GREEN SEAL
Issued for all Federal Reserve Banks 24.00

TWENTY DOLLAR NOTES (1915-1918)
FEDERAL RESERVE BANK NOTES
(ALL HAVE BLUE SEALS)
(Large Size) **NOTE NO. 103**

Face Design:
Portrait of
President
Cleveland left,
name of bank
and city center,
blue seal right.

Back Design:
Locomotive
and steamship,
similar to note
No. 98.

BANK & CITY	SERIES	GOV'T SIGNATURES	BANK SIGNATURES	A.B.P.	GOOD	V.FINE	UNC.
☐ Atlanta	1915	Teehee-Burke	Bell-Wellborn	55.00	100.00	500.00	2300.00
☐ Atlanta	1918	Elliott-Burke	Bell-Wellborn	55.00	100.00	500.00	2300.00
☐ Chicago	1915	Teehee-Burke	McLallen-McDougal	55.00	100.00	500.00	2300.00
☐ St. Louis	1918	Teehee-Burke	Attebery-Wells	55.00	200.00	750.00	3600.00
☐ Kansas City	1915	Teehee-Burke	Anderson-Miller	55.00	100.00	600.00	2300.00

BANK & CITY	SERIES	GOV'T SIGNATURES	BANK SIGNATURES	A.B.P.	GOOD	V.FINE	UNC.
☐Kansas City	1915	Teehee-Burke	Cross-Miller				
				60.00	100.00	600.00	2300.00
☐Dallas	1915	Teehee-Burke	Hoopes-Van Zandt				
				60.00	100.00	600.00	2300.00
☐Dallas	1915	Teehee-Burke	Gilbert-Van Zandt				
				69.00	115.00	600.00	2300.00
☐Dallas	1915	Teehee-Burke	Talley-Van Zandt				
				69.00	115.00	600.00	2300.00

SERIES OF 1988A,
SIGNATURES OF VILLALPANDO-BRADY, GREEN SEAL

BANK	UNC.	BANK	UNC.
☐Boston	23.00	☐Chicago	23.00
☐New York	23.00	☐St. Louis	23.00
☐Philadelphia	23.00	☐Minneapolis	23.00
☐Cleveland	23.00	☐Kansas City	23.00
☐Richmond	23.00	☐Dallas	23.00
☐Atlanta	23.00	☐San Francisco	23.00

SERIES OF 1990,
SIGNATURES OF VILLALPANDO-BRADY, GREEN SEAL

BANK	UNC.	BANK	UNC.
☐Boston	22.00	☐Chicago	22.00
☐New York	22.00	☐St. Louis	22.00
☐Philadelphia	22.00	☐Minneapolis	22.00
☐Cleveland	22.00	☐Kansas City	22.00
☐Richmond	22.00	☐Dallas	22.00
☐Atlanta	22.00	☐San Francisco	22.00

SERIES OF 1993,
SIGNATURES OF WITHROW-BENTSEN, GREEN SEAL

BANK	UNC.	BANK	UNC.
☐Boston	21.00	☐Chicago	21.00
☐New York	21.00	☐St. Louis	21.00
☐Philadelphia	21.00	☐Minneapolis	21.00
☐Cleveland	21.00	☐Kansas City	21.00
☐Richmond	21.00	☐Dallas	21.00
☐Atlanta	21.00	☐San Francisco	21.00

SERIES OF 1995,
SIGNATURES OF WITHROW-BENTSEN, GREEN SEAL

BANK	UNC.	BANK	UNC.
☐Boston	20.00	☐Chicago	20.00
☐New York	20.00	☐St. Louis	20.00
☐Philadelphia	20.00	☐Minneapolis	20.00

☐Cleveland	20.00	☐Kansas City	20.00
☐Richmond	20.00	☐Dallas	20.00
☐Atlanta	20.00	☐San Francisco	20.00

TWENTY DOLLAR NOTES (1929)
FEDERAL RESERVE BANK NOTES

(Small Size) **NOTE NO. 103A**

Face Design:
Portrait of
President
Jackson center,
name of bank
and city left,
blue seal right.

Back Design: The White House.

BANK	A.B.P.	V.FINE	UNC.	BANK	A.B.P.	V.FINE	UNC.
☐Boston	22.00	30.00	85.00	☐Chicago	18.00	30.00	80.00
☐New York	22.00	30.00	70.00	☐St. Louis	18.00	30.00	80.00
☐Philadelphia	22.00	30.00	70.00	☐Minneapolis	18.00	30.00	80.00
☐Cleveland	22.00	30.00	70.00	☐Kansas City	18.00	30.00	80.00
☐Richmond	22.00	30.00	75.00	☐Dallas	18.00	30.00	375.00
☐Atlanta	22.00	30.00	82.00	☐San Francisco	24.00	40.00	190.00

FIFTY DOLLAR NOTES

ORDER OF ISSUE

FIFTY DOLLAR NOTES (1862-1863)
UNITED STATES NOTES
(ALSO KNOWN AS LEGAL TENDER NOTES)

(Large Size)

NOTE NO. 104

Face Design: Portrait of Hamilton to left.

Back Design

SERIES	SIGNATURES	SEAL	A.B.P.	GOOD	V.FINE	UNC.
☐ 1862	Chittenden-Spinner*	Red	1300.00	2800.00	9000.00	18,000.00
☐ 1862	Chittenden-Spinner**	Red	1300.00	2800.00	8500.00	18,000.00
☐ 1863	Chittenden-Spinner**	Red	1300.00	2800.00	8500.00	18,000.00

*First Obligation: Similar to note No. 33.
**Second Obligation: Shown above.

FIFTY DOLLAR NOTES (1869) UNITED STATES NOTES
(ALSO KNOWN AS LEGAL TENDER NOTES)
(Large Size)   **NOTE NO. 105**

Face Design: Portrait of Henry Clay to right.

Back Design

SERIES	SIGNATURES	SEAL	A.B.P.	GOOD	V.FINE	UNC.
☐1869	Allison-Spinner	Red	2000.00	2800.00	15,000.00	30,000.00

Only twenty-four pieces of this note remain unredeemed.

FIFTY DOLLAR NOTES (1874-1880)
UNITED STATES NOTES

(Large Size)   **NOTE NO. 106**

Face Design: Franklin to left.

Back Design

SERIES	SIGNATURES	SEAL	A.B.P.	GOOD	V.FINE	UNC.
☐1874	Allison-Spinner	Sm. Red	300.00	700.00	4400.00	12,000.00
☐1875	Allison-Wyman	Sm. Red	300.00	650.00	4000.00	8500.00
☐1878	Allison-Gilfillan	Sm. Red	300.00	650.00	4000.00	8500.00
☐1880	Bruce-Gilfillan	Lg. Brown	330.00	550.00	2200.00	6800.00
☐1880	Bruce-Wyman	Lg. Brown	330.00	550.00	2200.00	6800.00
☐1880	Rosecrans-Jordan	Lg. Red	330.00	550.00	2000.00	5200.00
☐1880	Rosecrans-Hyatt	Lg. Red	330.00	550.00	2000.00	5400.00
☐1880	Rosecrans-Hyatt	Lg. Red	330.00	550.00	2000.00	5400.00
☐1880	Rosecrans-Huston	Lg. Red	330.00	550.00	2000.00	5400.00
☐1880	Rosecrans-Huston	Lg. Brown	330.00	550.00	2000.00	5200.00
☐1880	Tillman-Morgan	Sm. Red	330.00	550.00	2000.00	4600.00
☐1880	Bruce-Roberts	Sm. Red	330.00	550.00	2000.00	4600.00
☐1880	Lyons-Roberts	Sm. Red	330.00	550.00	2000.00	4600.00

FIFTY DOLLAR NOTES (1875) NATIONAL BANK NOTES
FIRST CHARTER PERIOD (Large Size)   **NOTE NO. 107**

Face Design: Washington crossing Delaware left,
Washington at Valley Forge, right.

Back Design: Embarkation of the pilgrims.

SERIES	SIGNATURES	SEAL	A.B.P.	V.FINE	UNC.
☐Original	Chittenden-Spinner	Red w/r	1900.00	3200.00	12,000.00
☐Original	Colby-Spinner	Red w/r	1900.00	3200.00	12,000.00
☐Original	Allison-Spinner	Red w/r	1900.00	3200.00	12,000.00
☐1875	Allison-New	Red w/s	1800.00	3000.00	10,500.00
☐1875	Allison-Wyman	Red w/s	1800.00	3000.00	10,500.00
☐1875	Allison-Gilfillan	Red w/s	1800.00	3000.00	10,500.00
☐1875	Scofield-Gilfillan	Red w/s	1800.00	3000.00	10,500.00
☐1875	Bruce-Gilfillan	Red w/s	1800.00	3000.00	10,500.00
☐1875	Bruce-Wyman	Red w/s	1800.00	3000.00	10,500.00
☐1875	Rosecrans-Huston	Red w/s	1800.00	3000.00	10,500.00
☐1875	Rosecrans-Nebeker	Red w/s	1800.00	3000.00	10,500.00
☐1875	Tillman-Morgan	Red w/s	1800.00	3000.00	10,500.00

FIFTY DOLLAR NOTES (1882) NATIONAL BANK NOTES
SECOND CHARTER PERIOD (Large Size)   **NOTE NO. 108**

First Issue (Brown seal and brown back)
Back Design: of note No. 108
Face Design: Similar to note No. 107.

SERIES	SIGNATURES	SEAL	A.B.P.	GOOD	V.FINE	UNC.
☐1882	Bruce-Gilfillan	Brown	168.00	280.00	575.00	3500.00
☐1882	Bruce-Wyman	Brown	168.00	280.00	575.00	3500.00
☐1882	Bruce-Jordan	Brown	168.00	280.00	575.00	3500.00
☐1882	Rosecrans-Jordan	Brown	168.00	280.00	575.00	3500.00
☐1882	Rosecrans-Hyatt	Brown	168.00	280.00	575.00	3500.00
☐1882	Rosecrans-Huston	Brown	168.00	280.00	575.00	3500.00
☐1882	Rosecrans-Nebeker	Brown	168.00	280.00	575.00	3500.00
☐1882	Rosecrans-Morgan	Brown	300.00	500.00	1300.00	4000.00
☐1882	Tillman-Morgan	Brown	168.00	280.00	550.00	3500.00
☐1882	Tillman-Roberts	Brown	168.00	280.00	550.00	3500.00
☐1882	Bruce-Roberts	Brown	168.00	280.00	550.00	3500.00
☐1882	Lyons-Roberts	Brown	168.00	280.00	550.00	3500.00
☐1882	Vernon-Treat	Brown	360.00	600.00	1300.00	3600.00

FIFTY DOLLAR NOTES (1882) NATIONAL BANK NOTES
SECOND CHARTER PERIOD (Large Size)   **NOTE NO. 108A**

Second Issue (Blue seal, green back with date "1882–1908")
Face Design: Washington crossing Delaware left,
Washington at Valley Forge right.

Back Design

SERIES	SIGNATURES	SEAL	A.B.P.	GOOD	V.FINE	UNC.
☐1882	Rosecrans-Huston	Blue	150.00	250.00	700.00	3000.00
☐1882	Rosecrans-Nebeker	Blue	150.00	250.00	700.00	3000.00
☐1882	Tillman-Morgan	Blue	150.00	250.00	700.00	3000.00
☐1882	Tillman-Roberts	Blue	150.00	250.00	700.00	3000.00
☐1882	Bruce-Roberts	Blue	150.00	250.00	700.00	3000.00
☐1882	Lyons-Roberts	Blue	150.00	250.00	700.00	3000.00
☐1882	Vernon-Treat	Blue	150.00	250.00	700.00	3000.00
☐1882	Napier-McClung	Blue	150.00	250.00	700.00	3000.00

FIFTY DOLLAR NOTES (1902) NATIONAL BANK NOTES
THIRD CHARTER PERIOD (Large Size)   NOTE NO. 109

First Issues (Red seal and numbers)
Face Design: Portrait of Sherman left. Name of bank center. Treasury Seal and numbers.

SERIES	SIGNATURES	SEAL	A.B.P.	GOOD	V.FINE	UNC.
☐1902	Lyons-Roberts	Red	210.00	325.00	1900.00	7200.00
☐1902	Lyons-Treat	Red	210.00	325.00	1900.00	7200.00
☐1902	Vernon-Treat	Red	210.00	325.00	1900.00	7200.00

Second Issue (Treasury Seal)
   Numbers remain blue, date "1902–1908" added on back.

☐1902	Lyons-Roberts	Blue	40.00	75.00	150.00	1325.00
☐1902	Lyons-Treat	Blue	40.00	75.00	150.00	1325.00
☐1902	Vernon-Treat	Blue	40.00	75.00	150.00	1325.00
☐1902	Vernon-McClung	Blue	40.00	75.00	150.00	1325.00
☐1902	Napier-McClung	Blue	40.00	75.00	150.00	1325.00
☐1902	Napier-Thompson	Blue	40.00	75.00	150.00	1325.00
☐1902	Napier-Burke	Blue	40.00	75.00	150.00	1325.00
☐1902	Parker-Burke	Blue	40.00	75.00	150.00	1325.00
☐1902	Teehee-Burke	Blue	40.00	75.00	150.00	1325.00

Third Issue (Treasury Seal)
   Numbers remain blue, date "1902–1908" removed from back.

☐1902	Lyons-Roberts	Blue	40.00	85.00	275.00	1275.00
☐1902	Lyons-Treat	Blue	40.00	85.00	275.00	1275.00
☐1902	Vernon-Treat	Blue	40.00	85.00	275.00	1275.00
☐1902	Vernon-McClung	Blue	40.00	85.00	275.00	1275.00
☐1902	Napier-McClung	Blue	40.00	85.00	275.00	1275.00
☐1902	Napier-Thompson	Blue	40.00	85.00	275.00	1275.00
☐1902	Napier-Burke	Blue	40.00	85.00	275.00	1275.00
☐1902	Parker-Burke	Blue	40.00	85.00	275.00	1275.00
☐1902	Teehee-Burke	Blue	40.00	85.00	275.00	1275.00
☐1902	Elliott-Burke	Blue	40.00	85.00	275.00	1275.00
☐1902	Elliott-White	Blue	40.00	85.00	275.00	1275.00

SERIES	SIGNATURES	SEAL	A.B.P.	GOOD	V.FINE	UNC.
☐1902	Speelman-White	Blue	60.00	75.00	250.00	1200.00
☐1902	Woods-White	Blue	60.00	75.00	250.00	1200.00

FIFTY DOLLAR NOTES (1929) NATIONAL BANK NOTES
(Small Size)
NOTE NO. 110

Face Design: Portrait of President Grant center. Bank left, brown seal right. Brown serial numbers, black Charter Numbers.

Back Design: The Capitol.

SERIES	SIGNATURES	SEAL	A.B.P.	V.FINE	UNC.
☐1929, Type I*	Jones-Wood	Brown	60.00	100.00	275.00
☐1929, Type II*	Jones-Wood	Brown	62.00	175.00	800.00

*See Page 78. Type I—Charter Number in black. Type II—Similar. Charter Number added in brown.

FIFTY DOLLAR NOTES (1878-1880)
SILVER CERTIFICATES

(Large Size)   **NOTE NO. 111**

Face Design: Portrait of Edward Everett.

Back Design

SERIES	SIGNATURES	SEAL	A.B.P.	GOOD	V.FINE
☐1878	Varied	Red			VERY RARE
☐1880	Scofield-Gilfillan	Brown	1800.00	3000.00	9300.00
☐1880	Bruce-Gilfillan	Brown	1800.00	3000.00	9300.00
☐1880	Bruce-Wyman	Brown	1800.00	3000.00	9300.00
☐1880	Rosecrans-Huston	Brown	1800.00	3000.00	9300.00
☐1880	Rosecrans-Nebeker	Red	1800.00	3000.00	11,000.00

FIFTY DOLLAR NOTES (1891) SILVER CERTIFICATES
(Large Size)
NOTE NO. 111A

Face Design: Portrait of Edward Everett

Back Design

SERIES	SIGNATURES	SEAL	A.B.P.	GOOD	V.FINE	UNC.
☐1891	Rosecrans-Nebeker	Red	250.00	475.00	2000.00	6800.00
☐1891	Tillman-Morgan	Red	250.00	475.00	2000.00	6800.00
☐1891	Bruce-Roberts	Red	250.00	475.00	2000.00	6800.00
☐1891	Lyons-Roberts	Red	250.00	475.00	2000.00	6800.00
☐1891	Vernon-Treat	Red	250.00	475.00	2000.00	6800.00
☐1891	Parker-Burke	Blue	250.00	475.00	2000.00	6800.00

FIFTY DOLLAR NOTES (1882) GOLD CERTIFICATES
(Large Size)   **NOTE NO. 112**

Face Design: Portrait of Silas Wright to left.

Back Design: Bright yellow color.

SERIES	SIGNATURES	SEAL	A.B.P.	GOOD	V.FINE	UNC.
☐1882	Bruce-Gilfillan	Brown	495.00	825.00	3750.00	15,000.00
☐1882	Bruce-Wyman	Brown	495.00	825.00	3750.00	15,000.00
☐1882	Rosecrans-Hyatt	Red	495.00	825.00	3750.00	15,000.00
☐1882	Rosecrans-Huston	Brown	495.00	825.00	3750.00	15,000.00
☐1882	Lyons-Roberts	Red	270.00	450.00	825.00	5800.00
☐1882	Lyons-Treat	Red	270.00	450.00	825.00	5800.00
☐1882	Vernon-Treat	Red	270.00	450.00	825.00	5800.00
☐1882	Vernon-McClung	Red	270.00	450.00	825.00	5800.00
☐1882	Napier-McClung	Red	270.00	450.00	825.00	5800.00

FIFTY DOLLAR NOTES (1913) GOLD CERTIFICATES
(Large Size)
NOTE NO. 113

Face Design: Portrait of President Grant.

Back Design: Bright yellow color.

SERIES	SIGNATURES	SEAL	A.B.P.	GOOD	V.FINE	UNC.
☐1913	Parker-Burke	Gold	126.00	210.00	600.00	3400.00
☐1913	Teehee-Burke	Gold	126.00	210.00	600.00	4100.00
☐1922	Speelman-White	Gold	102.00	170.00	450.00	1400.00

FIFTY DOLLAR NOTES (1928) GOLD CERTIFICATES
(Small Size) **NOTE NO. 114**

Back Design: Same as note No. 110.

SERIES	SIGNATURES	SEAL	A.B.P.	GOOD	V.FINE	UNC.
☐1928	Woods-Mellon	Gold	48.00	80.00	100.00	650.00

FIFTY DOLLAR NOTES (1891) TREASURY OR COIN NOTES
(Large Size) **NOTE NO. 114A**

Face Design: Portrait of William H. Seward. Only twenty-five pieces remain unredeemed.
Back Design: Green.

SERIES	SIGNATURES	SEAL	A.B.P.	GOOD	V.FINE	UNC.
☐1891	Rosecrans-Nebeker	Red	3000.00	6000.00	16,000.00	RARE

FIFTY DOLLAR NOTES (1914)
FEDERAL RESERVE NOTES

(Large Size)

NOTE NO. 115

SERIES OF 1914,
SIGNATURES OF BURKE-McADOO, RED SEAL AND
RED SERIAL NUMBERS

CITY	A.B.P.	GOOD	V.FINE	UNC.	CITY	A.B.P.	GOOD	V.FINE	UNC.
☐ Boston	67.00	150.00	600.00	1600.00	☐ Chicago	100.00	175.00	650.00	1750.00
☐ NYC	67.00	150.00	600.00	1600.00	☐ St. Louis	100.00	175.00	650.00	1750.00
☐ Phila	67.00	150.00	600.00	1600.00	☐ Minneap	100.00	175.00	650.00	1750.00
☐ Cleveland	67.00	150.00	600.00	1600.00	☐ Kans. C.	100.00	175.00	650.00	1750.00
☐ Richmd	67.00	150.00	600.00	1600.00	☐ Dallas	100.00	175.00	650.00	1750.00
☐ Atlanta	67.00	150.00	600.00	1600.00	☐ San Fran.	100.00	175.00	650.00	1750.00

SERIES OF 1914, BLUE SEAL AND BLUE SERIAL NUMBERS.
This note was issued with various signatures for each bank.*

BANK	A.B.P.	GOOD	V.FINE	UNC.	BANK	A.B.P.	GOOD	V.FINE	UNC.
☐ Boston	55.00	70.00	140.00	600.00	☐ Chicago	42.00	70.00	225.00	900.00
☐ NYC	55.00	70.00	140.00	600.00	☐ St. Louis	42.00	70.00	225.00	900.00
☐ Phila	55.00	70.00	140.00	600.00	☐ Minneap.	42.00	70.00	225.00	900.00
☐ Cleveland	55.00	70.00	140.00	600.00	☐ Kans. C.	42.00	70.00	225.00	900.00
☐ Richmd	55.00	70.00	140.00	600.00	☐ Dallas	42.00	70.00	225.00	900.00
☐ Atlanta	55.00	70.00	140.00	600.00	☐ San Fran.	42.00	70.00	225.00	900.00

*Signatures: Burke-McAdoo, Burke-Glass, Burke-Huston, White-Mellon.

FIFTY DOLLAR NOTES (1928)
FEDERAL RESERVE NOTES

(Small Size)   **NOTE NO. 116**

Face Design: Portrait of President Grant center. Black
Federal Reserve Seal with number to left. Green Treasury
Seal to right.
Back Design: Same as note No. 110.

SERIES OF 1928,
SIGNATURES OF WOODS-MELLON, GREEN SEAL

	A.B.P.	UNC.
Issued for all Federal Reserve Banks	75.00	125.00

(Small Size)   **NOTE NO. 116A**
SERIES OF 1928A,
SIGNATURES OF WOODS-MELLON, GREEN SEAL
The letter replaces numeral in Federal Reserve Seal.

Issued for all Federal Reserve Banks	75.00	115.00

(Small Size)   **NOTE NO. 116B**
SERIES OF 1934,
SIGNATURES OF JULIAN-MORGENTHAU, GREEN SEAL

Issued for all Federal Reserve Banks	68.00	95.00

SERIES OF 1934A,
SIGNATURES OF JULIAN-MORGENTHAU, GREEN SEAL

Issued for all Federal Reserve Banks except Philadelphia	67.00	90.00

SERIES OF 1934B,
SIGNATURES OF JULIAN-VINSON, GREEN SEAL

Issued for all Federal Reserve Banks except Boston and New York	67.00	100.00

SERIES OF 1934C,
SIGNATURES OF JULIAN-SNYDER, GREEN SEAL

Issued for all Federal Reserve Banks except San Francisco	67.00	90.00

SERIES OF 1934D,
SIGNATURES OF CLARK-SNYDER, GREEN SEAL

	A.B.P.	UNC.
Issued for Cleveland, St. Louis, Minneapolis, Kansas City, San Francisco	67.00	85.00

FIFTY DOLLAR NOTES (1950)
FEDERAL RESERVE NOTES
(Small Size)

NOTE NO. 116C

SERIES OF 1950,
SIGNATURES OF CLARK-SNYDER
The Federal Reserve and Treasury Seals are now smaller.

	UNC.
Issued for all Federal Reserve Banks	75.00

SERIES OF 1950A, SIGNATURES OF PRIEST-HUMPHREY
Issued for all Federal Reserve Banks except Minneapolis	74.00

SERIES OF 1950B, SIGNATURES OF PRIEST-ANDERSON
Issued for all Federal Reserve Banks except Atlanta and Minneapolis	70.00

SERIES OF 1950C, SIGNATURES OF SMITH-DILLON
Issued for all Federal Reserve Banks except Atlanta	73.00

SERIES OF 1950D, SIGNATURES OF GRANAHAN-DILLON
Issued for all Federal Reserve Banks	70.00

SERIES OF 1950E, SIGNATURES OF GRANAHAN-FOWLER
Issued for New York, Chicago, San Francisco	82.00

FIFTY DOLLAR NOTES (1963)
FEDERAL RESERVE NOTES
("IN GOD WE TRUST" ADDED ON BACK)
(Small Size)

NOTE NO. 116D

SERIES OF 1963, NO NOTES WERE PRINTED; SERIES OF 1963A, SIGNATURES OF GRANAHAN-FOWLER
Issued for all Federal Reserve Banks	65.00

FIFTY DOLLAR NOTES (1969)
FEDERAL RESERVE NOTES
(WORDING IN GREEN TREASURY SEAL CHANGED FROM LATIN TO ENGLISH)
(Small Size)

NOTE NO. 116E

SERIES OF 1969, SIGNATURES OF ELSTON-KENNEDY
Issued for all Federal Reserve Banks	62.00

SERIES OF 1969A, SIGNATURES OF KABIS-CONNALLY
Issued for all Federal Reserve Banks	62.00

SERIES OF 1969B, SIGNATURES OF BANUELOS-CONNALLY
Issued for Boston, New York, Philadelphia, Richmond, Atlanta, Chicago, Dallas	60.00

SERIES OF 1969C, SIGNATURES OF BANUELOS-SHULTZ UNC.

Issued for all Federal Reserve Banks — 60.00

SERIES OF 1974, SIGNATURES OF NEFF-SIMON

Issued for all Federal Reserve Banks — 60.00

SERIES OF 1977, SIGNATURES OF MORTON-BLUMENTHAL

Issued for all Federal Reserve Banks — 60.00

SERIES OF 1977A, SIGNATURES OF MORTON-MILLER

Issued for all Federal Reserve Banks — 60.00

SERIES OF 1981, SIGNATURES OF BUCHANAN-REGAN

Issued for all Federal Reserve Banks — 61.00

SERIES OF 1981A, SIGNATURES OF ORTEGA-REGAN

Issued for all Federal Reserve Banks — 61.00

SERIES OF 1985, SIGNATURES OF ORTEGA-BAKER

Issued for all Federal Reserve Banks — 60.00

SERIES OF 1988, SIGNATURES OF ORTEGA-BAKER

Issued for all Federal Reserve Banks — 60.00

SERIES OF 1990, SIGNATURES OF VILLALPANDO-BRADY

BANK	UNC.	BANK	UNC.
☐Boston	56.00	☐Chicago	56.00
☐New York	56.00	☐St. Louis	56.00
☐Philadelphia	56.00	☐Minneapolis	56.00
☐Cleveland	56.00	☐Kansas City	56.00
☐Richmond	56.00	☐Dallas	56.00
☐Atlanta	56.00	☐San Francisco	56.00

SERIES OF 1993, SIGNATURES OF WITHROW-BENTSEN, GREEN SEAL

BANK	UNC.	BANK	UNC.
☐Boston	52.00	☐Chicago	52.00
☐New York	52.00	☐St. Louis	52.00
☐Philadelphia	52.00	☐Minneapolis	52.00
☐Cleveland	52.00	☐Kansas City	52.00
☐Richmond	52.00	☐Dallas	52.00
☐Atlanta	52.00	☐San Francisco	52.00

SERIES OF 1995, SIGNATURES OF WITHROW-BENTSEN, GREEN SEAL

BANK	UNC.	BANK	UNC.
☐Boston	50.00	☐Chicago	50.00
☐New York	50.00	☐St. Louis	50.00
☐Philadelphia	50.00	☐Minneapolis	50.00
☐Cleveland	50.00	☐Kansas City	50.00
☐Richmond	50.00	☐Dallas	50.00
☐Atlanta	50.00	☐San Francisco	50.00

FIFTY DOLLAR NOTES (1918)
FEDERAL RESERVE BANK NOTES

(Large Size)

NOTE NO. 117

Face Design: Portrait of President Grant to left, Federal Reserve Bank in center, blue seal right.

Back Design: Female figure of Panama between merchant ship and battleship. Plates were made for all twelve Federal Reserve Districts. Only St. Louis bank issued. Less than thirty notes are known today.

CITY	SERIES	GOV'T SIGNATURES	BANK SIGNATURES	A.B.P.	FINE	UNC.
☐St. Louis	1918	Teehee-Burke	Attebery-Wells	2400.00	4000.00	11,000.00

FIFTY DOLLAR NOTES (1929)
FEDERAL RESERVE BANK NOTES
(Small Size)
NOTE NO. 117A

Face Design:
Portrait of
Grant center,
name of bank
left, brown
serial numbers,
black letter for
Federal Reserve
District.

Back Design:
Same as note
No. 110.

BANK	SERIES	SIGNATURES	SEAL	A.B.P.	V.FINE	UNC.
☐New York	1929	Jones-Woods	Brown	66.00	110.00	150.00
☐Cleveland	1929	Jones-Woods	Brown	66.00	110.00	150.00
☐Chicago	1929	Jones-Woods	Brown	66.00	110.00	150.00
☐Minneapolis	1929	Jones-Woods	Brown	60.00	120.00	185.00
☐Kansas City	1929	Jones-Woods	Brown	60.00	100.00	160.00
☐Dallas	1929	Jones-Woods	Brown	60.00	150.00	300 00
☐San Francisco	1929	Jones-Woods	Brown	69.00	175.00	250.00

ONE HUNDRED
DOLLAR NOTES

ORDER OF ISSUE

ONE HUNDRED DOLLAR NOTES (1862-1863)
UNITED STATES NOTES
(ALSO KNOWN AS LEGAL TENDER NOTES)

(Large Size)   **NOTE NO. 118**

Face Design: Eagle with spread wings left, three discs with "100," red seal numbers.

Back Design: Green, two variations of the wording in obligation.

SERIES	SIGNATURES	SEAL	A.B.P.	GOOD	V.FINE	UNC.
☐1862	Chittenden-Spinner*	Red	1000.00	2500.00	8500.00	25,000.00
☐1862	Chittenden-Spinner**	Red	1000.00	2000.00	7500.00	24,000.00
☐1863	Chittenden-Spinner**	Red	1000.00	2500.00	8000.00	24,000.00

*First Obligation: Similar to note No. 33.
**Second Obligation: Shown above.

ONE HUNDRED DOLLAR NOTES (1869-1880)
UNITED STATES NOTES
(Large Size)   **NOTE NO. 119**

Face Design: Portrait of President Lincoln.

Back Design: No. 119.

Back Design: No. 119A.

SERIES	SIGNATURES	SEAL	A.B.P.	GOOD	V.FINE	UNC.
☐1869	Allison-Spinner	Red	2000.00	4000.00	16,500.00	48,000.00

The following notes have a modified back design.
(Small Size)   **NOTE NO. 119A**

SERIES	SIGNATURES	SEAL	A.B.P.	GOOD	V.FINE	UNC.
☐1875	Allison-New	Sm. Red	1200.00	2800.00	10,000.00	30,000.00
☐1875	Allison-Wyman	Sm. Red	1200.00	3800.00	20,000.00	50,000.00
☐1878	Allison-Gilfillan	Sm. Red	1200.00	2800.00	10,000.00	30,000.00
☐1880	Bruce-Gilfillan	Lg. Brown	500.00	1100.00	8500.00	20,000.00
☐1880	Bruce-Wyman	Lg. Brown	500.00	1100.00	7500.00	20,000.00
☐1880	Rosecrans-Jordan	Lg. Red	500.00	1000.00	6500.00	19,000.00
☐1880	Rosecrans-Hyatt	Lg. Red	1500.00	3000.00	20,000.00	50,000.00
☐1880	Rosecrans-Hyatt	Lg. Red	500.00	1000.00	14,500.00	38,000.00
☐1880	Rosecrans-Huston	Lg. Red	500.00	1000.00	8500.00	20,000.00
☐1880	Rosecrans-Huston	Lg. Brown	600.00	1500.00	11,000.00	36,500.00
☐1880	Tillman-Morgan	Sm. Red	500.00	900.00	5500.00	15,000.00
☐1880	Bruce-Roberts	Sm. Red	500.00	900.00	5500.00	15,000.00
☐1880	Lyons-Roberts	Sm. Red	500.00	900.00	5500.00	15,000.00

ONE HUNDRED DOLLAR NOTES (1966) U.S. NOTES
(ALSO KNOWN AS LEGAL TENDER NOTES)
(Small Size) **NOTE NO. 119B**

Face Design: Portrait of Franklin, red seal, red serial numbers.

Back Design: Independence Hall.

SERIES	SIGNATURES	SEAL	V.FINE	UNC.
☐1966*	Granahan-Fowler	Red	110.00	200.00
☐1966A	Elston-Kennedy	Red	150.00	650.00

*This is the first note to be issued with the new Treasury Seal with wording in English instead of Latin.

ONE HUNDRED DOLLAR NOTES (1875)
NATIONAL BANK NOTES
(ALL HAVE RED SEAL)
FIRST CHARTER PERIOD (Large Size) **NOTE NO. 120**

Face Design: Perry leaving the Lawrence, left.

Back Design: Border green, center black, signing of the Declaration of Independence.

SERIES	SIGNATURES	SEAL	A.B.P.	GOOD	V.FINE
☐Original	Chittenden-Spinner	Red	960.00	1750.00	4000.00
☐Original	Colby-Spinner	Red	960.00	1750.00	4000.00
☐Original	Allison-Spinner	Red	960.00	1750.00	4000.00
☐1875	Allison-New	Red	960.00	1500.00	3600.00
☐1875	Allison-Wyman	Red	960.00	1500.00	3600.00
☐1875	Allison-Gilfillan	Red	960.00	1500.00	3600.00
☐1875	Scofield-Gilfillan	Red	960.00	1500.00	3600.00
☐1875	Bruce-Gilfillan	Red	960.00	1500.00	3600.00
☐1875	Bruce-Wyman	Red	960.00	1500.00	3600.00
☐1875	Rosecrans-Huston	Red	960.00	1500.00	3600.00
☐1875	Tillman-Morgan	Red	960.00	1500.00	3600.00

ONE HUNDRED DOLLAR NOTES (1882)
NATIONAL BANK NOTES

SECOND CHARTER PERIOD (Large Size)   **NOTE NO. 120A**

First Issue (Brown seal and brown backs.)

Face Design: Similar to note No. 120.

Back Design: Similar to note No. 39

SERIES	SIGNATURES	SEAL	A.B.P.	GOOD	V.FINE	UNC.
☐1882	Bruce-Gilfillan	Brown	300.00	500.00	1700.00	6000.00
☐1882	Bruce-Wyman	Brown	300.00	500.00	1700.00	6000.00
☐1882	Bruce-Jordan	Brown	300.00	500.00	1700.00	6000.00
☐1882	Rosecrans-Jordan	Brown	300.00	500.00	1700.00	6000.00
☐1882	Rosecrans-Hyatt	Brown	300.00	500.00	1700.00	6000.00
☐1882	Rosecrans-Huston	Brown	300.00	500.00	1700.00	6000.00
☐1882	Rosecrans-Nebeker	Brown	300.00	500.00	1700.00	6000.00
☐1882	Rosecrans-Morgan	Brown	300.00	500.00	1700.00	6000.00
☐1882	Tillman-Morgan	Brown	300.00	500.00	1700.00	6000.00
☐1882	Tillman-Roberts	Brown	300.00	500.00	1700.00	6000.00
☐1882	Bruce-Roberts	Brown	300.00	500.00	1700.00	6000.00
☐1882	Lyons-Roberts	Brown	300.00	500.00	1700.00	6000.00

SECOND CHARTER PERIOD (Large Size)   **NOTE NO. 121**

Second Issue (Blue seal, green back with date "1882–1908")

Face Design: Similar to note No. 120.

Back Design: Green with date "1882–1908" center.

SERIES	SIGNATURES	SEAL	A.B.P.	V.FINE	UNC.
☐1882	Rosecrans-Huston	Blue	780.00	1300.00	4700.00
☐1882	Rosecrans-Nebeker	Blue	780.00	1300.00	4700.00
☐1882	Tillman-Morgan	Blue	780.00	1300.00	4700.00
☐1882	Tillman-Roberts	Blue	780.00	1300.00	4700.00
☐1882	Bruce-Roberts	Blue	780.00	1300.00	4700.00
☐1882	Lyons-Roberts	Blue	780.00	1300.00	4700.00
☐1882	Vernon-Treat	Blue	780.00	1300.00	4700.00
☐1882	Napier-McClung	Blue	780.00	1300.00	4700.00

This note was also issued with (value) ONE HUNDRED DOL-LARS on the back. Very rare.

ONE HUNDRED DOLLAR NOTES (1902)
NATIONAL BANK NOTES
THIRD CHARTER PERIOD (Large Size) **NOTE NO. 122**

Face Design: Portrait of John J. Knox left.

Back Design: Male figures with shield and flags.
First Issue (Red seal)

SERIES	SIGNATURES	SEAL	A.B.P.	GOOD	V.FINE	UNC.
☐ 1902	Lyons-Roberts	Red	390.00	650.00	1800.00	7500.00
☐ 1902	Lyons-Treat	Red	390.00	650.00	1800.00	7500.00
☐ 1902	Vernon-Treat	Red	390.00	650.00	1800.00	7500.00

Second Issue*
   Design is similar to previous note. Seal and serial numbers are now blue; back of note has date "1902–1908" added.

SERIES	SIGNATURES	SEAL	A.B.P.	GOOD	V.FINE	UNC.
		Blue	125.00	150.00	400.00	1200.00

Third Issue*
   Design continues as previous notes. Seal and serial numbers remain blue, date "1902–1908" removed from back.

SERIES	SIGNATURES	SEAL	A.B.P.	GOOD	V.FINE	UNC.
		Blue	84.00	140.00	350.00	1200.00

* The notes of the **Second and Third Issue** appeared with various signatures: Lyons-Roberts, Lyons-Treat, Vernon-Treat, Vernon-McClung, Napier-McClung, Parker-Burke, Teehee-Burke, Elliott-Burke, Elliott-White, Speelman-White, Woods-White.

ONE HUNDRED DOLLAR NOTES (1929)
NATIONAL BANK NOTES

(Small Size)   **NOTE NO. 123**

Face Design: Portrait of Franklin center. Name of bank and city left. Brown seal right.

SERIES SIGNATURES	SEAL	A.B.P.	V.FINE	UNC.
☐ 1929 Type I Jones-Woods	Brown	100.00	125.00	400.00
☐ 1929 Type II Jones-Woods	Brown	120.00	200.00	700.00

ONE HUNDRED DOLLAR NOTES (1878)
SILVER CERTIFICATES

SERIES	SIGNATURES	SEAL	A.B.P.	GOOD	V.FINE	UNC.
☐ 1878	Scofield-Gilfillan-White	Red				UNIQUE
☐ 1878	Scofield-Gilfillan-Hopper	Red		NO SPECIMENS KNOWN		
☐ 1878	Scofield-Gilfillan-Hillhouse	Red		NO SPECIMENS KNOWN		
☐ 1878	Scofield-Gilfillan-Anthony	Red				UNIQUE
☐ 1878	Scofield-Gilfillan-Wyman (printed signature of Wyman)	Red		NO SPECIMENS KNOWN		
☐ 1878	Scofield-Gilfillan	Red				VERY RARE
☐ 1880	Scofield-Gilfillan	Brown		EXTREMELY RARE		
☐ 1880	Bruce-Gilfillan	Brown	1100.00	3000.00	13,500.00	32,500.00
☐ 1880	Bruce-Wyman	Brown	1100.00	3000.00	13,500.00	32,500.00
☐ 1880	Rosecrans-Huston	Brown	1100.00	3000.00	14,000.00	34,000.00
☐ 1880	Rosecrans-Nebeker	Brown	1100.00	3000.00	14,000.00	35,000.00

ONE HUNDRED DOLLAR NOTES (1891)
SILVER CERTIFICATES

(Large Size)

NOTE NO. 124

Face Design: Portrait of President Monroe.

SERIES	SIGNATURES	SEAL	A.B.P.	GOOD	V.FINE	UNC.
☐1891	Rosecrans-Nebeker	Red	400.00	1000.00	6000.00	15,000.00
☐1891	Tillman-Morgan	Red	400.00	1000.00	6000.00	15,000.00

This note was also issued in the Series of 1878 and 1880. They are very rare.

ONE HUNDRED DOLLAR NOTES (1882-1922)
GOLD CERTIFICATES

(Large Size)

NOTE NO. 125

Face Design: Portrait of Thomas H. Benton.

SERIES	SIGNATURES	SEAL	A.B.P.	GOOD	V.FINE	UNC.
☐1882	Bruce-Gilfillan	Lg. Brown	480.00	800.00	6000.00	RARE
☐1882	Bruce-Wyman	Lg. Brown	480.00	800.00	6000.00	RARE
☐1882	Rosecrans-Hyatt	Lg. Red	480.00	800.00	6000.00	RARE
☐1882	Rosecrans-Huston	Lg. Brown	480.00	800.00	6000.00	RARE
☐1882	Lyons-Roberts	Sm. Red	195.00	325.00	550.00	6200.00
☐1882	Lyons-Treat	Sm. Red	195.00	325.00	550.00	6200.00
☐1882	Vernon-Treat	Sm. Red	195.00	325.00	550.00	6200.00
☐1882	Vernon-McClung	Sm. Red	195.00	325.00	550.00	6200.00
☐1882	Napier-McClung	Sm. Red	195.00	325.00	550.00	6200.00
☐1882	Napier-Thompson	Sm. Red	195.00	325.00	550.00	6200.00
☐1882	Napier-Burke	Sm. Red	195.00	325.00	550.00	6200.00
☐1882	Parker-Burke	Sm. Red	195.00	325.00	550.00	6200.00
☐1882	Teehee-Burke	Sm. Red	195.00	325.00	550.00	6200.00
☐1922	Speelman-White	Sm. Red	195.00	325.00	550.00	3000.00

ONE HUNDRED DOLLAR NOTES (1928)
GOLD CERTIFICATES

(Small Size)   **NOTE NO. 126**

Face Design: Portrait of Franklin center. Yellow seal to left. Yellow numbers.

SERIES	SIGNATURES	SEAL	A.B.P.	GOOD	V.FINE	UNC.
☐1928	Woods-Mellon	Gold	115.00	110.00	160.00	700.00

ONE HUNDRED DOLLAR NOTES (1890-1891)
TREASURY OR COIN NOTES.

(Large Size)   **NOTE NO. 127**

Face Design: Portrait of Commodore Farragut to right.

Back Design: Large "100," called "Watermelon Note."

Back Design: ONE HUNDRED in scalloped medallion.

SERIES	SIGNATURES	SEAL	A.B.P.	GOOD	V.FINE	UNC.
☐1890	Rosecrans-Huston	Brown	3000.00	7500.00	18,000.00	RARE
☐1890	Rosecrans-Nebeker	Red	3000.00	10,000.00	26,000.00	RARE

ONE HUNDRED DOLLAR NOTES (1914)
FEDERAL RESERVE NOTES

(Large Size)   **NOTE NO. 128**

Face Design: Portrait of Franklin in center.
Back Design: Group of five allegorical figures.
SERIES OF 1914,
SIGNATURES OF BURKE-McADOO, RED SEAL
AND RED SERIAL NUMBERS

CITY	A.B.P.	GOOD	V.FINE	UNC.	CITY	A.B.P.	GOOD	V.FINE	UNC.
☐ Boston	120.00	200.00	750.00	2400.00	☐ Chicago	135.00	225.00	775.00	2500.00
☐ NYC	120.00	200.00	750.00	2400.00	☐ St. Louis	135.00	225.00	775.00	2500.00
☐ Phila	120.00	200.00	750.00	2400.00	☐ Minneap	135.00	225.00	775.00	2500.00
☐ Cleveld	120.00	200.00	750.00	2400.00	☐ Kansas C	135.00	225.00	775.00	2500.00
☐ Richmd	120.00	200.00	750.00	2400.00	☐ Dallas	135.00	225.00	775.00	2500.00
☐ Atlanta	120.00	200.00	750.00	2400.00	☐ San Fran	135.00	225.00	775.00	2500.00

SERIES OF 1914, DESIGN CONTINUES AS PREVIOUS NOTE, BLUE
SEAL AND BLUE SERIAL NUMBERS

This note was issued with various signatures for each bank (Burke-McAdoo, Burke-Glass, Burke-Huston, White-Mellon).

BANK	A.B.P.	V.FINE	UNC.	BANK	A.B.P.	V.FINE	UNC.
☐ Boston	120.00	220.00	575.00	☐ Chicago	150.00	250.00	675.00
☐ New York	120.00	220.00	575.00	☐ St. Louis	150.00	250.00	675.00
☐ Philadelphia	120.00	220.00	575.00	☐ Minneapolis	150.00	250.00	675.00
☐ Cleveland	120.00	220.00	575.00	☐ Kansas City	150.00	250.00	675.00
☐ Richmond	120.00	220.00	575.00	☐ Dallas	150.00	250.00	675.00
☐ Atlanta	120.00	220.00	575.00	☐ San Francisco	150.00	250.00	675.00

ONE HUNDRED DOLLAR NOTES (1928)
FEDERAL RESERVE NOTES

(Small Size)

NOTE NO. 129

Face Design: Portrait of Franklin, black Federal Reserve Seal left with number, green Treasury Seal right.

SERIES OF 1928,
SIGNATURES OF WOODS-MELLON, GREEN SEAL

CITY	A.B.P.	V.FINE	UNC.	CITY	A.B.P.	V.FINE	UNC.
☐ Boston	110.00	140.00	195.00	☐ Chicago	90.00	150.00	200.00
☐ New York	110.00	140.00	195.00	☐ St. Louis	90.00	150.00	200.00
☐ Philadelphia	110.00	140.00	195.00	☐ Minneapolis	90.00	150.00	200.00
☐ Cleveland	110.00	140.00	195.00	☐ Kansas City	90.00	150.00	200.00
☐ Richmond	110.00	140.00	195.00	☐ Dallas	90.00	150.00	200.00
☐ Atlanta	110.00	140.00	195.00	☐ San Francisco	90.00	150.00	200.00

SERIES OF 1928A,
SIGNATURES OF WOODS-MELLON, GREEN SEAL

The number is in black and the Federal Reserve Seal is changed to a letter.

(Small Size)

NOTE NO. 129A

CITY	A.B.P.	V.FINE	UNC.	CITY	A.B.P.	V.FINE	UNC.
☐ Boston	110.00	145.00	200.00	☐ Chicago	96.00	160.00	225.00
☐ New York	110.00	145.00	200.00	☐ St. Louis	96.00	160.00	225.00
☐ Philadelphia	110.00	145.00	200.00	☐ Minneapolis	96.00	160.00	225.00
☐ Cleveland	110.00	145.00	200.00	☐ Kansas City	96.00	160.00	225.00
☐ Richmond	110.00	145.00	200.00	☐ Dallas	96.00	160.00	235.00
☐ Atlanta	110.00	145.00	200.00	☐ San Francisco	96.00	160.00	225.00

SERIES OF 1934*,
SIGNATURES OF JULIAN-MORGENTHAU, GREEN SEAL
SERIES OF 1934A*,
SIGNATURES OF JULIAN-MORGENTHAU, GREEN SEAL

*The above two notes were issued for all Federal Reserve Districts. Average prices are: A.B.P. $110, V. Fine $120, and UNC. $185.

SERIES OF 1934B*.
SIGNATURES OF JULIAN-VINSON, GREEN SEAL

SERIES OF 1934C*,
SIGNATURES OF JULIAN-SNYDER, GREEN SEAL
SERIES OF 1934D*,
SIGNATURES OF CLARK-SNYDER, GREEN SEAL

*Not all Districts issued these series. Average prices are: A.B.P. $110, V. Fine $120, and UNC. $185.

ONE HUNDRED DOLLAR NOTES (1950)
FEDERAL RESERVE NOTES

(Small Size)   **NOTE NO. 129C**
All of the following notes have green seals.
SERIES OF 1950, SIGNATURES OF CLARK-SNYDER

	UNC.
Issued for all Federal Reserve Banks	150.00

SERIES OF 1950A, SIGNATURES OF PRIEST-HUMPHREY

Issued for all Federal Reserve Banks	140.00

SERIES OF 1950B, SIGNATURES OF PRIEST-ANDERSON

Issued for all Federal Reserve Banks	140.00

SERIES OF 1950C, SIGNATURES OF SMITH-DILLON

Issued for all Federal Reserve Banks	146.00

SERIES OF 1950D, SIGNATURES OF GRANAHAN-DILLON

Issued for all Federal Reserve Banks	146.00

SERIES OF 1950E, SIGNATURES OF GRANAHAN-FOWLER

Issued for New York, Chicago, San Francisco only	185.00

ONE HUNDRED DOLLAR NOTES (1963)
FEDERAL RESERVE NOTES

NOTE NO. 129D
SERIES OF 1963 (NO NOTES WERE PRINTED FOR THIS SERIES)
SERIES OF 1963A ("IN GOD WE TRUST" ADDED ON BACK)
SERIES OF 1963B, SIGNATURES OF GRANAHAN-FOWLER

Issued for all Federal Reserve Banks	135.00

ONE HUNDRED DOLLAR NOTES (1969)
FEDERAL RESERVE NOTES

NOTE NO. 129E
SERIES OF 1969 (ENGLISH WORDING IN GREEN TREASURY SEAL)
SERIES OF 1969, SIGNATURES OF ELSTON-KENNEDY

Issued for all Federal Reserve Banks	130.00

SERIES OF 1969A, SIGNATURES OF KABIS-CONNALLY

Issued for all Federal Reserve Banks	125.00

SERIES OF 1969B (NO NOTES WERE PRINTED)
SERIES OF 1969C, SIGNATURES OF BANUELOS-SHULTZ

Issued for all Federal Reserve Banks	120.00

SERIES OF 1974, SIGNATURES OF NEFF-SIMON UNC.
Issued for all Federal Reserve Banks — 120.00

SERIES OF 1977, SIGNATURES OF MORTON-BLUMENTHAL
Issued for all Federal Reserve Banks — 120.00

SERIES OF 1977A, SIGNATURES OF MORTON-MILLER
Issued for all Federal Reserve Banks — 120.00

SERIES OF 1981, SIGNATURES OF BUCHANAN-REGAN
Issued for all Federal Reserve Banks — 110.00

SERIES OF 1981A, SIGNATURES OF ORTEGA-REGAN
Issued for all Federal Reserve Banks — 110.00

SERIES OF 1985, SIGNATURES OF ORTEGA-BAKER
Issued for all Federal Reserve Banks — 110.00

SERIES OF 1988, SIGNATURES OF ORTEGA-BAKER
Issued for all Federal Reserve Banks — 110.00

SERIES OF 1990,
SIGNATURES OF VILLALPANDO-BRADY, GREEN SEAL

BANK	UNC.	BANK	UNC.
☐Boston	108.00	☐Chicago	108.00
☐New York	108.00	☐St. Louis	108.00
☐Philadelphia	108.00	☐Minneapolis	108.00
☐Cleveland	108.00	☐Kansas City	108.00
☐Richmond	108.00	☐Dallas	108.00
☐Atlanta	108.00	☐San Francisco	108.00

SERIES OF 1993,
SIGNATURES OF WITHROW-BENTSEN, GREEN SEAL

BANK	UNC.	BANK	UNC.
☐Boston	104.00	☐Chicago	104.00
☐New York	104.00	☐St. Louis	104.00
☐Philadelphia	104.00	☐Minneapolis	104.00
☐Cleveland	104.00	☐Kansas City	104.00
☐Richmond	104.00	☐Dallas	104.00
☐Atlanta	104.00	☐San Francisco	104.00

SERIES OF 1995,
SIGNATURES OF WITHROW-BENTSEN, GREEN SEAL

BANK	UNC.	BANK	UNC.
☐Boston	100.00	☐Chicago	100.00
☐New York	100.00	☐St. Louis	100.00
☐Philadelphia	100.00	☐Minneapolis	100.00
☐Cleveland	100.00	☐Kansas City	100.00
☐Richmond	100.00	☐Dallas	100.00
☐Atlanta	100.00	☐San Francisco	100.00

ONE HUNDRED DOLLAR NOTES (1929)
FEDERAL RESERVE BANK NOTES
(ISSUED ONLY IN SERIES OF 1929)

(Small Size)   **NOTE NO. 129F**

Face Design: Portrait of Franklin, brown seal and numbers.

Back Design

BANK & CITY	SIGNATURES	SEAL	A.B.P.	V.FINE	UNC.
☐New York	Jones-Woods	Brown	90.00	150.00	225.00
☐Cleveland	Jones-Woods	Brown	90.00	150.00	250.00
☐Richmond	Jones-Woods	Brown	90.00	150.00	250.00
☐Chicago	Jones-Woods	Brown	90.00	150.00	225.00
☐Minneapolis	Jones-Woods	Brown	90.00	150.00	225.00
☐Kansas City	Jones-Woods	Brown	90.00	150.00	275.00
☐Dallas	Jones-Woods	Brown	90.00	150.00	275.00

FIVE HUNDRED, ONE THOUSAND, FIVE THOUSAND, AND TEN THOUSAND DOLLAR NOTES

(Production of notes in denominations above one hundred dollars was discontinued in 1969.)

SPECIAL REPORT:
UNCUT SHEETS

As very few notes exist in the form of full uncut sheets, this is a limited area for the collector. Also, the prices are high, well out of range for most hobbyists.

Uncut sheets available on the market are of Small Size Notes exclusively. In most instances it is not known precisely how they reached public hands. Some were undoubtedly presented as souvenir gifts to Treasury Department officials. In any event, uncut sheets have never been illegal to own, since the notes they comprise are precisely the same as those released into general circulation.

The sheets differ in the number of notes, from a low of six in National Currency sheets to a high of eighteen for some sheets of United States (Legal Tender) Notes and Silver Certificates. Others have twelve notes. These differences are due entirely to the printing method being used at their time of manufacture. Any given note was always printed in sheets of the same size, with the same number of specimens per sheet. If you have an uncut sheet with twelve notes, it means that all notes from the series were printed twelve to a sheet.

The condition standards for uncut sheets are the same as those for single notes. Obviously, an uncut sheet did not circulate as money, but some specimens became worn or damaged as a result of careless storage, accident, or other causes. These impaired sheets do turn up in the market, but there is not much demand for them. Almost every buyer of uncut sheets wants Uncirculated condition. Quite often an uncut sheet will be framed when you buy it. This should be considered a plus, as the frame has probably kept the sheet in immaculate condition. Just to be entirely safe, however, it is wise to examine the reverse side of the sheet for possible staining or other problems.

The following prices were current for uncut sheets in Uncirculated grade at publication time. Gem Uncirculated sheets in absolutely pristine condition command higher prices than those shown.

SILVER CERTIFICATES

DENOMINATION	SERIES	NO. OF NOTES PER SHEET	CURRENT PRICE RANGE IN UNC. CONDITION
$1	1928	12	1700.00–5000.00
$1	1934	12	4300.00–6500.00
$5	1934	12	2000.00–3600.00
$10	1934	12	3000.00–4000.00
$1	1935	12	750.00–2200.00
$5	1953	18	2000.00–3200.00
$10	1953	18	4000.00–5000.00

UNITED STATES NOTES (LEGAL TENDER NOTES)

DENOMINATION	SERIES	NO. OF NOTES PER SHEET	CURRENT PRICE RANGE IN UNC. CONDITION
$1	1928	12	20,000.00 & UP
$2	1928	12	1500.00–3600.00
$5	1928	12	2000.00–3600.00
$2	1953	18	1000.00–2000.00
$5	1953	18	1500.00–2800.00

NATIONAL CURRENCY

DENOMINATION	SERIES	NO. OF NOTES PER SHEET	CURRENT PRICE RANGE IN UNC. CONDITION
$5	1929	6	1000.00–2500.00
$10	1929	6	1100.00–2800.00
$20	1929	6	1200.00–2400.00
$50	1929	6	4000.00–8000.00

MULES
(MIXED PLATE NUMBERS)

All U.S. currency has plate numbers on the face and back. These plate numbers are in the lower right corner somewhat close to the fine scroll design. They refer to the number of the engraved plate used to print the sheet of notes. Each plate can be used for about 100,000 impressions. It is then destroyed and a new plate with the next number in sequence is put into use.

During the term of Treasury officials Julian and Morgenthau, the plate numbers were changed from almost a microscopic to a larger size, far easier to read. Due to this improvement the series designation then in use was an advance on United States Notes, Silver Certificates, and Federal Reserve Notes. The signatures remained Julian-Morgenthau. National Currency and Gold Certificates were not affected, as these were discontinued earlier.

During the changeover period in printing, plates were sometimes mixed up, producing a note with a large number on one side and a small number on the other side. Notes of this variety are called "mules," or "mule notes." This is from a term applied to coins struck with the obverse or reverse die of one year and the opposite side from a die of another year.

Many collectors are eager to add one or more of these mule notes to their collection. Some of the most common mule notes are:

$2 UNITED STATES NOTES
1928-C, 1928-D

$5.00 UNITED STATES NOTES
1928-B, 1928-C, 1928-D, 1928-E

$1 SILVER CERTIFICATES
1935, 1935-A

$5 SILVER CERTIFICATES
1934, 1934-A, 1934-B, 1934-C

$10 SILVER CERTIFICATES
1934, 1934A

Mules were also issued in the Federal Reserve Note Series. However, these are not as popular with collectors as the United States Notes and Silver Certificates because of the higher denominations and the twelve districts involved.

The schedule below shows some of the most common mule notes and their values in new condition. The combination of the prefix and suffix letters of the serial numbers on notes is known as "Blocks." For instance: A—A Block, B—A Block.

			UNC.
$2 UNITED STATES NOTE	1928-D	B—A	550.00
		C—A	80.00
		*—A	90.00
$5 UNITED STATES NOTE	1928-B	E—A	125.00
		*—A	575.00
	1928-C	E—A	100.00
		*—A	135.00
$1 SILVER CERTIFICATE	1935	N—A	
		Thru	175.00
		P—A	
	1935-A	M—A	
		Thru	85.00
		V—A	
		C—B	85.00
$5 SILVER CERTIFICATE	1934-A	D—A	
		Thru	90.00
		G—A	
		*—A	175.00
$10 SILVER CERTIFICATE	1934	A—A	95.00
		*—A	140.00
	1934-A	A—A	225.00

Front　　　　　**SIZES DIFFERENT**　　　　　**Back**

INTRODUCTION TO
UNITED STATES
FRACTIONAL CURRENCY

Events following the outbreak of the Civil War resulted in a shortage of circulating coinage. Trade was hampered as many merchants, especially in large cities, were unable to make change and only customers presenting the exact amount for a purchase could buy—but they were generally as short on coins as the shop proprietors. Various attempts were made to solve this problem by issuing credit slips (which most customers didn't care for), tokens (which they also didn't care for), and using postage stamps as money. Finally, in 1862, the government stepped in, recognizing that the economy was being seriously hurt, and issued a series of small paper notes as equivalents of coinage denominations. They carried designs adapted from the current postage stamps of the day and were known as Postage Currency or Postal Currency. The more popular title is now Fractional Currency. There were five separate issues of Fractional Currency, three of which occurred during the Civil War and two thereafter, the final one as late as 1874. That a need existed for coin substitutes as late as the 1870s demonstrates the drain placed upon coinage during the war and the long period of recovery. A total of six denominations were issued, from 3¢ to 59¢, comprising 23 designs and more than 100 varieties. Because of its small size and lack of visual impact, Fractional Currency was long shunned by collectors. In recent years it has enjoyed an unprecedented surge of popularity, which, if continued, promises to drive prices beyond present levels. All told, more than $360,000,000 worth of Fractional Currency was circulated. It would be extremely plentiful today but for the fact that most notes were redeemed, leaving only about

$2,000,000 outstanding. This is what collectors have to work with, and a good deal of these are badly preserved.

FIRST ISSUE—Postage Currency August 21st, 1862
5-10-25-50
SECOND ISSUE—Fractional Currency October 10th, 1863
5-10-25-50
THIRD ISSUE—Fractional Currency December 5th, 1864
3-5-10-15-25-50
FOURTH ISSUE—Fractional Currency July 14th, 1869
10-15-25-50
FIFTH ISSUE—Fractional Currency February 26th, 1874
10-25-50

THE FRACTIONAL CURRENCY SHIELD

Fractional currency shields were sold by the Treasury Department in 1866. Specimen notes printed only on one side were used. Very Good–condition shields are valued at $3000 to $3500. Choice condition shields in contemporary frames can sell for $4200. Shields with pink, green, or other backgrounds are more valuable.

FRACTIONAL CURRENCY NOTES

The following notes may be collected by issue or by denomination. We list them here by denomination for convenience. Also, since most of these notes were hastily cut from large sheets, the margin size can vary. Specimens with larger than normal margins command premium prices.

THREE-CENT NOTES

THIRD ISSUE

NOTE NO. 142

Face Design:
Portrait of
President
Washington.

Back Design:
Large "3"
green.

	A.B.P.	GOOD	V.FINE	UNC.
☐With Light Portrait	6.00	7.00	19.00	70.00
☐With Dark Portrait	6.50	8.00	20.00	100.00

FIVE-CENT NOTES

FIRST ISSUE

NOTE NO. 143

Face Design:
Portrait of
President
Jefferson,
brown.

**Back
Design:**
"5" black.

	A.B.P.	GOOD	V.FINE	UNC.
☐Perforated edges, monogram ABNCO on back	4.00	6.00	20.00	110.00
☐Perforated edges, without monogram on back	5.00	7.00	26.00	130.00
☐Straight edges, monogram ABNCO on back	4.50	6.00	10.00	75.00
☐Straight edges, without monogram on back	7.00	11.00	21.00	155.00

FIVE-CENT NOTES

SECOND ISSUE

NOTE NO. 144

Face Design:
Portrait of
President
Washington.

Back Design:
Shield and brown, "5"s.

	A.B.P.	GOOD	V.FINE	UNC.
☐ Value only in bronze on back	4.00	6.00	11.00	60.00
☐ Surcharges 18-63 on back	4.00	6.00	11.00	60.00
☐ Surcharges S-18-63 on back	6.00	10.00	12.50	80.00
☐ Surcharges R-1-18-63 on back, fiber paper	8.00	13.00	42.00	250.00

FIVE-CENT NOTES

THIRD ISSUE

NOTE NO. 145

Face Design:
Portrait of
Spencer M.
Clark.

Back Design:
Green or red.

	A.B.P.	GOOD	V.FINE	UNC.
☐ Without letter "A" on face, green back	5.00	8.00	20.00	115.00
☐ With letter "A" on face, green back	6.00	9.00	26.00	145.00
☐ Without letter "A" on face, red back	4.00	6.00	15.00	75.00
☐ With letter "A" on face, red back	4.00	6.00	16.00	75.00

This note was authorized to have the portraits of the explorers Lewis and Clark on the face. Mr. Spencer M. Clark, who was then head of the Bureau of Currency, flagrantly placed his own portrait on this note. This caused congress to pass legislation forbidding the likeness of any living person on U.S. currency.

TEN-CENT NOTES

FIRST ISSUE

NOTE NO. 146

Face Design:
Portrait of
President
Washington

Back Design:
"10," black.

	A.B.P.	GOOD	V.FINE	UNC.
☐ Perforated edges, monogram ABNCO on back	4.00	6.00	26.00	120.00
☐ Perforated edges, without monogram on back	4.00	6.00	28.00	140.00
☐ Plain edges, monogram ABNCO on back	4.00	5.50	11.00	65.00
☐ Plain edges, without monogram on back	6.00	11.00	36.00	155.00

TEN-CENT NOTES

SECOND ISSUE

NOTE NO. 147

Face Design:
Portrait of
President
Washington.

Back Design:
"10,"
green.

	A.B.P.	GOOD	V.FINE	UNC.
☐ Value only surcharge on back	4.00	7.00	13.00	65.00
☐ Surcharge 18-63 on back	4.00	7.00	14.00	65.00
☐ Surcharge S-18-63 on back	5.00	8.00	15.00	70.00
☐ Surcharge I-18-63 on back	9.00	21.00	42.00	215.00
☐ Surcharge O-63 on back	150.00	410.00	1100.00	2100.00
☐ Surcharge T-1-18-63 on back, fiber paper	7.00	14.00	65.00	230.00

TEN-CENT NOTES

THIRD ISSUE

NOTE NO. 148

Face Design:
Portrait of
President
Washington.

Back Design:
"10," green
or red.

	A.B.P.	GOOD	V.FINE	UNC.
☐ Printed signatures Colby-Spinner, green back	4.00	9.00	14.00	80.00
☐ As above, figure "1" near left margin on face	4.00	10.00	14.00	80.00
☐ Printed signatures Colby-Spinner, red back	4.00	10.00	21.00	150.00
☐ As above, figure "1" near left margin, red back	5.00	13.00	20.00	75.00
☐ Autographed signatures Colby-Spinner, red back	7.00	17.00	26.00	150.00
☐ Autographed signatures Jeffries-Spinner, red back	7.00	17.00	50.00	200.00

TEN-CENT NOTES

FOURTH ISSUE

NOTE NO. 149

Back Design:
Green with
TEN and
"10."

Face Design:
Bust of
Liberty.

	A.B.P.	GOOD	V.FINE	UNC.
☐Large red seal, watermarked paper	3.50	6.00	14.00	60.00
☐Large red seal, pink fibers in paper	3.50	6.00	15.00	60.00
☐Large seal, pink fibers in paper, right end blue	4.00	6.50	18.00	68.00
☐Large brown seal	13.00	28.00	80.00	200.00
☐Small red seal, pink fibers, right end blue	4.00	7.00	24.00	100.00

TEN-CENT NOTES

FIFTH ISSUE

NOTE NO. 150

Face Design:
William
Meredith.

**Back
Design:**
Green.

	A.B.P.	GOOD	V.FINE	UNC.
☐Green seal, long narrow key	4.00	6.00	11.00	75.00
☐Red seal, long narrow key	3.00	5.00	10.00	60.00
☐Red seal, short stubby key	4.00	6.00	10.00	60.00

FIFTEEN-CENT NOTES
FACES AND BACKS PRINTED SEPARATELY
THIRD ISSUE

NOTE NO. 151

Face Design:
Sherman and
President
Grant.

**Back
Design:**
Green
or red.

	NARROW MARGIN	WIDE MARGIN
☐With printed signatures Colby-Spinner	200.00	320.00
☐With autographed signatures Colby-Spinner	1150.00	RARE
☐With autographed signatures Jeffries-Spinner	250.00	375.00
☐With autographed signatures Allison-Spinner	285.00	400.00
☐Green back	170.00	250.00
☐Red back	165.00	250.00

FIFTEEN-CENT NOTES

FOURTH ISSUE

NOTE NO. 152

Face Design:
Bust
of Columbia.

Back Design:
Green
with "15"s.

	A.B.P.	GOOD	V.FINE	UNC.
☐ Large seal, watermarked paper	6.00	11.00	22.00	125.00
☐ Large seal, pink fibers in paper	6.00	12.00	30.00	140.00
☐ Large seal, pink fibers in paper, right end blue	6.00	12.00	27.00	138.00
☐ Large brown seal	18.00	36.00	160.00	RARE
☐ Smaller red seal, pink fibers, right end blue	6.00	11.00	28.00	140.00

TWENTY-FIVE-CENT NOTES

FIRST ISSUE

NOTE NO. 153

Face Design:
Five 5¢
Jefferson
Stamps.

Back Design:
Black,
large "25."

	A.B.P.*	GOOD	V.FINE	UNC.
☐ Perforated edges, monogram ABNCO on back	5.00	10.00	30.00	165.00
☐ Perforated edges, without monogram on back	5.00	11.00	55.00	280.00
☐ Straight edges, monogram ABNCO on back	5.00	9.00	16.00	85.00
☐ Straight edges, without monogram on back	6.00	14.00	65.00	350.00

*A.B.P. (Average Buying Price): in better than good condition.

TWENTY-FIVE-CENT NOTES

SECOND ISSUE

NOTE NO. 154

Time and climatic condition have changed the purple color on the back of this note into many variations.

Face Design:
Portrait of
President
Washington.

Back Design:
Purple with
"25."

	A.B.P.	GOOD	V.FINE	UNC.
☐Value only surcharge on back	4.00	8.00	20.00	82.00
☐Surcharge 18-63 on back	6.00	12.00	20.00	90.00
☐Surcharge A-18-63 on back	6.00	11.00	20.00	90.00
☐Surcharge 1-18-63 on back	18.00	36.00	90.00	260.00
☐Surcharge 2-18-63 on back	6.00	11.00	25.00	115.00
☐Surcharge S-18-63 on back	8.00	15.00	25.00	115.00
☐Surcharge T-1-18-63 on back, fiber paper	10.00	15.00	25.00	220.00
☐Surcharge T-2-18-63 on back, fiber paper	7.00	15.00	25.00	210.00
☐Surcharge S-2-18-63, fiber paper				RARE

TWENTY-FIVE-CENT NOTES

THIRD ISSUE

NOTE NO. 155

All notes have printed signatures of Colby-Spinner.

Face Design:
Portrait of
Fessenden.

Back Design:
Green or
red with "25
CENTS."

	A.B.P.	GOOD	V.FINE	UNC.
☐Face—bust of Fessenden between solid bronze surcharges, fiber paper, back—green, surcharge M-2-6-5 in corners				
	100.00	185.00	410.00	1100.00
☐As above, with letter "A" in lower left corner of face				
	110.00	300.00	700.00	1800.00
☐Face—Fessenden, open scroll bronze surcharges, fiber paper, back—green, surcharges M-2-6-5 in corners				
	11.00	20.00	48.00	350.00
☐As above with letter "A" in lower left corner of face				
	8.00	17.00	45.00	250.00
☐Face—Fessenden, open scroll surcharges, plain paper, back—green, value surcharges only				
	7.50	14.00	30.00	150.00
☐As before, letter "A" in lower left corner of face, back—green, plain paper	10.00	17.00	42.00	150.00
☐Face—Fessenden, red back, value surcharge only	9.00	13.00	32.00	150.00
☐As above, letter "A" in lower left corner of face				
	9.00	13.00	30.00	150.00

TWENTY-FIVE-CENT NOTES

FOURTH ISSUE

NOTE NO. 156

Face Design:
Portrait of
President
Washington
and Treasury Seal.

**Back
Design:**
Green.

	A.B.P.	GOOD	V.FINE	UNC.
☐Large seal, plain watermarked paper	4.00	7.50	20.00	85.00
☐Large seal, pink silk fiber in paper	4.00	7.50	20.00	85.00
☐Large seal, pink fibers in paper, right end blue	4.00	7.50	21.00	85.00
☐Large brown seal, right end blue	35.00	70.00	280.00	1100.00
☐Smaller red seal, right end blue	4.00	8.00	20.00	75.00

TWENTY-FIVE-CENT NOTES

FIFTH ISSUE

NOTE NO. 157

Face Design:
Portrait of
Walker and
red seal.

**Back
Design:**
Black.

	A.B.P.*	GOOD	V.FINE	UNC.
☐With long narrow key in Treasury Seal.	4.00	6.00	11.00	50.00
☐With short stubby key in Treasury Seal	4.00	6.00	11.00	50.00

A.B.P. *(Average Buying Price): in better than good condition.*

FIFTY-CENT NOTES

FIRST ISSUE

NOTE NO. 158

Face Design:
Five 10¢
Washington
stamps.

**Back
Design:**
Green.

	A.B.P.	GOOD	V.FINE	UNC.
☐Perforated edges, monogram ABNCO on back	8.00	11.00	76.00	250.00
☐Perforated edges, without monogram on back	10.00	18.00	70.00	310.00
☐Straight edges, monogram ABNCO on back	6.00	9.00	25.00	110.00
☐Straight edges, without monogram	11.00	18.00	80.00	310.00

FIFTY-CENT NOTES

SECOND ISSUE

NOTE NO. 159

Face Design:
Portrait of
President
Washington.

**Back
Design:**
Red.

	A.B.P.	GOOD	V.FINE	UNC.
☐ Value surcharge only on back	44.00	100.00	350.00	1000.00
☐ Surcharge 18-63 on back	7.00	9.00	35.00	175.00
☐ Surcharge A-18-63 on back	6.00	9.00	26.00	175.00
☐ Surcharge I-18-63	6.00	9.00	26.00	175.00
☐ Surcharge O-1-18-63, fiber paper	7.00	18.00	60.00	250.00
☐ Surcharge R-2-18-63, fiber paper	10.00	16.00	46.00	250.00
☐ Surcharge T-1-18-63, fiber paper	7.00	14.00	46.00	250.00
☐ Surcharge T-18-63, fiber paper	45.00	90.00	190.00	500.00

FIFTY-CENT NOTES

THIRD ISSUE

NOTE NO. 160

Face Design:
Justice with
sword,
shield,
scales.

**Back
Design:**
Green
or red.

The following notes have printed signatures of Colby-Spinner and have green backs.

	A.B.P.	GOOD	V.FINE	UNC.
☐ Value surcharge and S-2-6-4 on back, fiber paper				
			VERY	RARE
☐ Value surcharge and A-2-6-5 on back, fiber paper				
	16.00	32.00	75.00	500.00
☐ As above with "1" and letter "A" on face, A-2-6-5 on back				
	26.00	75.00	350.00	1600.00
☐ As above with "1" only on face, A-2-6-5 on back				
	16.00	32.00	75.00	425.00
☐ As above with letter "A" only on face, A-2-6-5 on back				
	16.00	37.00	80.00	425.00
☐ A-2-6-5 on back, narrowly spaced, plain paper				
	7.00	10.00	35.00	375.00
☐ As above, numeral "1" and letter "A" on face				
	11.00	22.00	70.00	450.00

	A.B.P.	GOOD	V.FINE	UNC.
☐As above, numeral "1" only on face	6.00	12.00	35.00	370.00
☐As above, letter "A" only on face	11.00	18.00	41.00	400.00
☐A-2-6-5 on back, widely spaced, plain paper	10.00	18.00	41.00	410.00
☐As above, numeral "1" and letter "A" on face				
	10.00	30.00	100.00	550.00
☐As above, numeral "1" only on face	7.00	13.00	50.00	450.00
☐As above, letter "A" only on face	6.00	12.00	50.00	450.00
☐Without position letters or back surcharges	6.00	12.00	33.00	410.00
☐As above with numeral "1" and letter "A" on face				
	15.00	26.00	50.00	450.00
☐As above with numeral "1" only on face	5.00	11.00	30.00	410.00
☐As above with letter "A" only on face	6.00	12.00	36.00	400.00

The following notes have printed signatures of Colby-Spinner and red backs.

	A.B.P.	GOOD	V.FINE	UNC.
☐Value surcharge and S-2-6-4 on back, fiber	40.00	60.00	350.00	1200.00
☐As above, numeral "1" and letter "A"	125.00	350.00	700.00	RARE
☐As above, numeral "1" only on face	100.00	200.00	400.00	1600.00
☐As above, letter "A" only on face	95.00	200.00	500.00	1600.00
☐Value surcharge and A-2-6-5 on back, plain	7.00	16.00	45.00	425.00
☐As above, numeral "1" and letter "A"	15.00	31.00	70.00	450.00
☐As above, numeral "1" only on face	8.00	17.00	36.00	450.00
☐As above, letter "A" only on face	9.00	18.00	46.00	375.00
☐Value surcharge only on back, plain paper	9.00	18.00	42.00	425.00
☐As above, numeral "1" and letter "A" on face				
	13.00	26.00	55.00	510.00
☐As above, numeral "1" only on face	10.00	22.00	42.00	400.00
☐As above, letter "A" only on face	10.00	25.00	60.00	460.00

The following notes have autographed signatures of Colby-Spinner and red backs.

	A.B.P.	GOOD	V.FINE	UNC.
☐Value surcharge and S-2-6-4 on back, fiber	32.00	75.00	200.00	1100.00
☐Value surcharge and A-2-6-5 on back, fiber	14.00	24.00	80.00	600.00
☐Value surcharge only on back, plain paper	10.00	22.00	80.00	425.00

FIFTY-CENT NOTES

THIRD ISSUE

NOTE NO. 161

Face Design: Bust of Spinner with surcharges.
Back Design: Green or red.

The following notes have printed signatures of Colby-Spinner, and green backs.

	A.B.P.	GOOD	V.FINE	UNC.
☐ Value surcharge and A-2-6-5 on back	8.00	17.00	72.00	300.00
☐ As above, numeral "1" and letter "A" on face	20.00	39.00	110.00	650.00
☐ As above, numeral "1" only on face	6.00	17.00	42.00	350.00
☐ As above, letter "A" only on face	6.00	16.00	65.00	400.00
☐ Value surcharge only on back	6.00	10.00	35.00	375.00
☐ As above, numeral "1" and letter "A" on face	10.00	26.00	45.00	375.00
☐ As above, numeral "1" only on face	6.00	12.00	35.00	370.00
☐ As above, letter "A" only on face	6.00	12.00	35.00	400.00

TYPE II BACK DESIGN

	A.B.P.	GOOD	V.FINE	UNC.
☐ Value surcharge only on back	7.00	15.00	35.00	300.00
☐ Numeral "1" and letter "A" on face	18.00	35.00	75.00	350.00
☐ Numeral "1" only on face	8.00	15.00	42.00	315.00
☐ Letter "A" only on face	8.00	18.00	60.00	350.00

The following notes have a portrait of Spinner, printed signatures of Colby-Spinner, red backs, and are Type I.

	A.B.P.	GOOD	V.FINE	UNC.
☐ Value surcharge and A-2-6-5 on back	8.00	16.00	45.00	350.00
☐ As above with numeral "1" and letter "A"	18.00	39.00	130.00	400.00
☐ As above with numeral "1" only on face	10.00	15.00	45.00	330.00
☐ As above with letter "A" only on face	10.00	22.00	58.00	360.00

The following notes have autographed signatures, red backs, and are Type I.

	A.B.P.*	GOOD	V.FINE	UNC.
☐ Autographed signatures COLBY-SPINNER, back surcharged value and A-2-6-5	9.00	26.00	60.00	500.00
☐ Autographed signatures ALLISON-SPINNER, back surcharged value and A-2-6-5	9.00	26.00	75.00	610.00
☐ Autographed signatures ALLISON-NEW, back surcharged value and A-2-6-5	300.00	600.00	1000.00	2800.00

*A.B.P., (Average Buying Price): in better than good condition.

FIFTY-CENT NOTES

FOURTH ISSUE   **NOTE NO. 162**

Face Design:
Bust
of Lincoln.

Back Design:
Green.

	A.B.P.	GOOD	V.FINE	UNC.
☐ Plain paper	8.00	16.00	46.00	275.00
☐ Paper with pink fibers	8.00	16.00	52.00	285.00

FIFTY-CENT NOTES

FOURTH ISSUE   **NOTE NO. 163**

Face Design:
Bust
of Stanton.

Back Design:
Green
with "50."

	A.B.P.	GOOD	V.FINE	UNC.
☐ Red seal and signatures ALLISON-SPINNER, paper with pink fibers, blue ends	6.00	11.00	35.00	180.00

FIFTY-CENT NOTES

FOURTH ISSUE   **NOTE NO. 164**

Face Design:
Bust of
Samuel
Dexter.

Back Design:
Green with
"50."

	A.B.P.	GOOD	V.FINE	UNC.
☐ Green seal, pink fibers, blue ends	6.00	10.00	22.00	125.00

FIFTY-CENT NOTES

FIFTH ISSUE   **NOTE NO. 165**

Face Design:
Bust
of Crawford.

Back Design:
Green with
"50."

	A.B.P.*	GOOD	V.FINE	UNC.
☐ Signatures ALLISON-NEW, paper with pink fibers, blue ends	4.00	6.00	18.00	75.00

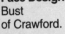

*A.B.P. (Average Buying Price): in better than good condition.

ERROR OR FREAK NOTES

Notes have been misprinted from time to time since the earliest days of currency. The frequency of misprintings and other abnormalities has increased in recent years due to heavier production and high-speed machinery. This has provided a major sub-hobby for note collectors. Freaks and errors have become very popular, their appeal and prices showing upward movement each year.

On the following pages we have pictured and described most of the more familiar and collectible Error Notes. Pricing is approximate only because many notes bearing the same general type of error differ in severity of error from one specimen to another. As a general rule, the less glaring or obvious errors carry a smaller premium value. Very valuable Error Notes include double denominations, or bills having the face of one denomination and reverse side of another.

Error and Freak Notes do turn up in everyday change. Specimens are located either in that fashion or from bank packs. As far as circulated specimens are concerned, some Error Notes have passed through so many hands before being noticed that the condition is not up to collector standards. This, of course, results in a very low premium valuation.

Values given below are for the specimens pictured and described. Different premiums may be attached to other specimens with similar errors, or notes showing the same errors but of different denominations.

MISMATCHED SERIAL NUMBERS

On ordinary notes, the serial number in the lower left of the obverse matches that in the upper right. When it fails to, even by the difference of a single digit, this is known as a "mismatched serial number." It occurs as the result of a cylinder or cylinders in the high-speed numbering machine becoming jammed. If more than one digit is mismatched, the value will be greater.

	V. FINE	UNC.
☐$1 Federal Reserve Note, Series 1969, signatures Elston-Kennedy	96.00	160.00

	V. FINE	UNC.
☐$1 Silver Certificate, Series 1957B, signatures Granahan-Dillon	90.00	150.00

	V. FINE	UNC.
☐$1 Federal Reserve Note, Series 1977A, signatures Morton-Miller	96.00	160.00

INVERTED THIRD PRINT

The inverted third print is also known as "inverted overprint." The Treasury Seal, District Seal, Serial Numbers, and District Number are inverted on the obverse side of the note, or printed upside-down, caused by the sheet of notes (having already received the primary design on front and back) being fed upside-down into the press for this so-called "third print." (The back design is the "first print," the front is the "second print," and these various additions comprise the "third print." It is not possible to print these third print items at the same time as the obverse design, since they are not standard on every bill. At one time the signatures were included in the third print, but these are now engraved directly into the plate and are part of the second print.)

Though very spectacular, inverted third print errors are not particularly scarce and are especially plentiful in 1974 and 1976 series notes.

	V. FINE	UNC.
☐ $5 Federal Reserve Note, Series 1974, signatures Neff-Simon	120.00	200.00

	V. FINE	UNC.
☐ $2 Federal Reserve Note, Series 1976, signatures Neff-Simon	306.00	510.00

	V. FINE	UNC.
☐$1 Federal Reserve Note, Series 1974, signatures Neff-Simon	132.00	220.00

	V. FINE	UNC.
☐$50 Federal Reserve Note, Series 1977, signatures Morton-Blumenthal	312.00	520.00

	V. FINE	UNC.
☐$20 Federal Reserve Note, Series 1974, signatures Neff-Simon	180.00	300.00

	V. FINE	UNC.
☐$10 Federal Reserve Note, Series 1974, signatures Neff-Simon	165.00	275.00

COMPLETE OFFSET TRANSFER

Offset transfers are not, as is often believed, caused by still-wet printed sheets coming into contact under pressure. Though very slight offsetting can occur in that manner, it would not create notes as spectacular as those pictured here, in which the offset impression is almost as strong as the primary printing. These happen as a result of the printing press being started an instant or so before the paper is fed in. Instead of contacting the paper, the inked plate makes its impression upon the machine bed. When the paper is then fed through, it picks up this "ghost" impression from the bed, in addition to the primary impression it is supposed to receive. Each successive sheet going through the press will acquire the impression until all ink is totally removed from the machine bed. But, naturally, the first sheet will show the transfer strongest, and the others will be weaker and weaker. Obviously, the market value of such notes depends largely on the strength of the offset impression. The heavier and more noticeable it is, the more valuable the note will be—all other things being equal.

	V. FINE	UNC.
☐ $5 Federal Reserve Note, Series 1977, signatures Morton-Blumenthal, offset of reverse side of face		
Dark	105.00	175.00
Light	57.00	95.00

	V. FINE	UNC.
☐ $1 Federal Reserve note, Series 1974, signatures Neff-Simon, offset of reverse side of face.		
Dark	70.00	175.00
Light	60.00	100.00

PARTIAL OFFSET TRANSFER

The most logical explanation for this error is that a sheet of paper fed into the press incorrectly became mangled or torn, and part of the inked plate contacted the printing press bed. Therefore, wet ink was left on those portions of the press bed not covered by paper. When the next sheet was fed through, it received the correct impression, plus it acquired a partial offset transfer by contacting this wet area of the press bed. Just as with offset transfers, the first sheet going through the press following an accident of this kind will receive the strongest transfer, and it will become gradually less noticeable on succeeding sheets.

	V. FINE	UNC.
☐ $1 Federal Reserve Note, Series 1969D, signatures Banuelos-Schultz, offset of a portion of reverse side on face		
Dark	36.00	60.00
Light	30.00	50.00

PRINTED FOLD

Notes showing printed folds occur as the result of folds in the paper before printing, which probably happen most often when the sheet is being fed into the press. If the sheet is folded in such a manner that a portion of the reverse side is facing upward, as shown here, it will receive a part of the impression intended for its obverse. Naturally the positioning of these misplaced portions of printing is very random, depending on the nature and size of the fold.

	V. FINE	UNC.
☐ $20 Federal Reserve Note, Series 1977, signatures Morton-Blumenthal, Federal Reserve District seal and District number printed on reverse	120.00	200.00

THIRD PRINT ON REVERSE

The cause of this error is obvious, the sheet having been fed through the press on the wrong side (back instead of front) for the third impression or "third print." In the so-called third print, the note receives the Treasury and Federal Reserve District seals, district numbers, and serial numbers.

	V. FINE	UNC.
☐ $1 Federal Reserve Note, third print on reverse	120.00	200.00

BOARD BREAKS

The terminology of this error is misleading. It suggests that the fernlike unprinted areas were caused by a broken printing plate. Actually they must have resulted from something—probably linty matter—sticking to the printing ink. The assumption reached by the public, when it encounters such a note, is that the blank streaks were caused by the paper being folded in printing. This, however, is not possible, as that would yield an error of a much different kind (*see* Printed Fold).

It should be pointed out that board breaks are easily created by counterfeiters by erasing portions of the printed surface, and that the collector ought to examine such specimens closely.

	V. FINE	UNC.
☐ $20 Federal Reserve Note, board breaks on reverse	60.00	100.00

MISSING SECOND PRINT

The "second print" is the front face, or obverse of the note—the "first print" being the reverse or back. A note with a missing second print has not received the primary impression on its obverse, though the back is normal and the front carries the standard third print matter (Treasury Seal, serial numbers, etc.). These errors, while they probably occur frequently, are so easily spotted by B.E.P. checkers that such notes are very scarce on the market.

	V. FINE	UNC.
☐ $10 Federal Reserve Note, missing second print	210.00	350.00

PRINTED FOLD

This note was folded nearly in half before receiving the third print, which fell across the waste margin on the reverse side. Had the note not been folded, this waste margin would have been removed in the cutting process. This note, when unfolded, is grotesque in shape.

	V. FINE	UNC.
☐ $1 Federal Reserve Note, printed fold with Federal Reserve District seal, district numbers, and serial numbers on reverse. (Naturally, this note lacks the "third print" matter, such as the Treasury Seal, that was supposed to appear on the righthand side of the obverse.)	120.00	200.00

V. FINE   UNC.

□ **$5 Federal Reserve Note.** Printed fold with entire Federal Reserve District seal, portion of another Federal Reserve District seal, and portion of two different serial numbers on the reverse. It may be hard to imagine how a freak of this nature occurs. This note was folded diagonally along a line bisecting the Lincoln Memorial building slightly to the right of center. The lefthand portion of the reverse side was thereby drawn down across the lefthand side of the obverse, extending well below the bottom of the note. It reached far enough down to catch the district seal intended for the note beneath it, as well as a bit of the serial number. This is why the two serial numbers are different; they were supposed to go on two different notes. Obviously, when something this dramatic happens in printing, not only one error note is created but several—at least—at the same time. Not all necessarily reach circulation, however.

240.00   400.00

THIRD PRINT BLACK INK MISSING OR LIGHT

Though the machinery used is ultramodern, U.S. currency notes are printed by the same basic technique used when printing was first invented more than 500 years ago. Ink is spread on the metal plates and these are pressed on the sheets as they go through the press. Because the inking is manually fed (as is the paper), an even flow is usually achieved. When an under-inked note is found, it is generally merely "light," giving a faded appearance. But sometimes the plate will be very improperly inked, due to mechanical misfunction or some other cause, resulting in whole areas being unprinted or so lightly printed that they cannot be seen without close inspection. These are not especially valuable notes but counterfeit specimens are frequently made.

	V. FINE	UNC.
☐$1 Federal Reserve Note, Series 1977, signatures of Morton-Blumenthal. Federal Reserve District seal and District numbers missing from lefthand side, remainder of "third print" material light but distinct. If the lefthand serial number was strong, there might be suspicion of this being a counterfeit.	48.00	80.00

THIRD PRINT GREEN INK MISSING OR LIGHT

In this case, the green, rather than the black, ink was applied too lightly to the printing plate.

	V. FINE	UNC.
☐$5 Federal Reserve Note, Series 1977, signatures of Morton-Blumenthal	30.00	50.00

NOTE FOLDED DURING OVERPRINT

This note was folded as it was being overprinted and failed to receive the District seal and District numbers at the left side of its obverse. This kind of error, like all involving missing portions of printing, has been extensively counterfeited.

	V. FINE	UNC.
☐$2 Federal Reserve Note, Series 1976, signatures of Neff-Simon	72.00	120.00

FAULTY ALIGNMENT

Notes of this kind were formerly called "miscut," and sometimes still are. "Faulty alignment" is a more inclusive term which encompasses not only bad cutting but accidents in printing. If the sheet shifts around in the press, it will not receive the printed impressions exactly where they should be. Even if the cutting is normal, the resulting note will be misaligned; the cutting machine cannot correct botched printing. It is very easy to determine where the fault lies. If one side of the note has its design higher than the opposite side, this is a printing error. If the misalignment occurs equally on both sides, the problem was in cutting. Since the two sides are not printed in the same operation, it would be a one-in-a-million chance for them to become equally misaligned.

The value of such notes depends upon the degree of misalignment. Collectors are especially fond of specimens showing a portion—even if very slight, as with the one pictured of an adjoining note.

	V. FINE	UNC.
☐$5 Federal Reserve Note, bottom left of reverse shaved (or "bled"), corresponding portion of adjoining note just visible at top. This ranks as a "dramatic" specimen.		
Slight	36.00	60.00
Dramatic	40.00	150.00

INSUFFICIENT PRESSURE

Under-inking of the printing plate is not the only cause of weak or partially missing impressions. If the press is not operating correctly and the inked plate meets the sheet with insufficient pressure, the result is similar to under-inking. This probably happens as a result of a sheet going through just as the press is being turned off for the day, or at other intervals. Supposedly all action ceases at the instant of turnoff, but considering the rapidity of this operation, it is likely that a random sheet could pass through and be insufficiently impressed. The note pictured here received normal "third print," as is generally the case with notes whose first or second print is made with insufficient pressure.

	V. FINE	UNC.
☐ $20 Federal Reserve Note, Series 1977, signatures of Morton-Blumenthal	105.00	175.00

PRINTED FOLD

This note, along with a large portion of the adjoining note, became folded after the second print. When it passed through the press to receive the third print or overprints (seals, serial numbers, etc.), these naturally failed to appear on the folded area.

	V. FINE	UNC.
☐ $1 Federal Reserve Note, printed fold with overprints partially missing		
Small	60.00	100.00
Large	90.00	210.00

DOUBLE IMPRESSION

Double impressions have traditionally been traced to the sheet of notes passing through the press twice, which would be the logical explanation. However, in considering the method by which currency is printed, it would seem more likely that double impression notes have not made two trips through the press. They probably result from the automatic paper feed jamming. The sheet just printed fails to be ejected, and the printing plate falls upon it a second time instead of on a fresh sheet. This does not merely create a strong impression, but a twin, or a ghost, impression, since the sheet is not positioned exactly the same way for the second strike. Though the paper feed may not be operating properly, there will still be some slight movement—enough to prevent the second impression from falling directly atop the first.

	V. FINE	UNC.
☐ $1 Federal Reserve Note, Series 1977A,		
signatures of Morton-Miller, double "second print" impression		
Partial	150.00	250.00
Complete	370.00	625.00

DOUBLE IMPRESSION OF OVERPRINTS ("DOUBLE THIRD PRINT")

This note is normal as far as the primary obverse and reverse printings are concerned. It received twin impressions of the overprints or "third print." This was not caused by jamming of the paper feed as discussed above. Naturally, the serial numbers are different, as the automatic numbering machine turns with every rise and fall of the press.

	V. FINE	UNC.
☐ $20 Federal Reserve Note, Series 1950, signatures of Priest-Humphrey, double impression of overprints.		
Partial	210.00	350.00
Complete	390.00	650.00

THIRD PRINT (OR OVERPRINTS) SHIFTED

Whenever the overprints (serial number, seals, etc.) are out of position, vertically or horizontally, this is known as "third print shifted" or "overprints shifted." In the example pictured, shifting is extreme. This is a premium value specimen which would command the higher of the two sums quoted. Normally, the overprinting on a "shifted" note fails to touch the portrait, or touches it only slightly. The cause of this kind of error is a sheet feeding incorrectly into the press for the overprinting operation. As striking and desirable as these notes are to collectors, they often go unnoticed by the public.

	V. FINE	UNC.
☐ $100 Federal Reserve Note, Series 1969C, signatures of Banuelos-Schultz, third print shifted.		
Slight	135.00	225.00
Dramatic	170.00	275.00

INK SMEARS

Ink smearing is one of the more common abnormalities of currency notes. Generally it can be attributed to malfunction of the automatic inking device which inks the printing plate. When performing properly, ink is applied at a steady, controlled pace to the printing plate. A very minor disorder in the machine can dispense enough extra ink to yield very spectacular "smeared notes," such as the one illustrated. The value of ink smear notes depends upon the area and intensity of the smear. They are quite easily faked, so the buyer should be cautious.

	V. FINE	UNC.
☐ $1 Federal Reserve Note, ink smear		
Small	24.00	40.00
Large	45.00	75.00

PRINTING FOLD

This note was crumpled along the right side prior to the third printing or application of overprints. Hence the "third print" matter on the lefthand side is normal, but portions of the overprint on the right appear on the note's reverse side.

	V. FINE	UNC.
☐ $20 Federal Reserve Note, Series 1977, signatures Morton-Blumenthal.	108.00	180.00

BLANK CREASE

It occasionally happens that a note becomes creased prior to the reverse or obverse printing in such a way that a small fold is created. During the printing procedure this fold hides a portion of the note's surface, which fails to receive the impression. These notes are actually double errors—the cutting machine cuts them without knowledge of the fold, and when the fold is opened out the bill is then of larger than normal size. Since "crease errors" are difficult to spot in the Bureau of Engraving and Printing's checking, they find their way into circulation in rather sizable numbers. It is difficult to place standard values on them because the price depends on the exact nature of the specimen. The wider the crease, the more valuable the note will be. Premium values are attached to notes with multiple creases that cause the blank unprinted area to fall across the portrait.

	V. FINE	UNC.
☐ Blank crease note, any denomination. Value stated is collector premium over and above face value. (If note has additional value because of series, signatures, etc., this too must be added.)		
Single crease	24.00	40.00
Multiple crease	24.00	42.00

MIXED DENOMINATION

The two notes pictured are normal in themselves, and if they were not owned together as a set, no premium value would be attached to them. The error (which may be dubious to term as such) lies with their serial numbers. The $5 Note has a serial number one digit higher than the $1, suggesting that it was fed into the printing machine intended to print overprints (or "third prints") on $1 bills. Even when this does happen (probably infrequently), it is very difficult to obtain "matching" notes of the kind illustrated, in which the serial numbers are only a single digit apart. Even if you had a $5 Note and $1 Note (or other combination of denominations) from sheets that were fed one after the other, the odds on getting one-digit-apart serial numbers are extremely small.

The value is given for an Uncirculated set only, as there would be no possibility of finding such matched notes except in a bank pack. Once released into circulation, they may never again be mated.

UNC.

☐ Mixed denomination pair from bank pack, $5 Federal
Reserve Note within pack of $1 Federal Reserve Notes   2000.00

BLANK REVERSE

U.S. currency has its reverse printed before the obverse—in other words, back before front. The only logical explanation for blank reverse notes is that blank paper found its way into the batch of sheets on which reverses had already been printed. They were then fed—without detection—into the press for application of the obverse. They continued to escape notice during printing of the overprints, and miraculously got into circulation.

	V. FINE	UNC.
☐ $100 Federal Reserve Note, blank reverse	240.00	400.00

	V. FINE	UNC.

☐ $20 Federal Reserve Note, Series 1977,
signatures of Morton-Blumenthal Blank reverse — 135.00 225.00

	V. FINE	UNC.

☐ $10 Federal Reserve Note, Series 1974,
signatures of Neff-Simon Blank reverse — 135.00 225.00

	V. FINE	UNC.

☐ $1 Federal Reserve Note, Series 1977,
signatures of Morton-Blumenthal Blank reverse — 120.00 200.00

DOUBLE DENOMINATION COUNTERFEIT

This is a counterfeit or faked error. We include it to show
the kind of work done by counterfeiters, and how such items
can be made to resemble genuine errors. This happens to
be a counterfeit of an error note that cannot exist in its genuine
state. Thus, there can be no hesitancy in proclaiming it a fake.
Anyone who is even slightly familiar with the way currency
is printed should instantly recognize this item as a fraud.

Nevertheless, fakers succeed in selling (often at high prices) specimens of this kind, probably because some collectors want the impossible for their albums. Genuine double or twin denomination notes have the obverse of one denomination and the reverse of a different denomination. They do not consist of two obverses or two reverses, such as the one pictured. The note illustrated carries four serial numbers. For it to be genuine, it would have had to pass through the "third print" (overprinting) process twice. Obviously it was made by gluing a $1 and $5 Note together. Much more deceptive paste-ups are created with the notes correctly paired so that the obverse of one and reverse of the other shows. Beware!

INVERTED OBVERSE

U.S. currency is printed reverse first. Therefore, when the back and front do not face in the same vertical direction (as they should), the note is known as an "inverted obverse." The term "inverted reverse" is never used. This, of course, results from the sheet being fed through upside-down for the obverse or second print. Though these specimens are scarce in Uncirculated condition, they often pass through many hands in circulation before being spotted. The uninformed public is not even aware that a note with faces in opposite directions is an error and has premium value.

	V. FINE	UNC.
☐ $2 Federal Reserve Note, Series 1976, signatures of Neff-Simon, inverted obverse	285.00	475.00

MISSING THIRD PRINT

This error is also known as "missing overprint." It consists of a note released into circulation without having gone through the "third print" operation.

	V. FINE	UNC.
☐ $1 Federal Reserve Note, Series 1977, signatures Morton-Blumenthal, missing third print	135.00	225.00

FOREIGN MATTER ON OBVERSE

Sometimes foreign matter, usually paper scraps of one kind or another, gets between the printing plate and the sheet. This naturally results in the area covered being blank on the note. Because of the extreme pressure exerted in printing, the foreign matter is occasionally "glued" to the note and travels with it into circulation. If the appendage is paper, it will normally be found to be of the same stock from which the note is made—apparently a shred from one of the sheet margins that worked its way into a batch of sheets awaiting printing. The value of such notes varies greatly, depending on the size of the foreign matter and its placement. It's rare to find notes in which foreign matter became attached before the first or second print. Nearly always, they found their way to the note after the second print and before the third.

	V. FINE	UNC.
☐ $1 Federal Reserve Note, Series 1974, signatures Neff-Simon, foreign matter on obverse	90.00	150.00

	V. FINE	UNC.
☐ $1 Silver Certificate, Series 1935E, signatures of Priest-Humphrey. Foreign matter on obverse. More valuable than the preceding because of the note's age and the foreign matter being larger.	270.00	450.00

MISSING PORTION OF REVERSE DESIGN
(DUE TO ADHERENCE OF SCRAP PAPER)

In this instance, the foreign matter got in the way of the first print, or reverse printing. It prevented the covered area from being printed, but it later became dislodged and is no longer present. What appears on the illustration to be a strip of paper on the note is really the blank unprinted area once covered by the strip. Obviously a note that merely had a random strip of paper attached, over a normally printed design, would have no collector interest.

	V. FINE	UNC.
☐ $1 Federal Reserve Note, missing portion of reverse design due to adherence of scrap paper	90.00	150.00

OVERPRINT PARTIALLY MISSING

The overprint or third print on this note is normal on the righthand side and missing entirely on the left. This was caused by the note being folded (more or less in half, vertically) immediately before overprinting. Had the lefthand side been folded over the face, this would have interfered with the overprints on the righthand side. Instead, this specimen was folded over the reverse side, or downward, with the result that the missing portion of overprint did not strike the note at all—it simply hit the printing press bed. The reverse side of this note is normal.

	V. FINE	UNC.
☐ $1 Federal Reserve Note, Series 1963A, overprint partially missing	72.00	120.00

THIRD PRINT OFFSET ON REVERSE

This note is normal on the obverse but carries an "offset" of the third print or overprints on its reverse. It would appear that the overprints are showing through to the reverse, as if the note were printed on very thin paper. Actually, this "mirror image" is caused by a malfunction in the printing or paper-feeding machinery. The inked plate for printing the overprints contacted the machine bed without a sheet of paper being in place. Therefore, as the next sheet came through it received the normal overprint on its face and picked up the offset impression on its reverse from the machine bed. Each successive sheet going through the press also received an offset, but it naturally became

fainter and fainter as the ink was absorbed. The value of a
note of this kind depends on the intensity of the impression.

	V. FINE	UNC.
☐$5 Federal Reserve Note, offset impression of overprints on reverse	105.00	175.00

CONFEDERATE MONEY

The Civil War Centennial of 1961–65 has generally been credited with sparking an interest in the collecting and study of Confederate or C.S.A. Notes. This, however, is not totally borne out by facts, as C.S.A. currency had advanced steadily in value since the 1940s. It rides a crest of popularity today surpassing the early 1960s. This is due in part to the exhaustive research carried out since that time and numerous books and articles published. Even today, some C.S.A. Notes would still appear to be undervalued based on their availability vs. regular U.S. issues.

History. It became apparent upon the outbreak of the Civil War that both sides would experience extreme coinage shortages, and each took to the printing of notes that could be exchanged in lieu of bullion or "real money" (which always meant coined money until the 1860s). The South suffered more serious difficulties than the North, as it did not have as many skilled printers or engravers at its command. Also, with the war being fought on its territory rather than the North's, there was an ever-present danger of sabotage to plants printing money or engaging in related activities. The Confederacy tried by all available means to satisfy the currency demand and succeeded in distributing quite a large quantity of notes. Its shortage was taken up by notes issued by private banks, individual states, counties, railroads, and private merchants. Merchant tokens, to take the place of rapidly disappearing small change, poured forth in abundance during this period. All told, the Confederate Congress authorized the printing of about one and a half billion dollars' worth of paper currency. It is impossible to determine the total actually produced, but it would appear that this figure was far surpassed. At the war's conclusion, these notes were worthless, as the C.S.A. no longer existed and the federal government refused to redeem them. Many were discarded as scrap, but a surprising number were held faithfully by their owners who believed "the South will rise again." The South did indeed rise, industrially and economically, and those old C.S.A. Notes rose, too. They still aren't spendable, but many are worth sums in excess of face value as collectors' pieces. Until about 1900, however, practically no value was placed on Confederate currency—even by collectors.

Designs. Some surprising designs will be observed, including mythological gods and goddesses that seem to relate very little to the Southern artistic or cultural climate of the 1860s. Many scholarly efforts have been made to explain away the use of such motifs, but the simple fact is that they appeared not so much by choice as by necessity. Southern printers, not having the facilities of their Northern counterparts, were compelled to make do with whatever engravings or "stock cuts" were already on hand, as inappropriate as they might have proved. However, a number of original designs were created reflecting unmistakably regional themes and at times picturing heroes or leaders of the Confederacy. Slaves at labor, used as a symbol of the South's economic strength and its supposed advantage over the North, where labor was hired, was a frequent motif. Sailors were also depicted, as well as railroad trains and anything else that appeared symbolic of Southern industry. Probably the most notable single design, not intended to carry the satirical overtones it now possesses, is "General Francis Marion's Sweet Potato Breakfast" on the $10 1861 issue note.

In general, the C.S.A. Notes are not so badly designed a group as might be anticipated in light of conditions. The designing was, in fact, several leagues improved over the printing, which often left much to be desired. George Washington is depicted—not for being the first U.S. President but as a native son of Virginia. Jefferson Davis, President of the C.S.A., is among the more common portraits. He became even more disliked in the North than he otherwise might have been because of his picture turning up on currency. But after the war he took a moderate stand

and erased the old ill feelings; he even had words of praise for Lincoln. Other individuals whose portraits (not necessarily very faithful) will be encountered are:

- John C. Calhoun, U.S. Senator who led the battle for slavery and Southern Rights (later called "states rights")
- Alexander H. Stephen, Davis' Vice-President of the C.S.A.
- Judah P. Benjamin, holder of various official titles in the Southern government
- C.G. Memminger, Secretary of the Treasury and Secretary of War
- Lucy Pickens, wife of South Carolina's governor and the only woman (aside from mythological types) shown on C.S.A. currency
- John E. Ward
- R.M.T. Hunter

Printers. The study of printers of C.S.A. Notes is complex, made no less so by the fact that some contractors produced only plates, others did only printing (from plates procured elsewhere), and some did both. The principal Southern printer was the lithography firm of Hoyer & Ludwig of Richmond, Virginia. Also located in Richmond were Keatinge & Ball, which did commendable, if not exactly inspired, work, and B. Duncan, who also worked in Columbia, South Carolina. Another firm involved in quite a bit of note printing was J.T. Paterson of Columbia. The so-called "Southern Bank Note Company" was a fictitious name used to disguise the origin of notes prepared in the North. Some early notes were marked "National Bank Note Co., New York," but it was subsequently decided to remove correct identification from the notes of this printer, undoubtedly on the latter's request (fearing prosecution for aiding the enemy).

Cancellations. Two varieties of cancels are commonly found on C.S.A. Notes. First is the Cut Cancel (CC), in which a knife or similar instrument has been used to make piercings in a design or pattern. Unless roughly executed, such cuts do not materially reduce a specimen's value. In the case of some notes, examples without cancellation are almost impossible to find. The COC, or Cut-Out Cancel, is more objectionable because, instead of merely leaving slits, a portion of the paper was removed. The reduction of value for a Cut-Out Cancel averages around 25 percent. These are considered "space fillers" if the issue is fairly common, but a rare note with a COC may be very desirable. Pen Cancellations (PC) are far less frequently encountered. These show the word "Canceled" written out by hand across the note's face, in ink. Unless the ink is heavy or blotchy, a Pen Cancel will not have too much bearing on value. As the note is not physically injured, it would seem to be the least offensive of the three varieties. Whenever a note is being sold, presence of a cancel, of whatever type, should be plainly spelled out. Some collectors are not interested in canceled specimens. In time, as the scarce issues become even scarcer, they will probably have to be accepted as a fact of life.

Signatures. The first six notes issued, the four from Montgomery and T5 & 6 from Richmond, were hand-signed by the Register and Treasurer themselves. Thereafter, because the Treasury Secretary felt hand signatures helped prevent counterfeiting, and because of the quantities of notes spewing forth, clerks were hired to sign "for Register" and "for Treasurer." There were about 200 different people who signed for each Treasury official, making for thousands of signature combinations. Mostly the clerks were women, many the wives or daughters of soldiers who had been killed in action. Since the notes were signed in Richmond through April of 1864 (when all operations were removed to Columbia, South Carolina), most of the signers were from there. Some moved to Columbia, and others were hired there.

It is most interesting to many people to find that they had relatives who signed Confederate money, and many people search for such notes. A complete listing of all the names from the Confederate Records appears in Colonel Criswell's extensive book, *Confederate and Southern States Currency*.

Condition Grades. While condition standards are basically the same for Confederate currency as other notes of their age, some allowance must be made for paper quality and deficiencies in printing and cutting. These matters have nothing to do with the preservation or wear and can be observed just as frequently in Uncirculated specimens as in those in average condition. Without a source of good paper, printers were obliged to use whatever was most easily and quickly obtainable. Often the paper was thin, or stiff, or contained networks of minute wrinkles which interfered with printing. Cutting was generally not done by machine, as in the North, but by hand with a pair of scissors—workers actually took the sheets and cut apart notes individually. When paper-cutting devices were employed, they were apparently not of the best quality. In any case, regular edges on C.S.A. Notes are uncommon, and their absence does not constitute grounds for classifying an otherwise perfect specimen in a condition grade below Uncirculated. When the occasional gem is located—a well-printed, well-preserved note on good paper, decently cut—its value is sure to be higher than those listed. The collector is not advised to confine himself to such specimens, as his activities would become seriously limited.

Uncirculated—UNC. An Uncirculated note shows no evidence of handling and is as close to "new condition" as possible. An Uncirculated specimen may, however, have pinholes or a finger smudge, which should be mentioned in a sales offering. If these are readily noticeable, the note deserves to be classified as "Almost Uncirculated." Crispness is hardly a criterion of uncirculation as this quality is expected in notes graded as low as Very Fine.

Almost Uncirculated—A.U. Similar to the above grade, but not quite as good as an Uncirculated specimen. The note bears no indication of having actually circulated but has minor flaws resulting from accident or mishandling, such an individuals' counting crinkles.

Extremely Fine—X.F. An X.F. note is on the borderline between Uncirculated and Circulated. It has not been heavily handled but may reveal several imperfections: a pinhole, finger smudge, counting crinkles, or a light wallet fold. The fold is not so heavy as to be termed a crease.

Very Fine—V.F. Has been in circulation but is not worn or seriously creased. It must still be clean and crisp, without stains or tears. Fine to Very Fine condition is considered the equivalent of "Average Circulated" but not "Average" condition (which is another term for poor).

Fine—F. A note that has been in circulation and shows it, but has no physical injuries or just slight ones.

Very Good—V.G. A well-circulated note bearing evidence of numerous foldings. It may possibly have creased corners and wrinkles as well as light staining, smudging, or pinholes, but major defects (such as a missing corner) would place it into an even lower category.

Good—G. Good notes have been heavily circulated, worn, possibly stained or scribbled on edges, could be frayed or "dog-eared." There may be holes larger than pin punctures, but not on the central portion of design. This is the lowest grade of condition acceptable to a collector, and only when nothing better is available. Unless very rare, such specimens are considered space-fillers only.

Average Buying Prices—A.B.P. The Average Buying Prices given here are the approximate sums paid by retail dealers for specimens in Good condition. As selling prices vary, so do buying prices, and in fact they usually vary a more. A dealer who is overstocked on a certain note is sure to offer less than one who has no specimens on hand. The dealer's location, size of operation, and other circumstances will also influence the buying price. We present these figures merely as approximate guides to what sellers should expect.

Type Numbers. Each Confederate Note pictured has a "Type" number as well as a "regular" Criswell catalog number. The Criswell numbers are listed in the beginning of each of the price listings, and the Type numbers appear immediately following in parantheses. These numbers are used for identification and are cross-referenced in Grover Criswell's publications.

FOR MORE INFORMATION

Considered to be the foremost authority on Confederate currency, Col. Grover Criswell has a variety of books available. His last release, *Confederate and Southern States Currency* ($75), covers all the currency issued by the

Confederate States Central Government, the Southern States, the Indian Territories, the Florida Republic and Territory, and the Republic and Independent Government of Texas. This edition also gives interesting discovery information that you are sure to enjoy. There are also current market values listed, as well as rarities. This is the best reference available for the serious collector, libraries, and the casual reader.

To order this book, or for a complete list of books that are available, write Criswell's Publications, Salt Springs, Florida 32134-6000, or call 904-685-2287.

CONFEDERATE STATES OF AMERICA—
1861 ISSUE, MONTGOMERY, ALABAMA
$1,000,000 authorized by "Act of March 9th."
Written dates "1861."
"NATIONAL BANK NOTE CO., NY"

TYPE 1

Face Design: Green and black, bears "Interest Ten Cents Per Day," 607 issued. John C. Calhoun left, Andrew Jackson right.

CRISWELL	NOTE	A.B.P.	GOOD	UNC.
□1	$1000	2500.00	4000.00	20,000.00

"NATIONAL BANK NOTE CO., NY"

TYPE 2

Face Design: Green and black, bears "Interest Five Cents Per Day," 607 issued. Cattle crossing a brook.

CRISWELL	NOTE	A.B.P.	GOOD	UNC.
□2	$500	2500.00	5000.00	22,000.00

CONFEDERATE STATES OF AMERICA—
1861 ISSUE
"NATIONAL BANK NOTE CO., NY"

TYPE
3

Face Design: Green and black, bears "Interest One Cent Per Day." Railway train, Minerva left.

CRISWELL	NOTE		A.B.P.	GOOD	UNC.
☐3	$100		1200.00	2600.00	12,000.00

"NATIONAL BANK NOTE CO., NY"

TYPE
4

Face Design: Green and black, bears "Interest Half A Cent Per Day." Negroes hoeing cotton.

CRISWELL	NOTE		A.B.P.	GOOD	UNC.
☐4	$50		1200.00	2500.00	19,000.00

CONFEDERATE STATES OF AMERICA—1861 ISSUE
"AMERICAN BANK NOTE CO., NY"
(Though ostensibly by the "SOUTHERN BANK NOTE CO.")

TYPE
5

Face Design: Green and black, red fibre paper, bears "Interest One Cent Per Day." Railway train, Justice left and Minerva right.

CRISWELL	NOTE	A.B.P.	GOOD	UNC.
☐5	$100	150.00	250.00	1000.00

TYPE
6

Face Design: Green and black, red fibre paper, bears "Interest Half A Cent Per Day." Pallas and Ceres seated on bale of cotton, Washington at right.

CRISWELL	NOTE	A.B.P.	GOOD	UNC.
☐6	$50	125.00	200.00	900.00

CONFEDERATE STATES OF AMERICA—1861 ISSUE
$20,000,000 authorized by "Act of May 16th, 1861"
(All lithographic date "July 25th, 1861")
"HOYER & LUDWIG, RICHMOND, VA"

TYPE
7

Face Design: Ceres and Proserpina flying, Washington left.

CRISWELL	NOTE	A.B.P.	GOOD	UNC.

TYPE
8

| ☐ 7-13 | $100 | 200.00 | 400.00 | 1000.00 |

Face Design: Washington, Tellus left.

CRISWELL	NOTE	A.B.P.	GOOD	UNC.
☐ 14-22	$50	35.00	60.00	180.00

CONFEDERATE STATES OF AMERICA—1861 ISSUE

TYPE
XXI

Face Design: Exists in a variety of colors.

CRISWELL	NOTE	A.B.P.	GOOD	UNC.
☐XXI	$20	35.00	75.00	175.00

The above type notes were bogus. For years it was thought they were a regular Confederate issue, and evidence exists that they were circulated as such. No collection of Confederate Notes is complete without one. There is no evidence as to who the printer was, but the authors have reason to believe he was located somewhere in Ohio. It is not a product of S.C. Upham, of Philadelphia, the well-known counterfeiter of Confederate Notes.

TYPE
9

Face Design: Large sailing vessel, "20" at left.

CRISWELL	NOTE	A.B.P.	GOOD	UNC.
☐23-33	$20	20.00	45.00	125.00

CONFEDERATE STATES OF AMERICA—1861 ISSUE

Face Design: Liberty seated by eagle, with shield and flag.

There are at least forty-two minor varieties of this note, including a supposed ten or eleven stars on shield. Usually the stars are so indistinct that a note may show from six to fifteen stars. The other differences are minute changes in the size of the "10" in the upper corners. We list only the major type.

CRISWELL	NOTE	A.B.P.	GOOD	UNC.
☐34-41	$10	30.00	75.00	800.00

TYPE
10

TYPE
11

Face Design: Liberty seated by eagle, sailor left.

CRISWELL	NOTE	A.B.P.	GOOD	UNC.
☐42-45	$5	100.00	750.00	8000.00

CONFEDERATE STATES OF AMERICA—1861 ISSUE
(Written date "July 25th, 1861")
"J. MANOUVRIER, NEW ORLEANS"

TYPE 12

Face Design: CONFEDERATE STATES OF AMERICA in blue on blue reverse.

CRISWELL	NOTE	A.B.P.	GOOD	UNC.
☐46-49	$5	200.00	800.00	5000.00

$100,000,000 authorized by "Act of Aug. 19th, 1861."
$50,000,000 authorized by "Act of Dec. 24th, 1861."
"HOYER & LUDWIG, RICHMOND, VA"

TYPE 13

(Lithographic date "September 2nd, 2d, & s, 1861")
Face Design: Negroes loading cotton, sailor left.

CRISWELL	NOTE	A.B.P.	GOOD	UNC.
☐50-58	$100	25.00	50.00	100.00

CONFEDERATE STATES OF AMERICA—1861 ISSUE

TYPE
14

Face Design: Moneta seated by treasure chests, sailor left.

CRISWELL	NOTE	A.B.P.	GOOD	UNC.
☐59-78	$50	20.00	40.00	80.00

"SOUTHERN BANK NOTE CO., NEW ORLEANS"

TYPE
15

Face Design: Black and red on red fibre paper. Railway train, Justice right, Hope with anchor left.

CRISWELL	NOTE	A.B.P.	GOOD	UNC.
☐79	$50	400.00	600.00	5000.00

CONFEDERATE STATES OF AMERICA—1861 ISSUE
"KEATINGE & BALL, RICHMOND, VA"

TYPE
16

Face Design: Black and green, red fibre paper. Portrait of Jefferson Davis.

CRISWELL	NOTE	A.B.P.	GOOD	UNC.
☐80-98	$50	35.00	75.00	400.00

"HOYER & LUDWIG, RICHMOND, VA"

TYPE
17

Face Design: Black with green ornamentation, plain paper. Ceres seated between Commerce and Navigation, Liberty left.

CRISWELL	NOTE	A.B.P.	GOOD	UNC.
☐99-100	$20	75.00	125.00	500.00

CONFEDERATE STATES OF AMERICA—1861 ISSUE
"HOYER & LUDWIG, RICHMOND, VA"

TYPE 18

Face Design: Large sailing vessel, sailor at capstan left.

CRISWELL	NOTE	A.B.P.	GOOD	UNC.
☐101-136	$20	15.00	30.00	80.00

"SOUTHERN BANK NOTE CO., NEW ORLEANS"

TYPE 19

Face Design: Black and red on red fibre paper. Navigator seated by charts, Minerva left, blacksmith right.

CRISWELL	NOTE	A.B.P.	GOOD	UNC.
☐137	$20	200.00	500.00	3000.00

CONFEDERATE STATES OF AMERICA—1861 ISSUE
"B. DUNCAN, COLUMBIA, SC"

TYPE
20

Face Design: Industry seated between cupid and beehive, bust of A. H.
Stephens left.

CRISWELL	NOTE	A.B.P.	GOOD	UNC.
☐139-140	$20	15.00	20.00	80.00

"B. DUNCAN, RICHMOND, VA"

CRISWELL	NOTE	A.B.P.	GOOD	UNC.
☐141-143	$20	15.00	20.00	85.00

"KEATINGE & BALL, COLUMBIA, SC"

TYPE
21

Face Design: Portrait of Alexander H. Stephens.

YELLOW-GREEN ORNAMENTATION

CRISWELL	NOTE	A.B.P.	GOOD	UNC.
☐144	$20	35.00	75.00	500.00

DARK-GREEN ORNAMENTATION

CRISWELL	NOTE	A.B.P.	GOOD	UNC.
☐145-149	$20	35.00	75.00	500.00

CONFEDERATE STATES OF AMERICA—1861 ISSUE
"SOUTHERN BANK NOTE CO., NEW ORLEANS"

TYPE 22

Face Design: Black and red, red fibre paper. Group of Indians, Thetis left, maiden with "X" at right.

CRISWELL	NOTE	A.B.P.	GOOD	UNC.
☐150-152	$10	60.00	100.00	450.00

"LEGGETT, KEATINGE & BALL, RICHMOND, VA"

TYPE 23

Face Design: Black and orange/red. Wagon load of cotton, harvesting sugar cane right. John E. Ward left.

CRISWELL	NOTE	A.B.P.	GOOD	UNC.
☐153-155	$10	100.00	200.00	950.00

CONFEDERATE STATES OF AMERICA—1861 ISSUE
"LEGGETT, KEATINGE & BALL, RICHMOND, VA"

**TYPE
24**

Face Design: Black and orange/red. R.M.T. Hunter left, vignette of child
right.

CRISWELL	NOTE	A.B.P.	GOOD	UNC.
☐156-160	$10	25.00	75.00	300.00

"KEATINGE & BALL, RICHMOND, VA"

CRISWELL	NOTE	A.B.P.	GOOD	UNC.
☐161-167	$10	25.00	75.00	300.00

"KEATINGE & BALL, RICHMOND, VA"

**TYPE
25**

Face Design: Hope with anchor, R.M.T. Hunter left, C. G. Memminger right.

CRISWELL	NOTE	A.B.P.	GOOD	UNC.
☐168-171	$10	25.00	75.00	275.00

CONFEDERATE STATES OF AMERICA—1861 ISSUE
"KEATINGE & BALL, RICHMOND, VA"

TYPE
26

Face Design: Hope with anchor, R.M.T. Hunter left, C.G. Memminger right.

Face Design: *Solid red "X" and "X" overprint.

CRISWELL NOTE	A.B.P.	GOOD	UNC.
☐173-184 $10	25.00	50.00	300.00

*There are three types of red "X" and "X" overprints. That section of the note on which the overprints appear is illustrated in double size.

Face Design: *Coarse lace "X" and "X" red overprint.

CRISWELL	NOTE		A.B.P.	GOOD	UNC.
☐189-210	$10		25.00	50.00	300.00

CONFEDERATE STATES OF AMERICA—1861 ISSUE

Face Design: Fine lace "X" and "X" red overprint.*

CRISWELL	NOTE		A.B.P.	GOOD	UNC.
☐211–214	$10		25.00	50.00	300.00

Face Design: Liberty seated by shield and eagle.

TYPE
27

CRISWELL NOTE	A.B.P.	GOOD	UNC.
☐221-229, $10	600.00	2500.00	25,000.00

CONFEDERATE STATES OF AMERICA—1861 ISSUE
"HOYER & LUDWIG, RICHMOND, VA"

Face Design: Ceres and Commerce with an urn.

TYPE
28

CRISWELL NOTE	A.B.P.	GOOD	UNC.
☐230-234 $10	15.00	25.00	225.00

"J. T. PATERSON, COLUMBIA, SC"

CRISWELL NOTE	A.B.P.	GOOD	UNC.
☐235-236 $10	15.00	30.00	225.00

"B. DUNCAN, RICHMOND, VA"

TYPE 29

Face Design: Negro picking cotton.

CRISWELL	NOTE	A.B.P.	GOOD	UNC.
☐237	$10	40.00	80.00	600.00

CONFEDERATE STATES OF AMERICA—1861 ISSUE
"B. DUNCAN, COLUMBIA, SC"

TYPE 30

Face Design: Gen. Francis Marion's "Sweet Potato Dinner." R. M. T. Hunter left, Minerva right.

CRISWELL	NOTE	A.B.P.	GOOD	UNC.
☐238	$10	20.00	35.00	175.00

NO ENGRAVER'S NAME

CRISWELL	NOTE	A.B.P.	GOOD	UNC.
☐239-241	$10	20.00	35.00	200.00

"SOUTHERN BANK NOTE CO., NEW ORLEANS"

TYPE
31

Face Design: Black and red on red fibre paper. Minerva left; Agriculture, Commerce, Industry, Justice, and Liberty seated at center; statue of Washington right.

CRISWELL	NOTE	A.B.P.	GOOD	UNC.
☐243-245	$5	60.00	100.00	500.00

CONFEDERATE STATES OF AMERICA—1861 ISSUE
"LEGGETT, KEATINGE & BALL, RICHMOND, VA"

TYPE
32

Face Design: Black and orange/red. Machinist with hammer, boy in oval left.

CRISWELL	NOTE	A.B.P.	GOOD	UNC.
☐246-249	$5	100.00	200.00	2000.00

"LEGGETT, KEATINGE & BALL, RICHMOND, VA"

TYPE
33

Face Design: Black and white note with blue-green ornamentation. C.G. Memminger, Minerva right.

CRISWELL	NOTE	A.B.P.	GOOD	UNC.
□250-256	$5	20.00	35.00	400.00

CONFEDERATE STATES OF AMERICA—1861 ISSUE
"KEATINGE & BALL, RICHMOND, VA"

TYPE
34

Face Design: C.G. Memminger, Minerva right.

CRISWELL	NOTE	A.B.P.	GOOD	UNC.
□262-270	$5	25.00	60.00	400.00

"HOYER & LUDWIG, RICHMOND, VA"

TYPE 35

Face Design: Loading cotton left, Indian princess right.

CRISWELL	NOTE	A.B.P.	GOOD	UNC.
☐271	$5	1000.00	2500.00	50,000.00

CONFEDERATE STATES OF AMERICA—1861 ISSUE
"HOYER & LUDWIG, RICHMOND, VA"

TYPE 36

Face Design: Ceres seated on bale of cotton, sailor left.

CRISWELL	NOTE	A.B.P.	GOOD	UNC.
☐272	$5	15.00	25.00	100.00

"J. T. PATERSON & CO., COLUMBIA, SC"

CRISWELL	NOTE	A.B.P.	GOOD	UNC.
☐274	$5	15.00	25.00	100.00
☐276-282	$5	15.00	25.00	100.00

CONFEDERATE STATES OF AMERICA—1861 ISSUE
"B. DUNCAN, RICHMOND, VA"

TYPE
37

Face Design: Sailor seated beside bales of cotton, C.G. Memminger left,
Justice and Ceres right.

CRISWELL	NOTE	A.B.P.	GOOD	UNC.
☐284	$5	25.00	50.00	250.00

"B. DUNCAN, COLUMBIA, SC"

CRISWELL	NOTE	A.B.P.	GOOD	UNC.
☐285	$5	25.00	50.00	300.00

"B. DUNCAN, COLUMBIA, SC"

TYPE
38

Face Design: Personification of South striking down Union, J.P. Benjamin
left. Dated "September 2, 1861" through an error. No Confederate Note less
than $5 was authorized in 1861.

CRISWELL	NOTE	A.B.P.	GOOD	UNC.
☐286	$2	100.00	285.00	3000.00

CONFEDERATE STATES OF AMERICA—1862 ISSUE
$165,000,000 Authorized by "Act of April 17th."
"HOYER & LUDWIG, RICHMOND, VA."

TYPE 39

Face Design: Railway train, straight steam from locomotive, milkmaid left. Bears "Interest at Two Cents Per Day."

CRISWELL	NOTE	A.B.P.	GOOD	UNC.
☐287-289	$100	25.00	45.00	60.00

Dated May 5 to May 9, 1862
J.T. PATERSON, COLUMBIA, S.C. (At Lower Left)

		A.B.P.	GOOD	UNC.
☐290-293	$100	15.00	25.00	50.00

VARIOUS WRITTEN DATES, MAY THROUGH OCTOBER, 1862
J.T. PATERSON, COLUMBIA, S.C. (At Lower Right)

		A.B.P.	GOOD	UNC.
☐294-296	$100	15.00	25.00	50.00

VARIOUS WRITTEN DATES, MAY THROUGH OCTOBER, 1862

TYPE 40

"J.T. PATERSON, COLUMBIA, S.C."
Face Design: Railway train, diffused steam from locomotive, milkmaid left Bears "Interest at Two Cents Per Day."

CRISWELL	NOTE	A.B.P.	GOOD	UNC.
☐298-309	$100	15.00	25.00	60.00

VARIOUS WRITTEN DATES, MAY THROUGH OCTOBER, 1862

CONFEDERATE STATES OF AMERICA—1862 ISSUE
"KEATINGE & BALL, COLUMBIA, S.C."
On the following notes there are two types of ornamental
scrolls in the upper right corners.

**TYPE
41**

Face Design: "Hundred" overprint in orange/red. Bears "Interest at Two
Cents Per Day." Negroes hoeing cotton, J.C. Calhoun left, Columbia right.

CRISWELL	NOTE	A.B.P.	GOOD	UNC.
☐310-314	$100	25.00	55.00	60.00

Dated "August 26th, 1862" (Date all written, scroll No. 1.)

☐315-324	$100	15.00	35.00	60.00

Written dates, AUG. to DEC. "1862." ("186" of date is engraved.)

☐325-331	$100	15.00	35.00	60.00

Dated January 1st to January 8th, 1863.

CONFEDERATE STATES OF AMERICA—1862 ISSUE
$5,000,000 authorized by "Act of April 18th, 1862"
$5,000,000 authorized by "Act of September 23rd, 1862"
"B. DUNCAN, COLUMBIA, S.C."

TYPE
42

Face Design: Personification of South striking down Union, J.P. Benjamin left.

CRISWELL	NOTE	A.B.P.	GOOD	UNC.
☐334-337	$2	10.00	25.00	100.00

TYPE
43

Face Design: "2" and "Two" in green overprint. Personification of South
striking down Union, J.P. Benjamin left.

CRISWELL	NOTE	A.B.P.	GOOD	UNC.
☐338	$2	15.00	35.00	300.00

CONFEDERATE STATES OF AMERICA—1862 ISSUE

TYPE
44

Face Design: Steamship at sea. Lucy Holcombe Pickens right. Liberty left.

CRISWELL	NOTE	A.B.P.	GOOD	UNC.
☐ 339-341	$1	12.00	35.00	100.00

TYPE
45

Face Design: "1" and "One" green overprint. Steamship at sea. Lucy Holcombe Pickens right. Liberty left.

CRISWELL	NOTE	A.B.P.	GOOD	UNC.
☐ 342-342A	$1	15.00	50.00	300.00

CONFEDERATE STATES OF AMERICA—1862 ISSUE
"HOYER & LUDWIG, RICHMOND, VA."
This is a Sept.2, 1861 note, dated through error "September 2, 1862." No engravers' name, appears, but it is a product of Hoyer & Ludwig, Richmond, VA.

TYPE 46

Face Design: Ceres reclining on cotton bales. R.M.T. Hunter at right.

CRISWELL	NOTE	A.B.P.	GOOD	UNC.
☐343-344	$10	10.00	25.00	250.00

(Essay Note, Printed Signatures.)
"KEATINGE & BALL, COLUMBUS, S.C."

TYPE 47

Face Design: Liberty seated on bale of cotton. R.M.T. Hunter right.

CRISWELL	NOTE	A.B.P.	GOOD	UNC.
☐345	$20		EXTREMELY RARE	

CONFEDERATE STATES OF AMERICA—1862 ISSUE
(Essay Note, Printed Signatures.)
"KEATINGE & BALL, COLUMBUS, S.C."

TYPE
48

Face Design: Ceres holding sheaf of wheat. R.M.T. Hunter right.

CRISWELL	NOTE	A.B.P.	GOOD	UNC.
☐346	$10		EXTREMELY RARE	

CONFEDERATE STATES OF AMERICA—1862 ISSUE
$90,000,000 authorized by "Act of Oct. 13th, 1862"
"KEATINGE & BALL, COLUMBIA S.C."

TYPE
49

Face Design: Fancy green reverse. Lucy Holcombe Pickens. George W.
Randolph right.

CRISWELL	NOTE	A.B.P.	GOOD	UNC.
☐347-349	$100	20.00	50.00	300.00

CONFEDERATE STATES OF AMERICA—1862 ISSUE
"KEATINGE & BALL, RICHMOND, VA." (THIRD SERIES)

TYPE
50

Face Design: Black and green. Ornate green reverse. Jefferson Davis.

CRISWELL	NOTE	A.B.P.	GOOD	UNC.
☐350-356	$50	25.00	75.00	400.00

"KEATINGE & BALL, COLUMBIA, S.C." (THIRD SERIES)

CRISWELL	NOTE	A.B.P.	GOOD	UNC.
☐357-362	$50	25.00	75.00	400.00

CONFEDERATE STATES OF AMERICA—1862 ISSUE
"KEATINGE & BALL, COLUMBIA, S.C."

TYPE
51

Face Design: Fancy blue reverse. State Capitol at Nashville, Tennessee.
A.H. Stephens.

CRISWELL	NOTE	A.B.P.	GOOD	UNC.
☐363-368	$20	15.00	50.00	150.00

CONFEDERATE STATES OF AMERICA—1862 ISSUE

TYPE 52

Face Design: Fancy blue reverse. State Capitol at Columbia S.C., R.M.T. Hunter. Printed on pink paper.

"B. DUNCAN."

CRISWELL NOTE	A.B.P.	GOOD	UNC.
☐369-375IB $10	12.00	30.00	85.00

"EVANS & COGSWELL"

CRISWELL NOTE	A.B.P.	GOOD	UNC.
☐376-378 $10	12.00	30.00	85.00

TYPE 53

Face Design: Fancy blue reverse. State Capitol at Richmond, VA., C.G. Memminger. Printed on pink paper.

There are many varieties of printers names on notes of this issue, though all have the same engraver's names. In general, the only valuable ones are those with two "Printers" names.

CRISWELL	NOTE	A.B.P.	GOOD	UNC.
☐ 379-390	$5	10.00	20.00	60.00

TYPE 54

Face Design: Judah P. Benjamin. Printed on pink paper.

CRISWELL	NOTE	A.B.P.	GOOD	UNC.
☐391-396	$2	10.00	20.00	80.00

TYPE 55

Face Design: Clement C. Clay. Printed on pink paper.

CRISWELL	NOTE	A.B.P.	GOOD	UNC.
☐397-401	$1	10.00	20.00	80.00

CONFEDERATE STATES OF AMERICA—1863
$50,000,000 authorized monthly, from April 1863 to January
1864, "By Act of March 23rd, 1863."

All notes of this year dated April 6th, 1863, but a red overprinted date
appears on all the $5, $10, $20, $50, and $100 denominations showing the
year and month of issue.

"KEATINGE & BALL, COLUMBIA, S.C."

TYPE
56

Face Design: Green reverse. Lucy H. Pickens. Two soldiers left. George W.
Randolph right.

CRISWELL	NOTE	A.B.P.	GOOD	UNC.
☐402-404	$100	25.00	50.00	100.00

"KEATINGE & BALL, RICHMOND, VA."

**TYPE
57**

Face Design: Green and black, ornate green reverse, Jefferson Davis.

CRISWELL	NOTE	A.B.P.	GOOD	UNC.
☐406-417	$50	20.00	40.00	100.00

CONFEDERATE STATES OF AMERICA—1863

**TYPE
58**

Face Design: Fancy blue reverse. State Capitol at Nashville, TN., A.H. Stephens.

CRISWELL	NOTE	A.B.P.	GOOD	UNC.
☐418-428	$20	10.00	20.00	50.00

**TYPE
59**

Face Design: Blue back. State Capitol at Columbia, S.C., R.M.T. Hunter.

CRISWELL	NOTE	A.B.P.	GOOD	UNC.
☐429-447	$10	10.00	25.00	40.00

Engravers' names on lower margin.

**TYPE
60**

Face Design: Fancy blue reverse. State Capitol at Richmond, VA. C.G.
Memminger.

CRISWELL	NOTE	A.B.P.	GOOD	UNC.
☐448-469	$5	10.00	20.00	50.00

Pink Paper.

**TYPE
61**

Face Design: Judah P. Benjamin

CRISWELL	NOTE		A.B.P.	GOOD	UNC.
□470-473	$2		15.00	40.00	225.00

TYPE
62

Face Design: Clement C. Clay. Pink Paper.

CRISWELL	NOTE	A.B.P.	GOOD	UNC.
☐474-484	$1	10.00	25.00	75.00

"ARCHER & DALY. RICHMOND, VA."

TYPE
63

Face Design: Bust of Jefferson Davis. Pink Paper.

CRISWELL	NOTE	A.B.P.	GOOD	UNC.
☐485-488	50 Cents	10.00	18.00	30.00

CONFEDERATE STATES OF AMERICA—1864

$200,000,000 was authorized by "Act of February 17th, 1864."
All notes of this year are dated "Feb. 17th, 1864."

The actual amount issued was probably ten times the figure given above and the amount printed even greater. Thus there are many minor varieties of each type including color variations, flourishes, and more signature combinations than any other year. The authors list only the **important** types. The most common Confederate Notes appear in this year.

"KEATINGE & BALL, COLUMBIA, S.C."

TYPE 64

Face Design: Reddish horizontal line background. Equestrian statue of Washington and Confederate flag at left. Gen. T.J. "Stonewall" Jackson right.

CRISWELL NOTE	A.B.P.	GOOD	UNC.
☐489-489A $500	100.00	150.00	300.00

"A CONFEDERATE COUNTERFEIT."

Same as $100 Note illustrated on the next page, but 1/4 inch narrower, and 1/4 inch shorter.
This note only exists in Serial Letter "D."

CRISWELL	NOTE	A.B.P.	GOOD	UNC.
☐ 492	$100	20.00	50.00	100.00

Although a counterfeit, this note was listed in Bradbeer as a genuine, and evidence exists proving that it was accepted as such in the Confederacy. It is an excellent copy, in some ways better engraved than the genuine, but is easily distinguishable by its small size. The authors list it herein with the regular issues because few collectors desire to be without one. It is by far the most popular Confederate counterfeit.

**TYPE
65**

Face Design: Reddish network background. Intricate blue reverse with
"Hundred" in large letters. Lucy Pickens. Two soldiers left. George W.
Randolph right.

CRISWELL	NOTE	A.B.P.	GOOD	UNC.
☐490-494	$100	25.00	40.00	85.00

**TYPE
66**

Face Design: Reddish network background. Intricate blue reverse with "Fifty"
in large letters. Jefferson Davis.

CRISWELL	NOTE	A.B.P.	GOOD	UNC.
☐495-503	$50	20.00	60.00	85.00

**TYPE
67**

Face Design: Reddish network background. Intricate blue reverse with
"Twenty" in large letters. State Capitol at Nashville, TN. A.H. Stephens right.

CRISWELL	NOTE	A.B.P.	GOOD	UNC.
☐504-539	$20	8.00	15.00	25.00

"KEATINGE & BALL, COLUMBIA, S.C."
("PTD. BY EVANS & COGSWELL" On left end)

**TYPE
68**

Face Design: Reddish network background. Intricate blue reverse with "Ten" in large letters. Horses pulling cannon. R.M.T. Hunter at right.

CRISWELL	NOTE	A.B.P.	GOOD	UNC.
☐540-553	$10	6.00	12.00	25.00

"KEATINGE & BALL, COLUMBIA, S.C."

**TYPE
69**

Face Design: Reddish network background. Intricate blue reverse with "Five" in large letters. State Capitol at Richmond, VA. C.G. Memminger at right.

CRISWELL	NOTE	A.B.P.	GOOD	UNC.
☐558-565	$5	6.00	12.00	25.00

**TYPE
70**

Face Design: Reddish network background. Judah P. Benjamin.

CRISWELL	NOTE	A.B.P.	GOOD	UNC.
☐566-571	$2	10.00	30.00	60.00

TYPE
71

Face Design: Reddish network background. Clement C. Clay.

CRISWELL	NOTE	A.B.P.	GOOD	UNC.
☐572-577	$1	12.00	20.00	100.00

"ENGRAVED BY ARCHER & HALPIN, RICHMOND, VA."

TYPE
72

Face Design: Bust of Jefferson Davis. Pink Paper.

CRISWELL	NOTE	A.B.P.	GOOD	UNC.
☐578-579	50 Cents	8.00	15.00	25.00

THE BLACKBOOKS!

The leading authorities on U.S. coins, paper money, and postage stamps!

All national bestsellers, these dynamic books are the *proven* annual guides for collectors in these fields for more than two decades!

- **COINS** — Every U.S. coin evaluated. . . features the American Numismatic Association Official Grading System!
- **PAPER MONEY**— Every government-issued note covered!
- **POSTAGE STAMPS** — Every U.S. stamp detailed. . . features a full-color, fast-find photo index arranged by the Scott numbering system!

DON'T LEAVE HOME WITHOUT THEM!

TURN YOUR PENNIES INTO PROFITS!

Discover in *One-Minute Coin Expert* how to find valuable coins in your pocket change. This top-grade book contains invaluable information, including

- how to handle and store your coins
- the best coins for starting a collection
- buying and selling tips
- how to grade coins
- top-ten coin picks for future price appreciation
- written by coin authority Scott Travers, seen on ABC's *Good Morning America*, CNN, and CNBC

HOUSE OF COLLECTIBLES
SERVING COLLECTORS FOR MORE THAN THIRTY YEARS

HOUSE OF COLLECTIBLES

THE OFFICIAL® IDENTIFICATION AND PRICE GUIDES TO

AMERICAN INDIAN ARROWHEADS
1st edition
John L. Stivers
876-37913-7 $17.50

ANTIQUE CLOCKS
3rd edition
876-37513-1 $12.00

ANTIQUE JEWELRY (ID)
6th edition
Arthur Guy Kaplan
876-37759-2 $21.00

ANTIQUE AND MODERN FIREARMS
7th edition
876-37908-0 $17.00

ANTIQUE AND MODERN TEDDY BEARS
1st edition
Kim Brewer and Carol-Lynn Rossel Waugh
876-37792-4 $12.00

ANTIQUES AND COLLECTIBLES
14th edition
Eric Alberta and Art Maier
876-37961-7 $15.00

ARTS AND CRAFTS
The Early Modernist Movement in American Decorative Arts, 1894–1923 (ID)
2nd edition
Bruce Johnson
876-37879-3 $12.95

THE BEATLES
Records and Memorabilia
1st edition
Perry Cox and Joe Lindsay, with an introduction by Jerry Osborne
876-37940-4 $15.00

BEER CANS
5th edition
Bill Mugrage
876-37873-4 $12.50

BOTTLES
11th edition
Jim Megura
876-37843-2 $14.00

CIVIL WAR COLLECTIBLES
1st edition
Richard Friz
876-37951-X $17.00

COLLECTIBLE TOYS
(ID), 5th edition
Richard Friz
876-37803-3 $15.00

COLLECTOR CARS
Robert Balderson
8th edition
676-60024-7 $17.00

COLLECTOR KNIVES
11th edition
C. Houston Price
876-37973-0 $17.00

COLLECTOR PLATES
6th edition
Rinker Enterprises
876-37968-4 $17.00

COMPACT DISCS
1st edition
Jerry Osborne
876-37923-4 $15.00

COUNTRY MUSIC RECORDS
1st edition
Jerry Osborne
676-60004-2 $15.00

ELVIS PRESLEY RECORDS AND MEMORABILIA
1st edition
Jerry Osborne
876-37939-0 $14.00

FINE ART
2nd edition
Rosemary and Michael McKittrick
876-37909-9 $20.00

FRANK SINATRA RECORDS AND CDs
1st edition
Vito R. Marino and Anthony C. Furfero
876-37903-X $12.00

GLASSWARE
1st edition
Mark Pickvet
876-37953-6 $15.00

HOUSE OF COLLECTIBLES cont'd

LIMITED EDITION COLLECTIBLES
1st edition
Susan K. Elliott and J. Kevin Samara
876-37927-7 $15.00

OLD BOOKS
1st edition
Marie Tedford and Pat Goudey
876-37915-3 $15.00

OLD BOOKS & AUTOGRAPHS
7th edition
876-37313-9 $14.00

OLD WEST COLLECTIBLES
1st edition
R. C. House
876-37902-1 $12.95

ORIENTAL RUGS (ID)
1st edition
Joyce Ware
876-37882-3 $12.50

POSTCARDS (ID)
1st edition
Diane Allmen
876-37802-5 $9.95

POTTERY AND PORCELAIN
8th edition
Harvey Duke
876-37893-9 $15.00

RECORDS
11th edition
Jerry Osborne
876-37963-3 $20.00

ROCK AND ROLL—MAGAZINES, POSTERS, AND MEMORABILIA
(ID), 1st edition
David K. Henkel
876-37851-3 $12.50

STAR TREK® & STAR WARS® COLLECTIBLES
3rd edition
Sue Cornwell & Mike Kott
876-37831-9 $12.00

WATCHES
10th edition
Cooksey Shugart & Tom Engle
876-37808-4 $18.00

THE OFFICIAL BECKETT PRICE GUIDES TO

BASEBALL CARDS
16th edition, 1997
Dr. James Beckett
676-60003-4 $6.99

BASKETBALL CARDS
5th edition, 1996
Dr. James Beckett
876-37970-6 $6.99

FOOTBALL CARDS
15th edition, 1996
Dr. James Beckett
876-37969-2 $6.99

HOCKEY CARDS
5th edition, 1996
Dr. James Beckett
876-37971-4 $6.99

BECKETT GREAT SPORTS HEROES

MICHAEL JORDAN
876-37979-X $15.00

MICKEY MANTLE
876-37982-X $15.00

JOE MONTANA
876-37981-1 $15.00

SHAQUILLE O'NEAL
876-37980-3 $15.00